DAVE RAMSEY'S COMPLETE GUIDE TO MONEY

The Handbook of Financial Peace University

Peace

Philippians 4:7

This publication is designed to provide accurate and authoritative information with regard to the subject matter covered. It is sold with the understanding that the publisher is not engaged in rendering financial, accounting, or other professional advice. If financial advice or other expert assistance is required, the services of a competent professional should be sought.

Editors: Allen Harris, Jennifer Gingerich, Darcie Clemen

Cover design: Chris Sandlin

Interior design: Thinkpen Design, Inc., www.thinkpendesign.com

ISBN: 978-1-937077-20-4

14 15 C&C Shenzhen 10 9 8 7

DEDICATION

To the millions of men and women across the country who have sat face to face and knee to knee with other families in *Financial Peace University* classes since 1994. Your passion, enthusiasm, and incredible successes are taking the message of Financial Peace to new heights, changing behaviors, breaking generational trends, and restoring hope for our nation's economy.

To Louis Falzetti, executive vice president of Financial Peace University, who stayed late after class one night to help me stack chairs and hasn't left my side in the sixteen years since. Your vision for what FPU could become turned my small, local class into a household name. Millions of families thank you—and so do I.

ACKNOWLEDGMENTS

Writing a book is a huge endeavor that goes far beyond the name of the guy on the cover. I'd like to thank the following people for leading the charge to make this book possible:

Allen Harris, my editor for this book, for helping me turn twenty years' worth of teaching, experience, and stories into a manual that anyone can use to win with money.

Darcie Clemen, Grace Clausing, Blair Moore, and Jennifer Gingerich for providing editorial and project management support.

Daniel Bell and Chris Sandlin for overseeing all graphics and cover art.

Louis Falzetti, Debbie LoCurto, Paul Boyd, Beth Tallent, Oksana Ballard, Brian Beaman, Russ Carroll, Jack Galloway, Heath Hartzog, Darrell Moore, and Brent Spicer for reviewing early drafts of this book to let me know what worked—*and* what didn't.

TABLE OF CONTENTS

INTRODUCTION

For the past couple of decades, I've been known as "that money guy on the radio," but if you had met me back in the late 1980s, you would have met a much different Dave Ramsey. At that time, I was climbing out of a huge financial hole, caused by some stupid, risky mistakes I had made in my real estate business. If *that* guy were to call in to *The Dave Ramsey Show* today, I'd chew him out for being so stupid with his money! But hey, we've got to start somewhere, right? I started at the bottom of a huge money pit.

As I got my life back on track, I went on a crusade to figure out how money works. I read everything I could get my hands on, talked to a ton of successful people, and discovered a new passion—my life's calling, really. In 1990, I started counseling people one on one, helping them sort through their own financial messes and sharing what I was learning through my own struggles. But within just a few years, I had become incredibly frustrated. I would run into people I had counseled a few months earlier, and they'd tell me they were in the middle of filing for bankruptcy. I'd say, "What? But we figured it out! We had a plan to get you back on track! What happened?"

And they'd say something like, "I know, Dave, but it just didn't work," or "The budget seemed okay, but we just couldn't stick to it," or "Yeah, but once we left your office, we just felt overwhelmed again and bankruptcy seemed easier." After this happened several times, a lightbulb went off in my head. In my early years of counseling, I had just been focusing on the math, but the math wasn't the problem. I realized that the real issue was people's *behaviors* around money, and that's something math alone can't fix.

I enjoyed one-on-one counseling, and I believed there was a place for that, but the truth is, broke people can't afford to pay for ongoing counseling as they clean up their messes. And beyond that, sitting with a counselor a couple of times a month didn't do much to address the behavior issues at the heart of the problem. So I started looking at other areas, to see how other places were doing it. I researched twelve-step programs, and then I really started looking at Weight Watchers as a model. You want to know a secret? Weight Watchers doesn't sell magic food. People lose weight because they know they've got to go to the group meeting and step on the scale on Tuesday night. That's the motivation that helps them walk past the donuts in the grocery store. *The accountability of a group environment causes people to change their behaviors.* It worked for weight loss, and I became convinced that it would work with money.

With that model of half-teaching, half-support group in mind, I got to work on a few lessons targeted at people considering bankruptcy. We called it *Life After Debt*, and I had high hopes. The first night, I set up one hundred chairs, expecting a big crowd. I had my overhead projector ready, and I was standing at the door in my bad suit and tie, waiting to greet the masses and change people's lives. Four people showed up. Only three of those four actually paid for the class. It was a humble start, but it was *still* a start.

A few more people showed up the next week, and a few more the week after that. As we grew and got to know the audience, we realized that this really wasn't just a class for people considering bankruptcy; it was a class for *everyone*. I pulled back and adjusted my perspective. It's great to help someone on the verge of bankruptcy, but wouldn't it be better if we helped people change their behaviors way before bankruptcy even became a thought? So we swapped out some of the bankruptcy material for investing and insurance lessons, and attendance kept going up. Then we added more nights and more classes, and even more people showed up. In time, I was teaching this class several nights a week, and we changed its name to something that better represented what we wanted to accomplish. *Life After Debt* was gone, and *Financial Peace University* was born. Within a few years, we outgrew what I was able to teach live and in person, so we put it on video. Now, almost twenty years later, more than one million families have gone through the class around the country.

We've tweaked the class a little bit over the years, but the central message hasn't changed at all. Information is important, but behavior is the key. Biblical, common-sense principles don't change. This stuff isn't rocket science; it's stuff my grandmother could have taught. The problem isn't really that we don't know or can't understand what to do. The problem is that we choose not to do it. I knew this approach would work that first night I taught the class, and the millions of men and women who have followed the program since then have proved me right.

The book in your hands takes the heart of the class and puts it into an easy-to-understand manual. This should be a book you read cover to cover, and then pull back out and refer to often. And if you're thinking about filing bankruptcy, taking out a loan, buying a new car, getting a cash value life insurance policy, loaning money to a friend, or making any other major financial decisions right now, stop! Don't do a thing until you read this book! Trust me—the information in these pages can save you a world of headaches and years of regret.

Sure, there are critics who like to push their glasses down to the tip of their noses as they shake their heads at our material and call it "simplistic" or "naive." That's fine. I didn't start this class or write this book for them. Why would I waste my time with a few dozen critiques from broke financial bozos when I could instead kick back with the thousands of thank-you and "We Did It!" letters we get every year from families who are winning like never before? Maybe someday soon, you can send me one of those letters, too, telling me how much your life has changed since you discovered genuine Financial Peace. I can't wait to read it, but we've got some work to do first.

1

SUPER SAVING

COMMON SENSE FOR YOUR DOLLARS AND CENTS

The water was so hot, it was almost burning my face—but I could barely feel it. All I really felt were the tears that wouldn't stop coming as I stood in the shower, crying like a baby. One thought kept repeating itself over and over in my head: *How in the world did I end up here?* Maybe that's a question you've asked yourself a time or two.

At that time, I was coming off a winning streak. I was the wonder kid of real estate. Still in my twenties, I had built up a $4 million portfolio in just a few years. My wife, Sharon, and I had been having all kinds of fun. Fancy jewelry. Luxury cars. Exotic vacations. We had it all. And then we lost it.

My success was a lie. It was propped up on a mountain of debt, and one day, one bank decided to knock me off that mountain. Over the next few years, that mountain of debt turned into an avalanche that just about wiped out me and my family. We lost everything, and I stood in the shower every morning with tears and dread knowing what I was going to have to face that day. I had played the money game, and I had lost.

For me, hitting rock bottom was the wake-up call I needed to get my financial act together. From that point on, I was on a quest to find out everything I could about God's and Grandma's ways of handling money, and for more than twenty years now,

I've been on a crusade to spread the news about what I found. Money really isn't that complicated, but most of what we hear in the media and from the "highbrow financial geniuses" is just plain wrong. If you really want to win with money, you just need to get your arms around a handful of simple, repeatable concepts.

The concepts are *simple*, but that doesn't mean the process is *easy*. It's not. That's because money is not just about math; it's about behavior. Personal finance is only 20 percent head knowledge. The other 80 percent—the bulk of the issue—is behavior. And it's our *behaviors* with money that can get us into the biggest trouble or lead us into the biggest successes. Behavior is the key to the whole deal, and we'll unpack how that plays out through all these different areas as we work through this book.

THE BABY STEPS

For years, I have taught people a process for getting out of debt and building wealth that I call the Baby Steps. I talk about the Baby Steps on my radio show, in my live events, all through our *Financial Peace University* class, and I've even written a book, *The Total Money Makeover*, that walks you step by step through the seven-step process. The book you're holding right now, though, is different. We'll talk about the Baby Steps a lot, and we'll check each step off the list as we work through this information, but this book is more of a practical, hands-on guide for navigating your way through some of the details like savings, investing, mutual funds, insurance, real estate, and all the other important parts of your financial plan that a lot of people either forget or ignore.

I'm not going to repeat everything you may have already read in *The Total Money Makeover*, but we are going to stick to the Baby Steps as "home base." Like I said, I've been teaching people this stuff for twenty years, and I know the Baby Steps work. I'm not going to change everything I've been teaching for two decades just to sell a new book!

JOIN THE CONVERSATION

After I got my $1,000 in the bank, I finally had some peace of mind, and I didn't feel like I had to freak out because something unexpected came up. IT WAS AWESOME!

—Alicia

www.facebook.com/financialpeace

Your Road Map for Success

Basically, the Baby Steps are your road map to win with money. Having a goal is great, but you need to know more than just where you want to end up; you need to know how to get from Point A to Point B. You might say, "I know my target. I want to have $1 million in my retirement account by the time I turn fifty." That's a great goal, but if you're sitting at age twenty-five with two car loans, no savings, maxed-out credit cards, a dead-end job, and no real plan, you're not going to make it. You need some step-by-step directions to get where you want to go.

So, let's take a quick look at the seven Baby Steps. You'll see these markers come up as we work through this book and the *Financial Peace University* class.

- **Baby Step 1:** Put $1,000 in a beginner emergency fund ($500 if your income is under $20,000 per year).
- **Baby Step 2:** Pay off all debt using the debt snowball.
- **Baby Step 3:** Put three to six months of expenses into savings as a full emergency fund.

- **Baby Step 4:** Invest 15 percent of your household income into Roth IRAs and pretax retirement plans.
- **Baby Step 5:** Begin college funding for your kids.
- **Baby Step 6:** Pay off your home early.
- **Baby Step 7:** Build wealth and give.

The Baby Steps work because of focus and priority. It's like eating an elephant; you can't do it all in one bite! But if you break it down into smaller steps and pour all of your attention, energy, and passion into *one thing at a time*, you can do anything.

This is where we're heading, but as we get there, we'll deal with all the other details that sneak up on us and derail our financial plan. Not anymore! This book is your guide through all things money—from the biggest deals to the smallest details. I want you to read it, work through all the lessons if you're in the *Financial Peace University* class, and then refer to this book often as you hit each new milestone in your financial walk. You ready? Then, let's get started.

PRIORITY NUMBER ONE: SAVE MONEY!

It took a near meltdown of the entire economy to get most people's attention about saving money. In the decade leading up to the 2008 financial mess, Americans flirted with a negative savings rate. That means, at times, the average American was spending more than he was making. All the money came in, and all the money went out—and then some. We were high on debt, high-risk loans, and crazy mortgages, and most people didn't have anything in the bank to catch them if they took a fall.

Gallup did a survey in the decade leading up to the 2008 crisis and found that only 32 percent of Americans would be able to cover a $5,000 emergency without borrowing money.[1] It doesn't take much to add up to $5,000, either. A car wreck, roof repair, or medical problem could hit $5,000 pretty quickly, and when that happens, seven out of ten respondents to the survey said they'd be charging up credit cards, taking out loans, or hitting up Mom and Dad for the money. They had no buffer between them and life.

Trust me, that's no way to live. I've been there; I've felt that pressure and there is no way I'm ever going back. So let's get started with the first step on the journey.

Baby Step 1: Put $1,000 in a Beginner Emergency Fund

This is your first priority, and you've got to do it *fast*! Today! Right now! Most people can come up with $1,000 in a month if they make it a priority. If you're making less than $20,000 a year, you can cut this down to $500, but get it done. Have a garage sale this weekend, eat rice and beans every meal for the next month, work extra hours. Do whatever it takes, but hit this goal fast!

The Pain of Change

In the grand scheme of life, $1,000 is not a lot of money. But this is often the hardest Baby Step for most people to take for one reason: it requires a change. A lot of the people I talk to every day have never had $1,000 in the bank before. When we start the process by putting that cash aside in the bank *just for emergencies*, they have to make a decision: *Am I going to actually take these steps? Am I done living the way I've been living? Am I willing to sacrifice to win?* That's no big deal for a lot of people, but I've seen tons of men and women face this decision and just walk away. They can't do it. Something in their spirits just won't let them mentally and emotionally make a commitment to change the behaviors that led them into a mess.

We don't always like change, do we? Sometimes, we're like a baby sitting in a poopy diaper. We think, *Sure it stinks, but it's warm and it's mine!* We get defensive of our mess even if it's not working. So when I tell people the first thing they need to do is put $1,000 in the bank and not touch it, it can be a deal-breaker. It requires you to look in the mirror and say, "You're the problem." When you do that emotionally, you'll start to win with money.

"Evil Rich People"

We need to deal with something before we get too far into the issue of saving money. I want you to have a big pile of money in the bank. I want you to be able to buy nice things, cover emergencies without stress and panic, and have some cash on hand to bless other people. But every time I talk about saving and building wealth, someone always comes up to me and says, "But if I save money and do the stuff you teach, I'll become one of those evil rich people." That's a total disconnect about how God wants us to handle our money.

Some people have a broken mind-set when it comes to wealth. They think that having money is somehow evil or wrong. That's a huge misreading of Scripture. The Bible doesn't say that money is the root of all evil; it says that *the love of money* is the root of all kinds of evil.[2] Money is amoral. It doesn't have morals. It's not good and it's not bad. It's the love of money that's the problem—and that's a human problem, not a money problem.

Money's like a brick. I can take a brick and throw it through someone's window, or I can take a brick and build a church or hospital. The brick doesn't care. It's just a brick. But when you put it into the hands of a human being, it takes on the character of that person. It does whatever the person holding it wants to do. But we get confused about this; sometimes we think, *Oh, that person has a big pile of bricks, so he must be evil. And that guy doesn't have any bricks, so he must be good.* But it's just a pile of bricks. Why are we putting morals and values on it?

I have met some rich people who are total greedy jerks, and so have you. I have also met some poor people who are total greedy jerks, and so have you. On the other hand, I've met some rich people who are some of the nicest, kindest, godliest people on the planet, and some poor people who are just as great. And I bet you have too. It's not about the money. You're not bad if you have some and you're not good if you don't. It's just bricks.

SAVING FOR AN EMERGENCY FUND

There are three basic reasons to save money. First, we save for an emergency fund. Second, we save for purchases. Third, we save for wealth building. Purchases and wealth building are fun, but we can't do any of that until we cover the basics—the emergency fund. This is a savings account set aside and never touched except for emergencies. You'll need to define what makes up an emergency for your family, too. Let me give you a clue: A new leather sofa or a vacation is *not* an emergency!

The emergency fund is your protection against life's unexpected events, and you are going to have a lot of them throughout your lifetime. They're not really "unexpected" if you think about it. You know they're coming; you just don't know when, what, or how much. But you can still be ready.

We already said that Baby Step 1 is a beginner emergency fund of $1,000. That's just to give you a little wiggle room as you work through Baby Step 2, which is getting out of debt (we'll cover that in chapter 4, *Dumping Debt*). Once you're out of debt, you go back to the emergency fund and fill it up.

Baby Step 3: Three to Six Months of Expenses in Savings

Notice that we're talking about *expenses*, not *income*. The goal here is to figure out from your budget how much it costs to keep your household running for a month. How much would you need to meet all of your obligations and pay your bills if your income suddenly dried up? Then, put three to six months of that in the bank.

Keep It Liquid

When we get to the investing chapters, we'll talk about liquidity. That's just a fancy financial term for "availability." You want to keep your emergency fund liquid, or available, when you need it. It's for emergencies, right? That means you won't usually have a week to wait for a bank or investment company to release the funds. You need to have instant access to the account.

However, do not think for a second that you can just keep your emergency fund in your regular checking account that you use for gas and groceries. If you mix your emergency fund with your other money, it will vanish. That's a little *too* liquid; it'll leak right out of your account! So you want it available, but separate. You need it off to the side where you won't accidentally dip into it, but where you can get to the money without any headaches or having to depend on banking hours.

I recommend keeping your emergency fund in a simple money market account with a good mutual fund company. This makes it available through basic check-writing privileges or

ATM access while keeping it separate from your regular bank account. This kind of account won't pay a great rate—somewhere in the neighborhood of CD (certificate of deposit) rates—but that's okay. Your emergency fund is there for your protection, not to make you money.

This is where a lot of people, mostly men, get confused. For most people, the full emergency fund is somewhere around $10,000–15,000. That's a lot of money, more money than most people have ever put in the bank. Sometimes, math nerds like me will start doing the math and figuring out how much we could be making with a $15,000 investment in a good mutual fund, instead of just having that much money sitting in a money market account. But the emergency fund is not an investment; it's insurance—and insurance *costs* you money.

Just Fix the Car

Years ago, I was doing a book signing and a lady came through the line that was, well, *glistening*, as we say in the South. It was the middle of summer, and it was hot outside. You get the idea. I saw her in line a few people back, and she just looked furious. When she finally got up to the table where I was signing, she said, "Dave, I'm so mad. I've been doing this stuff. I've been through *Financial Peace University*. I've worked my tail off to get out of debt and save up $12,000 in my emergency fund. And just now, on the way over here, my truck totally broke down and I had to get it towed. It's going to cost $1,000 to fix it. I'm so mad!"

I looked up and said, "What are you mad about? You've got $12,000 sitting in the bank. Just fix the car." Her whole face and posture changed. You could see the stress and tension melt off her shoulders. Even though she had a full emergency fund, she hadn't made the connection between unexpected expenses and actually having the cash on hand to handle them.

A lot of us, myself included, can understand that. Before I figured out how to handle money and my car broke down, I didn't just have a car crisis; I had a financial crisis too. It wasn't just, "My car's broke!" It was more like, "My car's broke—and so am I!" Actually having the money on hand, ready to go, to just fix the car is an incredible feeling. Even though this lady had done a fabulous job getting out of debt and saving up her emergency fund, it wasn't until she wrote a check for a $1,000 car repair that she *really* understood what it meant to have Financial Peace.

SAVING FOR PURCHASES

The second basic reason to save money is to make purchases. Since we're not borrowing money anymore, saving up for purchases is kind of a big deal!

The Sinking Fund Approach

I teach people to save up for big purchases using the sinking fund approach. For example, let's say your dining room furniture has fallen apart so bad that it can't take one more Thanksgiving dinner. No problem—you'll just run over to the furniture store and pick out a new set. If you're like most Americans, you'll find the one you want; pay the price that's on the sticker; agree to a rip-off, 90-days-same-as-cash scheme; sit at the financing desk, signing your life away for an hour; and have your stuff delivered the next day. Problem solved, right? Well, not really.

We'll talk about financing and 90-days-same-as-cash in chapter 6, *Buyer Beware*, but for now, here's the deal. A friend of mine in the financing business told me recently that almost nine out of ten people who take a 90-days-same-as-cash contract through his company actually *do not* pay off the loan in ninety days. Even if they've been making payments the whole time, as soon as they cross the ninety-day mark, they get charged back-interest dating all the way back to the date of purchase. That interest rate is somewhere around 24 percent. If you were in that deal and carried out those payments an average of twenty-four months, you'd have monthly payments of $211 and would end up paying $5,064 for your $4,000 dining-room set.

I don't care how good a deal you think you got on that furniture, you got robbed. You went in without a plan, half on impulse, got stuck in debt for two years, and ended up adding more than $1,000 to your furniture bill! I've got a better plan. Pay cash. That's pretty old-fashioned, isn't it? Find Grandma's cookie jar and stuff some money in it for a few months. That's how people *used* to pay for things!

Here's how I'd recommend buying that furniture. We'll use the sinking fund approach, which means I'm going to figure out how much I need to save, how long I have to save it, and how much that means I'll need to sock away every month. In the furniture example, if I saved $211 a month instead of making payments, I could buy that dining room set in eighteen months. You say, "But Dave, $211 times 18 is only $3,800." That's right. I've found that if you walk into a furniture store counting out hundred-dollar bills, you'll get a deal. So ultimately, you'll get that furniture with no debt and you'll save more than $1,000 on it. That's a good plan.

What if your kids really got this message early enough and applied it to buying cars? Starting with their first car at age sixteen, they could go their entire lives without a car payment. Most Americans can't even fathom that. You could retire a multi-millionaire just by avoiding car payments! Why don't they teach that in school?

SAVING FOR WEALTH BUILDING

The last thing we normally save money for is wealth building. We're going to cover this area in great detail later in chapter 9, *The Pinnacle Point*, and chapter 10, *From Fruition to Tuition*. There, you'll learn all about mutual funds, Roth IRAs, 401(k)s, annuities, college savings accounts, and everything else you need to know about building wealth. For now, we'll just cover some basics.

Discipline Is the Key

When it comes to saving money and building wealth over the long haul, nothing is more important than discipline. Putting money away every month, year after year, over the course of a few decades is a big deal! If you're twenty-two years old and just starting out in your career, you've probably got more than forty years until retirement! When you're looking out over a forty-, thirty-, or twenty-year span, it's easy to get distracted and let things creep in and steal the dollars you've marked for saving.

Discipline is hard, it hurts, and it requires sacrifice. Personally, I don't like discipline—but I *love* what discipline produces. When I'm disciplined with my diet and exercise, my body feels better. When I'm disciplined in doing the details in caring for my family and friends, my relationships are better. And when I'm disciplined in managing my money, I actually get to build some wealth and enjoy my money. This is really a biblical principle: "No discipline seems pleasant at the time, but painful. Later on, however, it produces a harvest of righteousness and peace for those who have been trained by it."[3]

Too many people skip the discipline and try to go straight to the enjoyment. That's a recipe for disaster. That's how so many people get hooked on playing the lottery or go broke in a horrible get-rich-quick scheme that falls apart. Wealth building is a marathon, not a sprint. There really aren't any shortcuts. That's why most people don't do it; if building wealth were easy, everyone would be rich!

What if you squeezed an extra $100 out of your budget every month? If you saved just $100 a month, every month, from age twenty-five to age sixty-five (your working lifetime) at the stock market average return of 12 percent, you'd retire with more than $1.1 million! You'd be a millionaire with just $100 a month! That's pizza and cable money for most people! Now, is it easy to find $100 in your budget? Sure, most people could figure out how to get an extra $100 out of their budget. But is it easy to do that every month like clockwork for forty years? No! As I said before, something else will sneak in and try to take away that money. It takes discipline to stick to your goals, but that little bit of discipline will take you a long way.

A Mathematical Explosion

There's another key to building wealth that can absolutely change your life if you get the concepts early. I'm talking about compound interest. Here's how it works. Say you have $1,000 in an investment making 10 percent. One year later, you'd have $1,100 in that account, right? That's your initial $1,000 investment plus one year of 10-percent growth, which is $100. So then you'd have $1,100 sitting in the account for another year at 10 percent, which would grow to $1,210 during the second year. It just keeps building from there. You'll keep earning 10 percent not on the original investment, but on its *current value*. So every year it's worth more, which means every year you'll earn more. That adds up pretty quickly until eventually, the compound interest just goes nuts. That's a great place to be!

I made this point in my first book, *Financial Peace*, using the example of Ben and Arthur:

> Ben, age nineteen, invests $2,000 per year compounded annually at 12 percent for eight years until he is twenty-six years old. For the next thirty-nine years, until he is sixty-five, Ben invests not one penny more.
>
> Arthur, age twenty-seven, invests $2,000 per year for thirty-eight years until he is sixty-five years old. His investment also earns 12 percent compound interest per year. At age sixty-five, will Arthur or Ben have the most money?[4]

Believe it or not, the guy who only saved for eight years with a total investment of only $16,000 beat the guy who saved for thirty-nine years and invested $76,000! Ben came out far ahead—$700,000 ahead—even though he saved fewer years and less money. Why? Because he started earlier. Because of compound interest, Ben's eight-year head start on Arthur pushed him past the $2 million mark at retirement! See the chart on the next page to see how all the numbers played out.

BEN vs. ARTHUR

BEN INVESTS	TOTAL	AGE	ARTHUR INVESTS	TOTAL
2,000	2,240	19	0	0
2,000	4,749	20	0	0
2,000	7,558	21	0	0
2,000	10,706	22	0	0
2,000	14,230	23	0	0
2,000	18,178	24	0	0
2,000	22,599	25	0 **ARTHUR STARTS LATE**	0
2,000	27,551	26	0	0
0	30,857	27	2,000	2,240
0	34,560	28	2,000	4,749
0 **BEN STOPS SAVING!**	38,708	29	2,000	7,558
0	43,352	30	2,000	10,706
0	48,554	31	2,000	14,230
0	54,381	32	2,000	18,178
0	60,907	33	2,000	22,599
0	68,216	34	2,000	27,551
0	76,802	35	2,000	33,097
0	85,570	36	2,000	39,309
0	95,383	37	2,000	46,266
0	107,339	38	2,000	54,058
0	120,220	39	2,000	62,785
0	134,646	40	2,000	72,559
0	150,804	41	2,000	83,506
0	168,900	42	2,000	95,767
0	189,168	43	2,000	109,499
0	211,869	44	2,000	124,879
0	237,293	45	2,000	142,104
0	265,768	46	2,000	161,396
0	297,660	47	2,000	183,004
0	333,379	48	2,000	207,204
0	373,385	49	2,000	234,308
0	418,191	50	2,000	264,665
0	468,374	51	2,000	298,665
0	524,579	52	2,000	336,745
0	587,528	53	2,000	379,394
0	658,032	54	2,000	427,161
0	736,995	55	2,000	480,660
0	825,435	56	2,000	540,579
0	924,487	57	2,000	607,688
0	1,035,425	58	2,000	682,851
0	1,159,676	59	2,000	767,033
0	1,298,837	60	2,000	861,317
0	1,454,698	61	2,000	966,915
0	1,629,261	62	2,000	1,085,185
0	1,824,773	63	2,000	1,217,647
0	2,043,746	64	2,000	1,366,005
0	2,288,996	65	2,000	1,532,166

$2,288,996
WITH ONLY A $16,000 INVESTMENT!

VS.

$1,532,166
ARTHUR NEVER CAUGHT UP!

The trick is, though, that you have to start *right now!* No matter how young or how old you are, all the time you have is all the time you have. You have to start where you are. So if you're under twenty-five, stop thinking you have all the time in the world. And if you're over forty, do not let regret keep you from getting this stuff going now. You have plenty of time left! It's never too late to start moving in the right direction!

YOU NEED A PLAN

You see, building wealth isn't really a mystery. We said it was hard, but that doesn't mean it's hard to *understand*. The stuff I teach is actually pretty simple intellectually; it's just *hard to do*. That's because it's easier to just drift through life without a plan, wandering from one thing to another. To really build wealth, though, you've got to know where you're going and have the discipline to do the things it takes to get there.

Turning the Key

If you don't make a plan for your money, someone else will. Let me tell you how it happens. Say you fight to pull your $1,000 emergency fund together this month. You take that $1,000 to a bank and open up a new account. By doing that, you have turned the key on the most sophisticated and well-funded marketing machine in history. That machine is called the financial institution. They spend more money promoting their product than any other service or product in history, and they do a very, *very* good job selling their stuff.

After you open that new account, you can expect to see a brand-new Visa card magically appear in your mailbox. It will probably come with a note that says something like, "Welcome to the family! We're excited about building a strong relationship with you!" Just what you want, right? A relationship with a bank. No thanks.

You look through the paperwork and see that your new card has an 18-percent interest rate on purchases, and you say, "Nobody lends money at 18 percent! How stupid! They must be crazy to think I'd borrow their money at 18 percent." And if you're like most Americans, you're saying this *as you put the card in your wallet*. And you think, *What a dumb idea. I'll tuck this plastic away in my wallet, though, just in case there's an emergency.*

And then over the course of the next month, the car breaks down. Emergency! And then the kids are screaming for a pizza. Emergency! And then you realize that your children grew over the summer and need some school clothes. Emergency! And then some kid has a birthday and needs some hunk of plastic from the toy store or he won't feel loved. Emergency!

All this stuff just rolls over and over, and a month later, the bill comes in the mail and your jaw drops. You yell through the house, "Who put $1,000 on the Visa? That was just for emergencies! What did we spend $1,000 on?" You look around, but you don't see a new HD television or a new computer. You don't have a new wardrobe, and you didn't take an exotic vacation to Hawaii. That $1,000 just disappeared. Life happened, and you didn't have a plan.

Guess who had a plan? Visa.

Here's what really happened in that situation. You took your $1,000 and loaned it to the bank at 6 percent (if you got an excellent savings rate). Then, the bank *loaned you back* your $1,000 at 18 percent. That's their business, and as I said, they are excellent at selling it to you.

It's Up to You

This book is going to challenge a lot of what you might have always thought about money. It will certainly challenge everything you see and hear in the world about how to handle your finances. If you really dig in and do this stuff, you're going to be totally weird because you'll be going against the cultural current. You'll be taking a stand and practically every store, business, ad campaign, and most of your friends will try to convince you why you're crazy.

I dealt with that a long time ago, and I'll be honest: that kind of pressure doesn't bother me a bit. After my wife, Sharon, and I went broke and started putting the pieces of our financial life back together, some things got clear in my head for the first time. I thought, *Who was it that taught me to borrow money?* It was my broke finance professor. I was talking about that with a friend once, and he said, "You know, a broke finance professor is like a shop teacher with missing fingers!" That's when I decided that I wasn't going to take financial advice from broke people anymore.

The bottom line is this: "Normal" in North America is broke. "Normal" is using credit cards, taking on a lifetime of car payments, and spending more than you make. "Normal" is living on a razor's edge, where any unexpected emergency can send you into panic mode. I finally figured out that I don't want to be "normal." I want to be weird!

Today, my motto is, "If you will live like no one else, later you can live like no one else." If you make some sacrifices, inject some discipline, and get intentional about winning with money, the future is wide open. You'll be blown away at the opportunities you'll have to serve and bless other people, and you'll be amazed at what life feels like without worrying about money all the time. It's a great place to be. If you're ready to find out for yourself, then keep reading. We've got a lot of ground to cover together.

WE DID IT!

I had heard of Dave Ramsey from my father, but that was the extent of it. When my husband and I decided to get married, our pastor was in one city, we were in another, and the wedding was in another—so getting together for pre-marriage counseling was not an option! Because we couldn't get together with our pastor, he recommended that we take Dave's *Financial Peace University* class in place of his traditional counseling, so we went to FPU at a local church.

My husband was still in school, and I had been working full-time at a low-paying job for a little over a year. At that time, we had roughly $3,500 in credit card debt. Between September and December, we were able to pay off all of the debt and even put $5,000 in savings! *How?* you may ask.

At the age of twenty-three, we did what most newlyweds would not have done. I remember it like it was yesterday. We were driving to our honeymoon with a bag full of cards stuffed with $3,000 of gift money. We decided that Dave would want us to use that cash to pay off the credit card debt—so we did. We didn't blow it like most kids our age would have, but I can *guarantee* we would have if we weren't in the middle of taking his class. *Financial Peace University* really helped us get a handle on where in the budget we had opportunities to save, and eventually those savings added up—BIG TIME!

Meredith
Jacksonville, TX

KEY POINTS

1. Saving must become a priority.
2. You must save for an emergency fund, major purchases, and wealth building.
3. Decide and agree with your spouse on what qualifies as an emergency.

QUESTIONS FOR REFLECTION

1. What keeps you from saving?
2. Why is Baby Step 1 the hardest step for many people? Is it that way for you?
3. Why do so many people use debt (credit cards, loans, home equity, etc.) for emergencies?
4. What does it mean to say that money is amoral? How is money like a brick?
5. What would constitute a financial emergency for your household? How would you cover such an emergency today?

2

RELATING WITH MONEY

NERDS AND FREE SPIRITS UNITE!

Money and relationships mess with each other. Bad relationships cause money messes. Money messes cause bad relationships. In fact, if you don't get your money under control, this one area can destroy your whole life! We need to really dig in here and see what money does in a marriage, what it does for single adults, how we need to talk to our kids about money, and how money can bless or wreck our friendships and every other relationship we have.

MARRIAGE AND MONEY

There's an old story about former president George H. W. Bush and his wife, Barbara, that I just love. Heck, I'm pretty sure it's not really true, but I still love it. As the story goes, George and Barbara Bush were in the presidential limo driving back from an event. They were driving on some out-of-the-way back roads, and the driver had to pull over for gas. The old service-station owner popped out of the door with his mouth gaping open at the sight of the president's limo sitting in front of his gas pump.

When Mrs. Bush saw him through the window, she jumped out of the car, ran up to him, and gave him a great big hug.

They talked for a few minutes, and then she got back in the limo. She turned to President Bush and said, "That's Harry, my old high school boyfriend!"

George got a big grin on his face, leaned back, and said, "So let me get this straight. If you had married him, you'd be the wife of a gas-station attendant. But instead, you married me, the most powerful man in the world, and you got to be the First Lady of the United States."

Barbara looked back at him with a sparkle in her eye and said, "Oh George, don't be silly! If I had married him, *he* would be president!" Truly, the woman makes the man—at least in my house!

Seriously, if there's one thing I've learned after more than two decades of marriage and after counseling thousands and thousands of married couples, it's this: marriage is hard! It takes a lot of time and hard work to get on the same page with a spouse. I mean, let's face it—I'm a pretty hardheaded guy. I make decisions fast and want to keep going forward without slowing down. This train is *moving*, so when you see me coming, you've got to get on board or get off the tracks!

My wife, Sharon, is different. She processes things a lot slower and always considers everybody's *feeeeeelings* before she can pull the trigger on a decision. If I'm not careful, I'll just roll right over her when it's time to make a decision. It's not that she doesn't want to contribute; she just goes about the whole process differently than I do.

Opposites Attract, But . . .

Every marriage consists of two totally different people. My friend, the late Larry Burkett, used to say, "Opposites attract. If two people just alike get married, one of you is unnecessary!"

One of you is burning up; the other is always cold. One of you is always late; the other is early for *everything*. One of you is a spender; the other is a saver. Those differences may be cute when you're dating, but they start to look a little different after a few years of marriage.

But those differences also add a lot of fun and spice to a healthy marriage—as long as you agree on the important stuff. Marriage counselors tell us that couples who can agree on four major issues have a much higher probability of a successful marriage. Those four things are religion (shared household faith), in-laws (boundaries, influence, etc.), parenting, and money. If you keep these four pillars standing strong in your marriage, you'll have a leg up on most of the couples you know.

Couples who aren't on the same page with their finances are destined for trouble—a *lot* of trouble. In fact, money fights and money problems are the number-one cause of divorce in North America. A Stanley and Markman study found that money is the one thing people say they argue about most in their marriage.[1] Another study by Citibank found that 57 percent of divorced couples said money fights were the primary reason they didn't get along.[2]

But if money has the potential to be the worst area of our marriages, then it has the same potential to be the *best* area of our marriages. Agreeing on money unlocks so many doors to a strong marriage because money is rarely *just* about money. How we handle money in our relationships involves power, priorities, dreams, passions, and ultimately, our value system. The checkbook is just a little window into the marriage. You can look through it to see how you're doing in most other areas. If you've got a weak marriage, it will show up in your money. If you've got a rock-solid marriage, it will show up in your money.

So if you're married and you have money fights, congratulations—you're normal. But if this is a real problem area for you, then you've got a huge opportunity to improve the relationship and maybe even reach agreement with your spouse about money. And seriously, once you agree on your money and how it impacts every part of your life, how much else is left to really fight about?

JOIN THE CONVERSATION

We now have a plan and that's such a wonderful thing! I'm even couponing to help save more money. Some people think that's weird of me to do, so I guess I know I'm on the right track!

—Andrea

www.facebook.com/financialpeace

Men, Women, and Money (Overgeneralizing)

After working with so many married couples over the years, I've found that men and women approach money in very different ways. I'm overgeneralizing here; of course, not all men and women will act this way, but there are some patterns that have proved themselves over and over.

Men, for example, use money like a scorecard and lose self-esteem when money problems pop up. Women, on the other hand, experience fear—my wife actually says *terror*—when money problems come up, because money represents security to them. This is why guys usually resist saving up three to six months of expenses as an emergency fund. Just having that much money sitting around doing nothing seems like a waste to men, but their wives will likely tell you it's the most important key to their financial plan.

And gender differences don't end with money. Author and counselor Dennis Rainey of FamilyLife explains that women are traditionally more verbal than men. I've heard him say men usually speak about 10,000–20,000 words a day, while women speak 30,000–50,000 words per day—with gusts up to 125,000! That's why a lot of guys come home from a busy day at work, hit the sofa, and don't say a word. They can't. They've already used up their quota.

In his book *Making Love Last Forever*, Gary Smalley lists five key differences he's noted in male and female behavior throughout his many years of research and counseling:

1. Men love to share facts; women love to express feelings.
2. Men connect by doing things; women connect by talking.
3. Men tend to compete; women tend to cooperate.
4. Men tend to be controlling; women tend to be agreeable.
5. Men tend to be independent; women tend to be interdependent.[3]

As I said, this is all an overgeneralization, but I can tell you without a doubt that this is how it is in my house!

Nerds, Free Spirits, and Budget Committee Meetings

So if men and women are so different, who is supposed to do the financial decision making in a marriage? BOTH! Handling money is not an either/or proposition; it's a both/and. Sure, one person is going to have a natural bent toward budgeting and working with numbers, but the decision making has to be done by both partners.

Every marriage has what I call a Nerd and a Free Spirit. Nerds like doing the budget, because it gives them control, and they feel like they are taking care of their loved ones. The Nerd doesn't have to wear a bow tie and a pocket protector; he or she just has a natural bent toward organization and numbers. A little spontaneity is okay with the Nerd; they just need to plan it out ahead of time!

The Free Spirit, on the other hand, isn't nearly as detailed. They see the Nerd's detailed plans, spreadsheets, and carefully calculated budgets and feel controlled, not cared for. Free Spirits are looking for a party, and the thought of a weekly budget summit is like death to them. They aren't necessarily sloppy or lazy, but they often appear irresponsible to the Nerd.

Each marriage also has a Spender and a Saver—and that is separate from the Nerd and Free Spirit. The Nerd is not always the Saver of the family. In my house, for example, I'm the Nerd and Sharon is the Free Spirit. But I'm also the Spender, and she's the Saver.

So let's see . . . Agreement on money is a key factor in a healthy marriage. Opposites attract. Men and women are different. Every marriage has a Nerd, Free Spirit, Spender, and Saver. Mix all this together, and it's really no surprise that money fights so often end in divorce. But there's a better way. I call it the Budget Committee Meeting. In a marriage, the committee has two members: the husband and the wife. Both have to be there, both have to participate, and both have to actively engage the process. If you have kids, it's okay to bring them into the discussion, but the kids don't get a vote. Mom and Dad always make the money decisions, and they do it *together*. I'll say it over and over: The key to winning with money in marriage is teamwork. If you're not working together on your plan, your plan's not working.

The Budget Committee meets once a month. The goal is to write out a budget before the month begins. We'll cover all the ins and outs of budgeting in chapter 3, *Cash Flow Planning*. For now, though, let me lay out a few rules for Nerds and Free Spirits for a successful Budget Committee Meeting. If you're enrolled in a *Financial Peace University* class, you can get a downloadable poster version of these rules in the online Member Resource Center to post on the fridge as a reminder.

Budget Committee Meeting: NERD RULES

1. Write up the budget draft beforehand. Then, bring it to the meeting, have your say, and shut up!
2. This is a meeting, not a weekend summit. You've only got the Free Spirit's attention for about seventeen minutes, so make them count!
3. You have to let the Free Spirit mess with your budget! This isn't your time to *tell* the Free Spirit what the budget is; this is your time to work with your spouse to make a budget you *both* agree on.

Budget Committee Meeting: FREE SPIRIT RULES

1. You must COME TO THE MEETING!
2. You have to talk in the meeting. This means *mature input*.
3. You need to change something on the Nerd's budget draft. This is not the Nerd's budget; it's your *family's* budget. Take some ownership by tweaking the Nerd's draft.
4. You can never again say these six words: "Whatever you want to do, honey." That's a cop-out. You've got to stick in there and make the budget work together.

If you're married, you probably heard the preacher say, "And now you are *one*." He didn't say, "And now you are a *joint venture.*" You're in this together, and you're going to win or lose as a team.

Tough Teamwork: Getting the Reluctant Spouse On Board

But what happens when one spouse isn't on board with the plan? One of the most common questions I get is, "How do I get my spouse to join me in working on the money?" This isn't a gender issue. A lot of men are frustrated with wives who act like spoiled little girls who want what they want, and they want it NOW! And a lot of women are frustrated and even angry at their passive, unassertive husbands who refuse to contribute to the money discussion. Whether the lone ranger is male or female, whoever is left shouldering the responsibility resents the other for making them carry it single-handedly. What should be an awesome husband-wife team effort becomes more like a parent-child struggle, with one "grown-up" trying to drag along a pouting, red-faced kid in an adult's body. That's a recipe for disaster—in your finances *and* in your marriage.

There are some ways to bring a reluctant spouse around, but before we get to those, here are some things you *don't* want to do. You don't want to nag and whine. That doesn't work, and it just makes you look like a child yourself. And don't beat them over the head with this book or start every sentence with "Dave Ramsey says . . ." I get a pile of hate mail every month from spouses who start off with, "Dave, I hate you, and I don't even know you. If I hear 'Dave says' one more time, I'm going to hit something!"

You don't want to be manipulative. If you're imagining you and me secretly working together to trick your spouse into talking about money, just cut it out. There are no games here; we're after open and honest communication. I just want you both to be on the same page, and that's not going to happen if you approach this as *us versus them*.

Last, you don't want to tell them how dumb they are. If you take an attack posture, they'll immediately get into the defensive position. Don't set this up like a battle; remember, you're trying to *end* the money fights!

So what are you supposed to do? First and foremost, you simply need to talk to your spouse. You didn't marry a mind reader, so don't expect your mate to immediately be on the same page with you if you haven't told him or her what page you're on! If they haven't picked up this book or gone to an FPU class with you yet, just sit them down and explain why you're so excited about what you're learning. Share the dreams and hopes you have for your family's money situation. Sometimes, one spouse's passion and excitement is all it takes to get the other spouse excited too.

If that's not enough to move the conversation forward, you're going to need to try a little harder. Take the time to write out exactly what you're concerned about in your current financial plan and how you believe life could be different for your family if both spouses were engaged in the process. Sometimes, the written word will get a spouse's attention more than a conversation.

You could also try the Valentine's approach: "Honey, the most romantic thing you could do for me is to sit down and work on the budget with me. On a scale of one to ten, dinner and a movie is a three, but working together to get out of debt is a nine."

Or the security approach: "Sweetie, what do you think it'd feel like if we had $10,000 in the bank just for emergencies? Can you even imagine that?"

Just get creative. Your spouse is your partner for life, so make sure he or she knows how important this is to you and how much you need him or her on board with you.

SINGLES AND MONEY

All over the country, in pretty much every *Financial Peace University* class, you'll find single adults in all kinds of situations. Some of them are young, just out of college, saddled with student loans, or just haven't married *yet*. Some are a little older and have either been single up to this point or maybe they've been through a divorce and are getting back on their feet financially and emotionally. Some are single parents trying to figure out how to teach their kids about money while working two jobs to support them. Some are over fifty and recently widowed, maybe with no idea how to support themselves or handle the money since their spouse passed.

Whatever the situation, I have a huge heart for single adults. They face unique challenges that us married folks have probably forgotten or just haven't faced yet. Those of us with a husband or wife to come home to have some built-in accountability; we've got someone waiting at the door when we get home, wondering where we've been and what we've bought! Singles have to be a little more proactive in inserting some accountability into their lives.

Single-Adult Trouble Spots

One of the biggest challenges that I've seen working with single adults of all ages is what I call "time poverty" and fatigue. That is, some of these men and women are cramming thirty-hour days into the eighteen or so hours they're awake. On one end of the spectrum, you've got young singles just starting their careers and pouring all their time and energy into that, and maybe going to school at night to get an extra lead on the competition. On the other end, you've got single parents who work all day, then pick up the kids, shuttle them to soccer practice, help with schoolwork, feed and bathe them, and drop them in bed before collapsing themselves. Add an active church life, some charity time, and maybe a friend or two to any of these situations, and that calendar is pretty much maxed out.

If there's no one else depending on your income, it's easy to let busyness keep you from even balancing your checkbook, let alone doing a written plan for your money every month. The problem with this is that, for all that activity, you're not going anywhere; you're just treading water. Plus, without a plan, fatigue leads to even greater expenses, because it's always easier to order a pizza and pay a dry cleaner than it is to cook at home and do your own laundry.

Another issue I've seen with some of the single adults I've worked with over the years is unplanned expenses due to loneliness. A single twentysomething called the radio show not too long ago. She had just graduated from school and had moved to a new city for a job. She hadn't found a church home yet, didn't have any friends, and spent a lot of nights in her apartment by herself. She said, "Dave, my restaurant expenses are killing me every month, but I can't help it. There are nights when the thought of sitting at my kitchen table all alone makes me want to cry, so I go out to eat and go see a movie. Even if I'm in a restaurant booth or theater seat by myself, at least I'm out in the world and get to be around other people."

The biggest challenge I see for single adults, though, is impulse buying. With no one at home to worry about, single adults can rationalize almost any expense, big or small! A new 72-inch plasma TV? "Sure, I owe it to myself!" The gang is going out for pizza? "Count me in!" A group is jetting down to the coast for the weekend? "Sounds like a blast!"

Now, I'm not saying all singles are this immature. But I am saying that single adults have to pay even more attention to impulse purchases, especially those brought on by stress or what I call the "I Owe It to Myself" syndrome. If you're single, you have a greater responsibility to manage your money, because no one is looking over your shoulder. It's up to you!

Single Parents

According to the Department of Commerce, 55 percent of single moms are considered poor.[4] Sometimes, I feel like I've met most of them, and they both inspire me and break my heart at the same time. I'll never forget one single mom who came up to me after I taught a live FPU class several years ago. She told me that she had been on my plan for a while and was just starting to get some traction. Things were tight, but she had a budget that was working—even though it was budgeted down to the wire with hardly any wiggle room.

She said, "Dave, for the first time in my life, I really started to feel a sense of hope. But then . . ." That "but then" was a train wreck. One Friday, she got up and got the kids ready for school. She was completely exhausted from a rough week, but was excited that it was Friday—she had made it to the end of the week. Then, driving the kids to school, she had a flat tire. She had to get out and change the flat on the interstate by herself, in the pouring rain, with the kids in the car. Because of the flat, she was late getting the kids to school, so they chewed her out. Then she walked into the office soaking wet and miserable, and her boss chewed her out for being late. She had to stay late to make up the hour, which meant she was late picking the kids up from after-school care. So they chewed her out again and charged her a fee. Once the kids were back in the car, they all started chanting, "McDonald's! McDonald's!"

She said, "Dave, I just didn't have anything left. I couldn't face the thought of going home and cooking dinner. So I wheeled through the ATM and took out a $20 bill and ran through the drive-thru." Now, twenty bucks may not be a big deal to you, but for this mom, living on a tightly balanced budget, it was huge. "That $20 caused me to bounce five checks. Those two Happy Meals cost me $157."

You don't deserve *that kind* of a break today. Those are the times, single moms or dads, when you've got to take a deep breath, drive the chanting kids home, and spread some peanut butter on some bread. Those are the moments that make or break you. You've got to live to fight another day.

Budgets and Buddies

The two best tips I can give a single adult at any age, whether they have kids or not, are to do a written budget every month and to find an accountability partner. A written plan, which we'll talk about in detail in the next chapter, gives the single person a sense of empowerment, *self*-accountability, and control. The empowerment comes from seeing a plan in action, breathing easier because you know you're going somewhere and not just living day to day. And that paper keeps you honest, too. Once you write down your budget for the month, you're done. You're the boss of your money and your budget until you write it down and mark it as final. After that, that piece of paper is in charge. It's like you telling future-you to behave!

Accountability relationships are also critical. Find someone with some experience, somebody with gray hair or no hair who has some cash in his or her pocket. Ask this person to walk with you, hold you accountable, help you with your budget, and talk about purchases with you. Think about a pastor, your favorite Sunday school teacher, or someone else who has helped and mentored you. Just remember, this is NOT your shopping buddy! In order for this to work, this has to be someone who loves you enough to hurt your feelings at times if that's what is needed to really help you.

KIDS AND MONEY

All the parents I've ever gone to church with love to quote Proverbs 22:6, "Train up a child in the way he should go, and when he is old he will not depart from it."[5] It's funny how many of them never carry that instruction over just one more verse to Proverbs 22:7, "The rich rules over the poor, and the borrower is the slave of the lender."[6] It's no accident that these two verses are side by side. Could it be that one of the most important things we can teach our kids is how to handle money? Absolutely!

Parents, you need to understand something: *someone* is going to teach your kids about money. It will either be you, or it will be a shady car dealer, a credit card pusher on your child's first day at college, a get-rich-quick infomercial pitchman, or just some clown who's after their money. If you want to protect your kids, you need to send them out into the world with some knowledge.

Following in Your Footsteps

When my oldest daughter, Denise, was in preschool, the brave (or crazy) teacher put her little feet in wet paint and then had her step onto some matting. Under those little prints she wrote, "I'm following in your footsteps." That's a sobering thought for most parents. I kept that plaque on my desk for years to remind me that my kids are watching me. They're going to do what I do. They're going to handle money the way I handle money. If I talk with my spouse, make a plan, spend, save, and give with some intentionality behind it, that's what they'll do. If I live paycheck to paycheck, buy whatever I want whenever I want it, and fan out credit cards like playing cards, that's what they'll do. Children learn by watching, so watch what they're watching.

Even though kids model your behavior, you can't just do your own thing and expect your children to catch on. They need some coaching; you have to be intentional about what you're teaching them. There are four main areas of money that children need to learn:

1. **Work.** Money comes from work, not from other people, the government, or dumb luck. From an early age, your kids need to feel that emotional connection between work and money. That's why my wife and I paid our

kids commissions, not allowances. You work; you get paid. You don't work; you don't get paid. It's true for parents—it should be true for kids.

2. **Save.** Teach your kids early on how to save up for purchases. If they learn how (and why) to save up for a Barbie today, they'll know how (and why) to save up for a car or house tomorrow—with no debt.

3. **Spend.** Let your kids have some fun with their money and experience the awesome feeling of buying something they want with money they saved. If you keep it all in the piggy bank and never let them enjoy it, they'll either grow up into miserable old misers *or* they'll rebel and become crazy, debt-ridden spenders once they hit college!

4. **Give.** Giving is the most fun you can have with your money. Nothing beats making a waitress's day with a $100 tip out of the blue! Just make sure your kids give *their own* money. If you hand Junior a quarter to drop in the offering plate on Sunday morning, he's just a courier for *your* money. He needs to know what it feels like to really give out of his own pocket.

Learning these four areas—especially giving—brings your kids a depth of confidence and character they'll never have otherwise. Without it, they'll become shallow, self-centered, and miserable adults.

Be Age-Appropriate

In the *Relating with Money* lesson of *Financial Peace University,* I show parents how to teach kids about money at any age. Age is important, though. Your four-year-old isn't ready for a checking account, and your high school senior is too old for a piggy bank. You've got to customize your coaching based on your kids' ages and maturity levels.

Ages 3–5: Quick Commissions and "Attaboys!"

Those of us with little kids know that for a four-year-old, "clean your room" means Mom and Dad put almost all toys away and the kiddo dropped the last one or two in the toy box. But that's okay! This is the time for teaching work and reward. A child this young can do simple chores, but then he needs an immediate "Attaboy!" and an instant commission payout. This is critical for him to see the work-pay connection and to feel the pride of doing a job well.

Use a clear container to teach savings so the child can watch the money grow. Every now and then, pull the money out, count it up, and head over to "Toys 'R' Them" so Junior can experience the pride of buying something with his own money. And don't hammer the topic of giving too much at this stage. Under six, the child is really too young for percentage-based, systematic giving. Let the giving be spontaneous and fun, and always watch out for opportunities to model spontaneous giving while your kids are watching.

Ages 6–12: Chore Charts and Envelopes

Sharon and I put a chore chart on our fridge for our kids when they were in the 6–12 range. We didn't make it too complicated; we weren't running a sweatshop with our children or anything. We planned on paying them $5 a week in commissions, so we gave each child five simple chores each week ($1 per chore). If the kid did the job, she got paid. If she did three of the five jobs, she got three bucks. Sure, your kids need to do some work around the house just as a matter of respect and participation, but if you don't pick out a few jobs to attach commissions to, you're missing out on a great opportunity to teach them about work and money.

When we paid the kids each week, we helped them divide their loot into three envelopes: giving, spending, and saving. So if my son did all five jobs, he got his five bucks. One dollar went in the Giving envelope, two into Spending, and two into Saving. That way, we were able to teach the basics of all three areas and had teachable moments about budgeting and planning every single week.

We created a product called *Financial Peace Junior* that pulls together the chore chart, envelopes, and several other teaching tools for parents with kids in the 3–12 range. You can find out more about that at daveramsey.com, or, if you're in an FPU class, you can find some information in the online resources for this lesson.

JOIN THE CONVERSATION

We're finally getting on the same page. We have gone through FPU and now have a Dave Ramsey Financial Counselor to help us. He has been a great blessing in keeping our feet to the fire.

—Scott

www.facebook.com/financialpeace

Ages 13–18: Cars and Debit Cards

Around age thirteen, savings became a big deal to our kids because we told them flat out that we were *not* going to buy them a car when they turned sixteen. If they wanted some wheels, they'd have to save up and buy their own. I did offer them a match on their savings, which we called 401DAVE, but they knew up front that Sharon and I would only match their own savings dollar for dollar. That matching plan worked for our family, but it may not work for yours. That's okay. And even if you do offer a match, I recommend putting a cap on how much you'll kick in. We didn't do that at first, and it almost cost us big-time when my middle kid saved up a huge pile on her own! And when it came time to buy, it was a great opportunity for me to go car shopping with them and teach them how to think through big purchases. We also didn't pay for their car insurance or basic repairs. We found that our kids drove cars differently if they were primarily responsible for them.

This was also the age when my kids got their own bank accounts with debit cards—NOT CREDIT CARDS! Their chores got a little harder and their commissions got a little higher. Once they were old enough, they also got jobs because that buy-a-car clock was ticking. After the first kid hit sixteen, the other two realized we were serious. Sharon and I matched our daughter's savings dollar for dollar, and not a penny more.

Instead of giving them cash like we'd done when they were younger, we paid their commissions by depositing the money directly into their accounts. We also stopped paying for things like clothes and sports fees with cash or checks and deposited all that money into their accounts, too. From there, it was up to them to manage and budget the money. If they wanted to go to the movies, buy school clothes, and pay their hockey or cheerleading fees, they had to do it themselves. The biggest lesson for them was to know that Mom and Dad weren't going to step in and rescue them if they bounced a check or overspent in one area. They had to learn how to manage it themselves. They made some mistakes, but they made them while they were still under our roof. So, when they all grew up and moved out, they (and we) were confident they'd be okay out in the "real world."

Boomerangs in the Basement

The "real world" is a kick in the pants for a lot of young adults, though. A recent Pew Research Center poll found that one in seven parents with grown children have had a kid move back in with them.[7] That's what we call "Boomerang Kids," as in, you throw them out, but they keep landing back on your doorstep. When grown kids returned home a hundred years ago, it was because Junior was there to work the family farm. Nowadays, it means Junior is out of work and needs a free bed. And that's eating up 10 percent of Mom and Dad's income![8]

Don't get me wrong; I love my kids and I'll always be there to help them no matter how old they are. But "helping" doesn't necessarily mean letting them stay in their childhood bedroom into adulthood. If they're out of college and still sleeping under their old Buzz Lightyear bedsheets, they really will stay there "to infinity and beyond!" And if you add free meals, free maid service, and free rein of your stuff, you could remove any motivation for them to get out there and find a job—*any job*—to pay some bills and get their adult life going for real. Can you say *codependency*?

This has become so prevalent in recent years that I'm honestly worried about the condition of this generation of men. The Census Bureau found that one-third of men ages 22–34 live with their parents![9] What?? A third of our nation's MEN— in the prime of their lives—live in their childhood bedrooms or their parents' basements! Are you kidding me? It's time for the eagle to leave the nest; otherwise that eagle will get comfortable and turn into a turkey pretty fast.

And parents, it may be time to kick some kids out—for their own good! We're not helping this generation by wrapping them in their old baby blankets. Instead, we're killing their future success and stealing their dignity! How will our kids ever experience the thrill of victory if we keep protecting them from the agony of defeat? Hey, some pain is good! It helps; it instructs; it directs. A pain-free life is a life without victory, risks, or hard-learned lessons that really make a man grow up.

Sure, there are some legitimate reasons for adult kids to come home again. Mom and Dad's house should always be a secure safety net if we take a bad fall. But I've never seen a daredevil fall, hit the safety net, and pitch a tent there. It's there to CATCH you, not to SHELTER you! I don't mean to be harsh here, but I've seen too many incredibly talented young men and women completely squander their full potential because they were "spared" the pressure to get out there and make something happen. So raise your kids right—then watch them fly away. And if they're scared to step out of the nest, well, it's nothing a little boot to the behind won't fix.

FAMILY, FRIENDS, AND MONEY

Dealing with Boomerang Kids isn't the only sensitive money situation we'll have, though. How many of us have parents, children, brothers, sisters, grandparents, or friends that we don't talk to much anymore because of money? Over the years on the radio and doing counseling, I've seen loans, inheritances, jealousy, and a ton of other financial issues completely destroy otherwise healthy relationships tens of thousands of times.

Young couples get into trouble with dumb decisions, and then they expect Mom and Dad to clean up the mess. Recent widows keep spending like normal after the breadwinner dies, and then they expect their adult kids to pay the credit card bills because "that's what a good daughter would do." A grand-mother loans Junior money for a new car, and then she never hears from Junior again. A buddy at work needs a quick $50 to make it until payday. A brother needs a $20,000 "investment" for a "no miss" business venture. Any of this sound familiar?

Are you a doormat if you give in to every request? Are you stingy if you don't? These things hit us every day from all sides, so we've got to learn some strategies to navigate our way through it. The first thing I recommend is for you to pick up the fabulous book *Boundaries* by Dr. Henry Cloud and Dr. John Townsend. They describe boundaries this way: "Just as homeowners set physical property lines around their land, we need to set mental, physical, emotional, [I'll add financial], and spiritual boundaries for our lives to help us distinguish what is our responsibility and what isn't."[10]

Giving a Drunk a Drink

The bottom line is that everything in my friends' and family's lives is *not* my responsibility. Whenever someone wants some-thing of mine—time, money, resources, etc.—I look carefully at the request. I always ask, "Will this truly help him, or will I just be giving a drunk a drink?"

I get several calls to my radio show every week from people asking me if they should give their brother/sister/mother/father/friend money. It's like they're all reading from the same script: "Dave, he told me that this is the last time. If I just pay this off for him, it will let him get back on his feet. It will bring him back up to zero, so he can start fresh. Sure, he's said that the past dozen times I've given him money, but he says he really means it this time. He hasn't listened to any of my advice or followed through with anything he said he'd do, but I have a responsibility to help him, right? I mean, he *is* family."

In a situation like that, I always answer the same way. First, I tell people to stop giving these needy friends and relatives an endless stream of money! If they don't change the behaviors that keep getting them into trouble, every dollar you give them in the name of "helping" actually hurts them, because it just enables their bad behavior.

Second, I tell people not to be scared to put conditions on a financial gift. You could give them money only if they agree to go through *Financial Peace University*. You could give them a copy of this book or another one of my books, *The Total Money Makeover*, and "pay" them to write you a book report. You could require that they submit three monthly budgets to you as you continue to help them through a transitional time. If they accuse you of butting in, just remind them that they are ASKING you to butt in by giving them money. If they want your help, they need to take *all* of your help, not just your money.

Third, I remind people that they can only help others if they have the cash on hand themselves. Never cosign a loan to "help" someone else, and never loan money to a friend or relative. That just keeps them in debt longer, strains the relationship, and keeps the cycle of destruction going.

Integrity and Value Systems

I also ask myself, "Does this fit within my value system?" For example, I don't borrow money, so of course I'm not going to cosign a loan for friend. It's not about the friend; it's that I believe debt is horribly destructive, so I can't help someone I care about go into debt. It goes against my value system. That doesn't make me mean or greedy. But I'm also not ashamed to be firm but fair in maintaining my boundaries. I'll try to help in other ways, but I can't violate my principles in the name of "helping."

Also note that when I choose to help people, I never loan them money. If I don't believe in debt, I'm certainly not going to become a lender. If I'm in a position to help, I just give the money. But it also means that even when I want to help, and even if the request is genuine and in line with my value system, I can't help them if I don't have the money. I'm not going to go into debt for myself, and I'm not going to go into debt for you. That's a matter of integrity.

Watching a Train Wreck Happen

What do you do with friends and relatives who are messing up their financial lives and don't ask for help? It's common for someone to go through *Financial Peace University* and then use these principles as a lens to analyze all the mistakes their friends are making. That's when they start using "Dave Ramsey says" like a club over the heads of unsuspecting friends, parents, brothers, and sisters! I've been doing this a long time, and I've never seen someone beaten into submission by a well-intentioned FPU graduate. My grandmother used to say, "Those convinced against their will are of the same opinion still."

So first, stop using my name as a weapon! Second, remember that you can't answer a question that hasn't been asked. If someone you love is goofing up with their money, don't barge into their business! Instead, you need to get them to ask for your help. That puts them in a position to actually listen to and receive your advice. Until they want your help, they'll just see you as intruding into their lives, and you'll risk losing the relationship.

There are a few ways I've found to get people to ask for my help. One of the best ways is to clean up your own financial life. Nothing speaks louder than a transformed life. If you used to be miserable and were under a pile of debt, but now you're debt-free and breathing easier than ever, your friends and family will notice. That testimony is powerful, and it will often bring you a lot of unexpected opportunities to talk to your friends about the change in your life.

Simple book recommendations go a long way, too. Read this book and *The Total Money Makeover* and just talk about what they mean to *you*. Stick to your own story, though; don't tell them what it could do for *them* unless they ask! And if you decide to buy a case of books as Christmas presents for everyone you know, at least put a note in each one telling them what the book meant to *you*. Otherwise, your Christmas gift might as well come with a card that says, "Hey, I just wanted you to know that we all see how badly you've screwed up with your money. Merry Christmas, you loser!"

JOIN THE CONVERSATION

We started our marriage with FPU, and it's been a very peaceful road so far, despite plenty of emergency spending situations (like when our car died and we had to buy a new one with cash).

—Jason

www.facebook.com/financialpeace

What Goes Around Comes Around

I've lived by these *Relating with Money* principles for more than twenty years, which means my own kids have been raised this way. Now that they're grown up, getting married, and stepping out into the world for themselves, it's been an incredible joy for Sharon and me to really see the fruit of this stuff in action. We applied it to our marriage, we instilled it in our children, we prepared them for adulthood as singles and then marrieds, and now we're watching our little birdies leave the nest and fly off. And we have no fears or doubts about where they'll land.

That's what I mean when I talk about "changing your family tree." No matter how far back in time your family has been screwing up with money, no matter how many generations deep the mess goes, all it takes is one person or couple to stand up and say, "Never again!" You have the chance to turn back the tide of generations of financial mistakes and carelessness. As Malcolm Gladwell might say, you can be *the tipping point*, the place where everything changes for your family for generations to come.

WE DID IT!

In 2000, we had three children graduate from college: one from undergraduate, one from law school, and one from graduate school. Free from nine years of triple tuition at private universities, I thought we were rich! For the next seven years I spent all the money that *had* been going for college. My husband had wanted us to live on a budget for thirty years, but I kept asking, "What does that mean?" We didn't have a clue!

Then in 2007, I signed up for a *Financial Peace University* class at our church. The very next week my husband fell and broke his shoulder and we were hit with $20,000 of medical expenses with no insurance. Suddenly, for the first time in my life, I was serious about a spending plan!

The great thing about FPU is that Dave "puts the cookies on the bottom shelf," which means I finally have the tools and understanding to plan a budget and get our debt and spending under control. Our communication in our marriage improved tremendously and we actually looked forward to discussing the monthly budget. It was difficult, but in twenty months we paid off $120,000 in debt! Now, three years later, our IRAs, taxes, and insurance are in order—and our house will be paid off this year! We're even taking a debt-free cruise this month for our thirty-eighth wedding anniversary to celebrate!

Thank you so much, Dave, for sharing your knowledge and your faith. God has used it to change our lives. To God be the glory!

Angela
Borger, TX

KEY POINTS

1. Men and women think differently about money.
2. Every marriage has a Nerd and a Free Spirit, and they must work *together*.
3. Singles should work with an accountability partner, someone with whom to discuss their finances, purchases, etc.
4. Parents must actively teach their kids about money with age-appropriate strategies.
5. Children must be taught from a young age that money comes from work, and that the three main uses of money are giving, saving, and spending.

QUESTIONS FOR REFLECTION

1. What advantages do singles have when it comes to controlling their cash flow? What are some disadvantages?
2. Why is it so important for married couples to agree on money management? Think in specifics *and* big picture.
3. Has financial stress ever caused you to make others (spouse, children, friends, etc.) believe money was more important to you than they were?
4. What are some practical ways to teach kids about money? How could you customize these methods to make them age-appropriate?
5. Reflect on this statement: "How you spend your money tells me who you are and what is important to you." How might this impact the way others see you?
6. In what ways could stress and fatigue impact your financial plan? Do you have specific examples?

3

CASH FLOW PLANNING

THE NUTS AND BOLTS OF BUDGETING

Tom called my radio show a while back to try to figure out why he couldn't make any headway with his family's finances. He was a pretty successful business owner and had several employees working for him. Profits were up, so his income had grown year over year for the past few years, but it seemed like every year he found himself deeper and deeper in debt.

He was frustrated. He could not understand why his income, debt, and stress were all going up at the same time! Doesn't more money automatically mean less debt and less money stress? Nope.

After talking for a couple of minutes, I said, "Tom, you obviously run a pretty good business. You have a budget for the business to track everything you have coming in and going out, right?" He said he did. I replied, "That's awesome. Now, do you have a budget for your home—a household budget?" Of course, he didn't.

Since I was talking to a business guy, I had to hit him where it hurts. I said, "Tom, let's pretend you run a company called You, Inc. And let's say you, as the owner of You, Inc., hired you to manage money for the company. If you managed money for You, Inc. the way you managed money for you now, would you fire you?" That did it.

BUDGET BASICS

Most people, even businesspeople who manage budgets all day at work, fail to bring that common-sense practice home with them. And without writing down what money's coming in and what money's going out every month, we'll never have any idea what's going on in our finances, and we'll never make any headway for the future. To win with money, we've got to embrace the dreaded B word: the *budget*.

Aiming at Nothing

Zig Ziglar says, "If you aim at nothing, you'll hit it every time." I love how Zig cuts right to the heart of the matter. If you don't have a target, if you don't have a goal in mind, then you'll never get where you want to go. Most people take a "Ready-Fire-Aim" approach to budgeting. They get the money, spend the money, and then wonder why they don't have any money. It's crazy!

My friend John Maxwell talks about this. In fact, he said my favorite quote of all time about budgeting: "A budget is just telling your money where to go, instead of wondering where it went." That might hit close to home with you. I've known countless people who have no idea where their money is going every month. They just fly by the seat of their pants week after week, and then look up at tax time and say something like, "What? We made $73,000 this year? Where did that $73,000 go?" They have no idea.

You cannot win with money by being passive. Money is active. It's going places; it's doing things all the time. It is flowing and has a certain current to it. That's why they call it *currency*! In his book *The Seven Habits of Highly Effective People*,

Stephen Covey says that effective people are *proactive*. That is, they *happen to things* instead of waiting around for *things to happen to them*. When it comes to personal finances, we've got to "happen" to our money. If we don't, the currency will just flow right over us and slip through our fingers.

JOIN THE CONVERSATION

Making a budget is easy! Sticking to it is HARD WORK!

—Stephanie

www.facebook.com/financialpeace

Consider the Cost

Jesus talked about budgeting in the Bible as a way to get the disciples to understand the cost of discipleship. He said, "For which of you, intending to build a tower, does not sit down first and count the cost, whether he has enough to finish it—lest, after he has laid the foundation, and is not able to finish, all who see it begin to mock him, saying, 'This man began to build and was not able to finish'?"[1] That's a real-world scenario, isn't it? It even includes your neighbors making fun of you!

Let's put that into today's terms. Imagine you were going to build a $400,000 home for your family. There's no way you'd just hand the builder a check for $400,000 and say something like, "Oh, I don't care what it looks like. Just throw something up with four walls over there, and let me know when it's done." No way! Instead, you'd have a gigantic stack of blueprints with every wall, shrub, fixture, pipe, outlet, and two-by-four drawn in perfect detail. You'd leave nothing at all to chance, because that would be a disaster.

However, the average family allows $400,000 to slip through their fingers every five or ten years. If your household income is $80,000 a year, five years of income for you is $400,000. If you don't have a plan in place telling every one of those dollars where to go and what to do, it's not much different than you just throwing a house together with no blueprint. You need a plan, and that plan is called a budget.

The Ground Rule . . . and Some Warnings

Starting this month and for the rest of your life, you need to do a written budget, or cash flow plan, every month. You're going to write down all of your expenses and all of your income on paper, on purpose, before the month begins. That statement freaks out all the Free Spirits; hey, it even freaks out a lot of Nerds! But doing this stuff on purpose is central to your long-term success. You will not win with money by accident!

I'll be honest: Your budget will not work the first month. You'll forget some things and have totally wrong numbers for certain categories. That's okay, and *it is going to happen*, so just expect it and don't let it derail you. Just plan on having one big Budget Committee Meeting at the start of the month and then a dozen "emergency" Budget Committee Meetings throughout the month as you make course corrections.

The second month, it will probably start working a little better, but will likely still be a bumpy ride. You'll have one month under your belt, so you'll be able to hone in on some of those amounts you allocated for food, gas, entertainment, and other things you've never tried to anticipate before. The third month, things will start to smooth out, but it still may not be perfect. But by then, you'll be on your way. It usually takes about three solid months of budgeting to get this right.

So whatever you do, *do not give up* when you get frustrated in the first ninety days. Budgeting is all about changing your behaviors with money, and behavior change takes time. Give yourself—and your spouse—some room to grow here, and do not expect an overnight miracle.

Along with the monthly budget, there's something else you have to do every month starting today: balance your checkbook. I am amazed at the number of people who don't know how to balance their checkbooks, or at least those who know how and still don't do it. Now, there's no shame if you just don't know how to do it. Again, that's a culture thing. The culture is telling you that nobody does this stuff, so a lot of people just never even think about it. But it's time to think about it.

If you honestly don't know how to balance—or reconcile—your checking account, it's easy to learn how. Most checkbook registers have the instructions right on them. Or, you can check out some of the resources at daveramsey.com or in the online bonus materials if you're in a *Financial Peace University* class. Again, I don't want to shame you if you don't know how to do it. The only shame would be if you go *another month* without learning! This is important!

Balancing your checkbook at least once a month keeps things in order and it prevents overdrafts on your account. Overdrafts are a sign of crisis living and sloppy, lazy money habits. But especially with the growing use of debit cards, overdrafts have become common—and the banks are racking up fees like crazy in "overdraft protection." In fact, the Center for Responsible Lending reported that overdraft fees alone brought in $10.3 billion for the banks in a single year recently.[2] If you turn those service fees into an annual interest rate, you'd see that these banks are charging the equivalent of 833 percent on thirty-day loans and up to 1,667 percent for fifteen-day loans. That's crazy, and even worse, it is 100 percent preventable—if you bother to balance your account regularly.

BUDGET OBJECTIONS

I've been teaching this stuff for a long time, and I talk to people about it on the radio for three hours every day, so I have heard every excuse in the book for why people don't do a cash flow plan. Everybody always thinks they have the one special reason why a budget won't work in their situation. Wrong! It works; it's just a matter of learning how to do it—and then *doing it*!

Why Don't We Do a Cash Flow Plan?

One reason people don't do a budget is because for many, it has a straitjacket connotation. That's why you'll never see me write a book called *Budgets Are Fun!* People just don't believe it. A lot of people would rather have a root canal than do a budget, or worse, read a book about budgeting! That's because many people see a budget as something restrictive, something that binds them up and takes away all their choices and freedom. That's a totally wrong view of a cash flow plan. Having a budget doesn't mean you can't order a pizza when you want one. It just means that you have a plan for your money. If you like pizza that much, then put a "Pizza" line on your budget! It's *your money*. I don't care what you do with it; I just want you to do it on purpose!

Another reason people don't do budgets is because a budget has been used to abuse them in the past. This is a tough one. A parent or a control-freak spouse has twisted their arm and beat them over the head with, "No! It's not in the budget! Get over it!" If you're doing that to a spouse, I have three words for you: *Cut it out!* You are not going to win over a reluctant spouse by turning the budget into a paper club. A budget is a method by which you make your money behave; it is *not* a method by which you make *other people* behave. Got it?

Of course, this doesn't mean that "anything goes," whether you have a budget or not. You still have to be responsible, and you still have to work together on your budget. If you want to make a big purchase, then work together to plan for it and determine if it is a wise purchase. We'll talk about those kinds of buying decisions in a later chapter.

One last reason why people often fail to do a budget is a big one: paralysis from fear of what they'll find. That's called *denial*. They're just afraid that if they actually balance the checkbook and write down all of their expenses, they'll have to face some things they don't want to face.

We had one guy in a *Financial Peace University* class who went home after the budgeting lesson and put everything on paper just like we taught. He came back the next week and said, "Well, Dave, we went home and we wrote it all down." I asked if anything specific jumped out at him. "Yessir. We found out that we've been spending $1,200 a month on restaurants. I now know why I don't have a retirement fund—I've been eating it!"

Those kinds of realizations may be a little scary, but guess what? Once that family figured out that they were literally eating $1,200 a month in restaurant meals, they immediately knew one big way they could turn their entire financial picture around. If they just cut that one budget item down to a reasonable $200 per month, they'd instantly have an extra $1,000 *every month*! What could you do with an extra grand a month? That's the same as giving yourself an instant $12,000 per year raise!

Why Some Budgets Don't Work

I want to be clear here: budgeting works. If you have a budget that's not working, it's not the budget's fault; it just means that you need to tweak how you're setting up the budget or, better yet, how well you're actually living on the budget. Some common reasons why budgets sometimes don't seem to work are:

1. You leave things out. Neither your spouse nor your budget can read your mind. If you forget to write something in the budget, then obviously you're going to have a problem when it comes time to pay for that thing. And *everybody* leaves *something* out of the budget sometimes. Maybe the kids have cheerleader fees that you forgot about, or maybe your car needs an oil change. You can plan for those things. It's not the budget's fault if you don't have "Oil Change" as a monthly budget item! Guess what? Cars need oil changes! It's not a surprise! That's why the budget forms in the back of this book are so detailed. We really go out of our way to try to help you anticipate all those little expenses that can

sneak up on you and derail the budget halfway through the month.

2. You overcomplicate your plan. Nerds, listen up. If you overcomplicate your cash flow plan, you're almost guaranteeing its failure. If it's a hundred pages long, or if it's a spreadsheet that requires a full ream of paper to print, it's doomed. You don't need an MBA to write out a budget, and you certainly don't need an MBA to read a budget. Keep it simple. That's a theme you'll hear from me over and over: those people who win with money over the long term do so by doing the same few simple things over and over again. It all starts with a budget that is easy to write out, understand, and live on.

3. You don't actually do it. Here's a shocker: if you don't actually do a budget, it won't work. But I have to tell people this over and over, because we live in a fast-paced, super-busy world. Days and weeks fly by, and it's easy to run into a new month without stopping to do a budget first. Never again! Remember, your goal is to write out the budget on paper, on purpose, *before the month begins*—every month!

4. You don't actually live on it. You can have the best budget in the world, but if it just stays in the realm of theory, it won't do you any good. It's like exercise. You can *think* about working out and *write out* a fantastic plan for how to get in shape, but if you never lace up your sneakers and actually *work out*, your excellent plan will fail miserably. Remember, we're dealing with behavior change, not math skills. The math stays on the paper, but the behavior is in how you actually apply the plan to your life.

BUDGET BENEFITS

You can see that I've heard all the excuses and complaints, but here's the deal: budgeting is crucial to your success. Your income is your responsibility. If you get to retirement with a mountain of debt and nothing to live on, it's no one else's fault. But beyond the obvious financial benefits to taking control of your money, there are a ton of other reasons to pull out the budget forms every month.

First Things First: The Four Walls

A written plan removes the "management by crisis" from your finances. You know what I'm talking about, right? We've already said that 70 percent of Americans are living paycheck to paycheck, just one missed payday away from disaster. When you're living on the razor's edge like that, with no plan at all for your money and no savings in the bank, it doesn't take much to qualify as a crisis. You could make $100,000 a year and still go into crisis mode if you need an unexpected $500 car repair!

No matter how blessed or distressed you are financially, your first priority every month is to cover what I call the Four Walls. Think of it as the four walls that hold your house together. They are food, shelter, clothing, and transportation. If you have food in your belly, a roof over your head, clothes on your back, and a way to get to work tomorrow, you'll live to fight another day.

Starting today, make a commitment to never allow anything or anyone to prevent you from covering these basics every month. You've got to take care of your family before you do anything else. The Bible says it this way: "If anyone does not provide for his own, and especially for those of his household, he has denied the faith and is worse than an unbeliever."[3] Your family comes first.

It's sad, but about a quarter of the people who come into our office for financial counseling are current with their credit cards but behind on their mortgage. How backward is that? I understand the reason, though. The credit card collectors start yelling at you if they even *think* you're going to be late with a payment. Mortgage companies act a little more dignified (at first, anyway), so they don't seem as intimidating. So what happens is that people put their houses in jeopardy in order to keep Visa and MasterCard off their backs. Never again! We'll cover this more later when we deal with collection practices.

Also, if you're sitting in a big mess right now and simply cannot afford to make even the minimum payments on your debts, don't lose hope! We'll deal with that situation in detail in chapter 5, *Credit Sharks in Suits*, where we'll talk about how to use the pro rata plan for working with creditors.

JOIN THE CONVERSATION

We were on the brink of divorce before we started doing a budget. Now, we have more communication and a happier marriage!

—**Bridgette**

www.facebook.com/financialpeace

The Money Stretcher

Managed money goes farther. It's the weirdest thing, but practically everyone who has gone through *Financial Peace University* or comes into our office for counseling says almost the same thing: "The first time we did a budget, it felt like we got a huge raise!" How does that happen? It's because when you write up a budget, you're accounting for every single dollar of your income. You know exactly what's coming in and exactly what needs to go out. You cut out all of those little expenses that fly into your wallet like moths and eat away at your money.

When you run your money through a budget, it just works harder. It has more muscle. It's like the guy who discovered he was spending $1,200 on restaurants every month. Once you cut out all the "spending by accident" stuff that most people never think about, you'll find money you never knew was there. You'll hear this from me a lot: your income is your most powerful wealth-building tool. But you'll only build that wealth and security if you free your income from accidental, careless spending and an endless cycle of debt payments.

No More Fights, Guilt, Shame, Fear, and Stress

Couples who actually agree on and live according to a written plan will automatically remove many of the money fights that plague so many marriages. Don't get me wrong, though; working on a budget together can actually *cause* a lot of marriage fights, so don't forget what we talked about in the last chapter! But long term, if you and your spouse work together on this money stuff, you're doing more than managing your income. You're coming together to agree on your goals, dreams, and priorities. I've heard from couples a million times that actually working on their finances saved their marriages. That's because it's not *just* about money. This is powerful stuff, and it has the power to create unity in your marriage. Don't miss that incredible opportunity.

A written plan will also remove a lot of the guilt, shame, and fear that may be associated with buying necessities for your family. I remember standing in the grocery store one day when Sharon and I were flat broke. I wrote a check for food and immediately got this sick feeling in the pit of my stomach, wondering if I had just spent the money that we needed to pay the electric bill. Sharon got that same feeling whenever she wrote a check for clothes that she or the kids needed. We felt like buying something we needed kept us from buying something else we needed, and it was a black cloud that followed us everywhere, every time we spent money.

You'll never have that feeling again once you start living on a written plan, because you'll know exactly how much money you have for food, and you'll know that the electric bill money is already budgeted. Everything is laid out in order, and you know precisely what's going on. It gives you this incredible sense of control and power in ways you'd never expect.

A budget will also remove the overdrafts, bounced checks, and overspending from your life. When you know how much you have to spend in each area—and when you actually live on that plan—all these things become nonissues. As a result, your stress level goes way down, because you really feel in control of your income and expenses.

THE BEST METHOD

When you sit down to do your budget, there's one crucial thing to remember: every month is different. There is no such thing as "the perfect month." That means you've got to do a fresh budget every single month. You can't just do a template of all your income and expenses and expect it to work every month. It won't. You've got to plan for each month, one month at a time.

Counting to Zero

One of my all-time favorite scenes of any movie is in *Jerry McGuire*. Remember the scene where Jerry is on the phone with his client, and he's about to lose him? He's willing to do anything it takes to keep that one client happy. What does Cuba Gooding Jr.'s character tell Jerry to do? What's the one thing he needed to hear? It's four simple words: "Show me the money!"

I make people stand up and shout that during my live events, and they all start out as hesitant and quiet as Jerry did in the movie. I tell them to shout it, and they just kind of whisper it and look down as they shuffle their feet. That's not good enough! I'll yell, "Say it again!" and they'll pick it up a little bit. I'll come back with, "Say it like you mean it!" and they'll start to scream. After four or five times, I'll hear up to ten thousand men and women yelling in unison, "SHOW ME THE MONEY!"

When you sit down to do a budget, that's what you're telling the paper. It should not be some calm, casual, half-thought-out, quiet discussion. You should sit down with your budget, calculator, and pencil and literally scream, "SHOW ME THE MONEY!" That's what your budget does; it shows you exactly where your money is, where it's going, what it's doing, and everything else. This is your financial well-being we're talking about here! Get excited! Make those dollars dance!

The best, easiest, and most powerful method is the zero-based budget. We've got forms in the back of this book that show you how to do it, and we even offer online budgeting software on daveramsey.com and in the online resources for our *Financial Peace University* class members. Whether you do it on paper or online with our software, the point is to be intentional about where every dime of your income is going.

The forms and online software have instructions to walk you through the budget, but I'll quickly cover the basics here. With a zero-based budget, your goal is to spend your income all the way down to zero before you ever even get paid. You'll write your income at the top of the page, and then you'll write every single expense for the month under it, including giving and saving. By the time you get to the bottom of the page, your income minus expenses should equal zero. If it doesn't, go back and adjust some numbers. Maybe you have some extra that could go toward clothing, or maybe it'd be nice to take your spouse out for a fancy meal at a restaurant. Again, it's *your* money; I don't care what you do with it, as long as you do it on purpose!

But if you're working the Baby Steps like we teach, then you know every cent of any extra money you have goes to Baby Step 1: saving up the $1,000 emergency fund first. After that, all the extra money goes toward Baby Step 2: the debt snowball. After that, everything you can squeeze out of the budget goes to Baby Step 3: filling up your full emergency fund of three to six months of expenses. If you're working through these first three Baby Steps, you already know where any "extra" money is going, so go back to the budget, adjust those categories, and write a zero at the bottom of the page.

Stuffing Envelopes for Fun and Profit

Back when Sharon and I went broke and we started putting our life back together, we were kind of stuck between our old ways of handling money and the new habits we were trying to form. After all, the old ways didn't really work out that well for us, did they? So we were doing monthly budgets and trying hard to live on them, but we kept getting into trouble. We had budgeted this much for food and this much for gas and this much for entertainment, but all that money was just sitting in one big lump in our checking account. That meant when we went to the store and wrote a check for groceries, we "kinda sorta" had an idea of how much we had left in the grocery budget, but not really. As a result, one of us was always overspending in an area, and the other one always got mad. We were budgeting, but we were still fighting about what we were spending!

Obviously, something had to change. Around that time, I learned about the cash-based envelope system from Larry Burkett. It was the first time I had ever heard of it, but Larry didn't create it—your grandmother did. This system has been around forever, but modern society has gotten too "sophisticated" for it. And by "sophisticated," I mean "broke" and "lazy."

Here's how the envelope system works. When you get paid, there are some expenses that can (or should) get zapped right out of your account. For example, retirement accounts and utility bills can be set up on auto-draft so you know that money's just gone. Other expenses require you to put a check in the mail or make a debit card payment online or by phone. These are things like doctor's bills. But there are a lot of things we pay for in person, purchases that actually require us to put a hand in a purse or pocket and pull out some form of payment. For most people, that's a credit card; for us, it's cash.

So, what Sharon and I did was identify those things in the budget that we could use cash for. For us, food, gas, and entertainment were no-brainers. We'd budget how much money we were going to spend on food for the month, and then when we got paid, we'd take that amount out of the bank in cash and put it in an envelope marked "FOOD." We didn't buy anything with that money except food, and we didn't buy food with any money except from that envelope. When the envelope was empty, we were done buying food. Overspending problem solved.

Clothing is another great opportunity for the envelope system. Ladies, if you're sick of your husband complaining that you're spending too much on clothes, then go to envelopes. Agree together on an appropriate amount for this budget category every month, put that cash in an envelope marked "CLOTHES," and you're done. Then you can buy whatever clothes you want—until the envelope is empty. She gets to shop, he's agreed to the boundaries, and no one is accusing the other of misbehaving. Everybody wins!

Dealing With an Irregular Income

I've been in sales most of my life, which means I've really never had a regular, consistent, this-much-every-two-weeks paycheck. Instead, I've always had what's called an *irregular income*. That just means my paycheck varies from check to check. If you're in sales or real estate, for example, you know exactly what I'm talking about. So when I talk about doing a zero-based budget every month, I get some pushback from people who have an irregular income. They sometimes think that just because they don't know exactly what they'll make for the month ahead, they don't have to do a budget. Not true!

We have a form in the back of this book designed specifically for those with an irregular income, but I'll go ahead and give you the nutshell version. If you're not sure how much you'll make each month, and if you don't know when you'll get your next commission check, your budget will look more like a list. At the top of the page, write down your first spending priority. Ask yourself, *If I only have enough money to do ONE THING this month, what would it be?* Write that at the top of the page. Then ask, *If I only have enough money to do ONE OTHER THING this month, what would it be?* Write that down. Continue this all the way down the paper until you've covered everything you could spend your money on (including debt payments, giving, saving, etc.).

Now, you're ready to get paid. When you get some money, you'll just work down the list. When the money's gone, you stop. Draw a line on the paper where the money runs out and carry those things into the next month's budget. An irregular income is no excuse for skipping the budget. In fact, not knowing how much you'll make or when you'll get paid makes your careful budgeting even more important!

FORMS FOR EVERYTHING

In the back of this book, you'll find a complete set of reproducible budget forms that walk you through pretty much every budgeting, retirement, insurance, and long- and short-term planning scenario. There are detailed instructions for the more complicated forms and overall instructions for how, when, and why to do the whole set. Spend some time getting to know the forms; they'll walk you and your spouse step by step through everything, and they'll probably remind you of some specific budget items that most people accidentally leave out of the budget at first.

I walk through the details of each of these forms in our *Financial Peace University* class, so if you're not in the class, you might want to check it out. And like I've said, we have a ton of budgeting resources available online in FPU's online resources for class members and at daveramsey.com.

I know budgeting isn't the most exciting topic in the world, so good for you for hanging with me all the way to the end of this chapter! Remember, though: personal finance is 80 percent behavior; it's only 20 percent head knowledge. All the books and forms and online resources in the world won't make a difference in your life unless you actually *do* this stuff! Don't just plow through this information. You need to slow down here, actually get the budget forms, and write out your budget. If this is all new to you, I challenge you to have your first complete monthly budget in place by the end of this week. I don't care what day of the month it is; you've got to start *sometime*! Today's the day!

I want to say this as clearly as possible: *You will never experience genuine Financial Peace—you will never win with money—until you do a budget.* The stuff I teach is not always easy or convenient, but if you do it, it absolutely works—every time.

WE DID IT!

When my husband and I first heard about Dave Ramsey, we were over $15,000 in debt, not counting our home mortgage. We also had $50,000 in debt on my husband's company. It was a nightmare! We tried to save money, but we had so many bills that we could never get ahead. When emergencies hit, I would cry myself to sleep worrying about where to get even $25 to pay a bill. Worst of all, I did all of the bill paying and my husband thought everything was "normal" about our way of living. We had cut back on everything and were living like paupers but still couldn't get ahead of the bills.

From the first lesson of *Financial Peace University*, I saw a change in my husband's views about money and we finally began to work as a team. We had our last real money fight during the second lesson, and we've had none since!

It's been six months since we completed the course. We have ZERO consumer debt and about $4,000 in savings, and we've also negotiated a way to get rid of our company debt. We have told everyone we meet about the course and know that those who take this class will see their financial lives in a brand-new light! Many thanks to Dave and his team!

Lauren
Lake City, MN

KEY POINTS

1. In order to win with money, you must spend all of your money on paper, on purpose—before the month begins. That's called a budget.
2. The envelope system is an effective way to manage key budget areas, such as groceries, entertainment, and gasoline.
3. Your budget will not work the first month! It usually takes about three months to really start running smoothly.
4. Use the forms in the back of this book or our online budget software to get your finances in order.

QUESTIONS FOR REFLECTION

1. What are some specific benefits of a written cash flow plan?
2. How can the written budget impact a marriage? How can it strengthen a single person?
3. If you have already been living on a budget, what are some specific ways it has helped you stay on target with your spending? If you've never lived on a budget, what concerns have prevented you from doing so?
4. How can the concept of the Four Walls (food, shelter, clothing, and transportation) empower you to prioritize your spending?
5. Have you ever allowed someone else (bill collector, salesperson, family member, etc.) to set your family's financial priorities? How did that happen, and how did it turn out?
6. In what budget areas could you immediately implement the envelope system? How do you feel about actually spending cash instead of using a credit or debt card for these purchases?

4

DUMPING DEBT

BREAKING THE CHAINS OF DEBT

I once heard the story of a clever English professor who wanted to teach her students the power of perspective. She walked into class and wrote the following on the board:

A WOMAN WITHOUT HER MAN IS NOTHING

She picked two volunteers from the class, one man and one woman. She brought them to the front of the room, handed each of them a marker, and asked them to provide the appropriate punctuation for the sentence she had written. The young man went first. He didn't pause at all as he walked up and made three quick marks making the sentence read:

A WOMAN, WITHOUT HER MAN, IS NOTHING.

He stepped back smiling, confident he had aced the assignment. Now it was the young woman's turn. She approached the board, shaking her head, and without hesitation she erased two of the guy's marks and replaced them with the following:

A WOMAN: WITHOUT HER, MAN IS NOTHING.

The lesson, of course, is that two people can *look* at the same thing but *see* two very different interpretations. It's all about our perspective; a simple change in perspective can fundamentally change our whole lives. That is exactly what I want to happen in how our country views debt.

A DIFFERENT PERSPECTIVE

The topic of debt is probably what I am best known for, but it's also the most challenging part of what I teach. My view of debt is completely perpendicular to every other message you get in our culture. We live in a world where it takes a total, national economic meltdown to get most people's attention about crazy mortgages and stupid credit card debt! If there's one good thing that's come from the national economic mess of 2008 and beyond, it's that some people are finally getting the message: debt is dumb!

The *Wall Street Journal* reported several years ago that 70 percent of Americans are living paycheck to paycheck. I've been using that figure for years, so I was curious if it had changed much in recent years. It hasn't. National Payroll Week's 2008 "Getting Paid in America" survey found that 70 percent of Americans would have difficulty meeting current financial obligations if their next paycheck was delayed by only one week.[1] That is heartbreaking. If you count ten homes on your street, seven of those families are living on a razor's edge, just one paycheck away from total financial disaster. The problem? Overspending and way too much debt.

The Greatest Marketing Job in History

Debt has been marketed to us in so many forms and so aggressively that to even imagine living without it requires a complete paradigm shift. That is, we have to totally change our way of thinking and do a full about-face when it comes to debt. The world wants us to believe that debt is a *service or reward* that is offered to help consumers. Lie! The truth is: debt is a product—the *most successfully marketed product in history.*

The banks and credit industry do such a fabulous job selling us on the idea of debt that we have gotten completely turned around on the issue. When you walk into a retail store and an aggressive salesperson runs up and asks, "Can I help you?" what's your gut reaction? Most of us put our guards up and instinctively say something like, "No thanks! I'm just looking!" Translation: "Get away from me! I'm just looking around, and if you're lucky, I'll buy your stuff."

But how do we approach debt? We run up to credit card sellers, fall down on bended knee, and plead, "Please! Please! Sell me your credit card! I *need* it!" And then, when they grant us the "blessing" of their product, we feel special. We think they've done us a favor by allowing us to buy from them. We feel like we've been *accepted*, like we've been granted access to an exclusive country club. "I'm special. My platinum card says so."

As a marketer, I have to give the industry some credit. They've done an amazing job of marketing their product. They've not only gotten nearly every American hooked on their goods, but they've done it in a way that makes the consumer feel special, accepted, and as though they've been done a favor. It's kind of scary how good a job they've done, in fact.

If you have a hard time viewing debt as a product that is sold and marketed, maybe this will help. In one recent year, the gross revenue for the entire credit card industry was more than $150 billion. That's more than the gross national product of

Egypt, Puerto Rico, and the Bahamas—*combined*. This is big, big money. It's their business, not a service. We've got to change our mind-set about debt and see it for what it is.

Our Parents' Lifestyle—Only Bigger, Better, and Faster

Sharon and I got married right out of college. We had some student loans and some more debt on a couple of little credit cards. We didn't have a lot of stuff, but that was okay. You know: "We don't have money, honey, but we've got love!" That was a good thing, because we *definitely* didn't have any money. We were broke!

Around that time, all my buddies were making fun of the car Sharon was driving, so I got embarrassed and went and got my wife a "safe," brand-new car . . . *that I wanted*. And we were huddled around a tiny little television in our apartment that started acting up, so I went down to the electronics store and bought a stereo television, which of course required a new stereo. Obviously, our little apartment didn't have enough furniture to hold that new stuff, so we had to get a new entertainment center to put it all in.

Soon, all our friends started buying houses, and our tiny, one-bedroom fleabag apartment started looking cramped. So, we bought a house with nothing down, because that's how much we had—*nothing*. They called it "creative financing," which is code for "too broke to buy a house."

That house we bought was in the same neighborhood that I grew up in. As I looked back on it later, it really struck me: we were trying to fast-track our way to the same standard of living as our parents. Financial expert and author Larry Burkett used to say that modern couples spend the first five to seven years of their marriage trying to attain the same standard of living as their parents—only it took their parents thirty-five years to get there.

That's how most couples start out these days. Out of school with some student loans, one or two car loans, a new house on crazy payments and no equity, a houseful of furniture on 90-days-same-as-cash, and a pretty lousy income. In fact, the average household income for a twenty-five-year-old couple is only $27,047.[2] With that kind of intense financial stress on a young marriage, is it any wonder why the divorce rate is so devastating for couples in their first few years of marriage? They're starting their lives together with a boat anchor around their necks. They don't stand a chance.

JOIN THE CONVERSATION

I figured out that credit cards are not for emergencies. That's what I have savings for. DUH!

—Jennifer

www.facebook.com/financialpeace

A HISTORY OF CREDIT

I bet this sounds like the start of most of the marriages you know. We usually forget, though, that debt has not always been a way of life. In the scope of American history, debt is still relatively new. Our great-grandparents pretty much believed debt was a sin! They thought it was morally wrong. As a matter of fact, I have an old Sears catalog from 1910 that says plain as day, "Buying on credit is folly!" Can you imagine Sears telling you that today?

Sears wasn't alone in the anti-debt stance, either. Have you ever wondered what the "J. C." stands for in J. C. Penney? It's named for the founder, James "Cash" Penney. He never allowed credit to be offered in any of his stores while he was alive. It was only after his death that credit cards and store credit slipped into J. C. Penney's business. And now, old James "Cash" is spinning in his grave.

Henry Ford hated debt so much that he didn't allow the use of credit at Ford Motor Company until ten years after the other carmakers were making car loans. With Henry long gone, Ford Motor Credit is now a huge part of the family business.

So our great-grandparents thought debt was a sin. Our grandparents weren't quite as strict, but they still thought it was really stupid and only borrowed on a few things. In 1950, Frank McNamara changed the whole financial landscape of the country with a little piece of plastic called Diner's Club. He had made deals with several restaurants in New York City, who all agreed to accept this single form of payment across all the different businesses as a "convenience" to the consumers. Right then and there, the credit card was born.

A few years later, in 1958, a little bank on the West Coast, called Bank of America, sent a mailing out to about sixty thousand of their customers that contained a similar piece of plastic called the BankAmericard. That same year, a new company emerged to "help" consumers make easy payments, and American Express was born. Now, of course, American *Excess* is a way of life, but then, our grandparents were a lot less trusting.

Our parents were more accepting, though, and they started borrowing on even more things. Credit cards started popping up more often, and in 1976, BankAmericard changed its name—to Visa. Heard of them? Ten years later, in 1986, Sears got into a big dispute with Visa, which resulted in Sears branching out and taking Visa on head-to-head with their new card, which they called Discover. Discover quickly became the most profitable division of Sears, so a while later, when Sears was in serious financial trouble, selling off the Discover brand was one of the things that saved them from bankruptcy.

I usually don't dive into the history of debt in this kind of detail, but I personally find it fascinating. Credit practically didn't exist, as we know it, just fifty years ago, but today, we can't imagine living without car loans and credit cards! The thought of actually paying with cash at a department store has become somewhat of a novelty. Can you imagine that in 1970, only about 15 percent of Americans had a credit card? Today, 77 percent of all adults have at least one card, and the average cardholder has more than seven cards![3] It feels like the Visa brand has been around since the dawn of time, but Visa as a household name is just a little over thirty years old. Again, that's some *incredible* marketing power.

BUSTING THE MYTHS

We weren't born to use debt. Our country was not founded on easy financing and 90-days-same-as-cash. The great fortunes in the history of America weren't built on cash-back bonuses and free airline miles. We've been sold a bill of goods, and it's a total lie. And if you tell a lie or spread a myth often enough, loud enough, and long enough, eventually the myth becomes accepted as truth. That's where we are with debt in America: trapped in the myth that credit is a normal, healthy part of life.

Along with that main lie, there are several other sub-myths, tricky little beliefs that individually may not look that bad, but when taken together can absolutely destroy your financial peace. I've gone into great detail with some of these myths in my book *The Total Money Makeover*. Here, I'm going to quickly review those and drop in a few more just for fun.

Myth: If I loan money to a friend or relative, I will be helping them.
Truth: The relationship will be strained or destroyed.

Proverbs 22:7 says, "The rich rules over the poor, and the borrower is the slave of the lender."[4] This is a verse you'll hear me repeat over and over, because it perfectly captures the biblical view of debt: "The borrower is the slave of the lender." That word "slave" isn't used carelessly in the inspired Word of God. This is serious business. If you loan your son $1,000, you immediately change the relationship. Thanksgiving dinner won't be the same, because it won't be a simple, loving time with family; it will be a master eating turkey with his slave. That's some foul bird.

It doesn't matter if you mean to or intend to, and it doesn't even matter if you believe me or not. It happens. It's not a choice you make; it's a biblical principle and a fact of life. The statistics prove the biblical point too. Bankrate.com reports that 57 percent of people have seen a friendship or relationship end because of loaning money, and 63 percent have seen someone skip out on repaying a friend or family member.[5] Do you want to inject some poison into your closest relationships? Then by all means, start loaning money.

Myth: By cosigning a loan, I am helping out a friend or relative.
Truth: The bank requires a cosigner because the person isn't likely to repay.

Remember, debt is the most marketed product in the history of the world. Banks go out of their way to put their services in front of the consumer in an all-out cage match with other banks just to get a shot at loaning us money. So if a bank goes through all that time, trouble, and expense to get someone to borrow money and then *turns that person down* for a loan, does it really take a genius to figure out why? They know the person won't pay the money back!

I am amazed at the number of parents and grandparents who fall into horrible cosigning deals! "Oh, they just don't know Junior the way I do." You're right! They know Junior better than you do in this area. They're not blinded by love or codependency, and they can see that Junior is a deadbeat waiting for a place to happen! I know, because I've been on the hook for a deadbeat twice. I've cosigned two loans in my life, and I personally repaid both of them. Heck, I've even had someone cosign a loan *for me* once, and *they* had to pay back that loan because I couldn't! I went back and repaid them later, but that's not the point! The point is, cosigning is a nightmare that will make you broke and destroy your relationships. The Bible is crystal clear on this: "It's stupid to guarantee someone else's loan."[6] Gotta love the Contemporary English Version, don't you?

Myth: Cash advance, rent-to-own, title pawning, and tote-the-note car lots are needed services for lower-income people to get ahead.

Truth: These are horrible, greedy ripoffs that aren't needed and benefit no one but the owners of these companies.

You can usually judge the economics of a neighborhood by the number of cash advance and rent-to-own businesses you see up and down the thoroughfares. If you're in a wealthy part of town, you really won't see any of these places. If you're in a poor part of town, you'll probably see them scattered every-where, even next door and across the street from each other. That should be your first sign that these are horrible businesses designed to keep people broke.

You might think that these businesses aren't in nice neigh-borhoods because "all those rich people" don't need their "ser-vices." Bull! The truth is, wealthy people wouldn't dream of using such a ripoff; it's not *because* they're rich; it's *why* they're rich. Wealthy people don't throw their money away. Cash advance is a poor man's activity. I don't want to be poor! If I want to be rich, I'm going to do what rich people do. If I want to stay broke, I'll do what broke people do. It's almost just that simple.

The "service fee" on that payday loan may not seem like that big a deal—until you see it as an annual rate. Would you defend a credit card company with an APR of 800 percent, or even up to 1,800 percent? Heck no! Then stop telling me a payday loan is a good idea. It's predatory lending at its worst, and it is one big reason why broke people get stuck in a downward spiral of uncontrollable debt. This is trash, plain and simple.

Myth: Playing the lottery and other forms of gambling will make me rich.
Truth: The lottery is a tax on the poor and on people who can't do math.

Have you ever seen a long line of people in business suits, fine dresses, and expensive jewelry at the lottery ticket counter? Me neither. If this was the way to get rich, I promise you'd see some rich people standing in line. As it is, though, all I ever see in that line are broke people. And it's sad, because I'm seeing them get even broker right in front of my eyes.

Texas Tech did a study on lottery players and found that people without high school diplomas spent $173 a month playing, while college graduates who played only spent $49.[7] That study makes me sick. I can't even process broke people spending $173 a month on the lottery, so let's just look at those paying $49. If you invest $50 a month at the stock market average of 12 percent, every month, from age twenty to age seventy, you will end up with $1,952,920—EVERY TIME! Not if you get lucky. Not if you pick the right numbers. Not if you score on a scratcher. EVERY TIME!

Another study found that people with incomes under $20,000 were twice as likely to play the lottery than those making over $40,000.[8] This is a tax on the poor! *But Dave, it's fun!* Throwing money in the toilet is fun? Then why don't you just cut out the middleman and flush your whole paycheck as soon as you get it? *But Dave, it helps fund our state's education.* That's fantastic: broke people paying for rich people's kids to go to college. There's a plan. Here's a better one: pay at the pump and skip the lottery line at the gas station. That's broke people behavior, plain and simple.

JOIN THE CONVERSATION

There's always extra money somewhere, and it can go toward the debt snowball!

—Ada

www.facebook.com/financialpeace

Myth: Car payments are a way of life, and you'll always have one.

Truth: The typical millionaire stays away from car payments by driving reliable used cars.

I hear this a hundred different ways every day: "You'll *always* have a car payment. Car payments are a way of life. You're always going to have a payment, so you might as well drive a nice car." That is one of the biggest lies in the debt industry, but it has been packaged so well that most people believe it. And trust me, if you go through life thinking you'll *always* have a car payment, there will be plenty of people who will *help you* to always have a car payment.

We Americans *love* our cars. We put our whole identity in them, like we're actually saying, "I'm a Lexus." We'll drop $600 a month on a payment just to impress someone at a stoplight that we'll never meet. That's crazy, and it's not at all how real millionaires behave. The average millionaire drives a nice, slightly used, two- or three-year-old car that they bought with cash, and they practically never drive a brand-new car off the lot.

People always say, "Well, Dave, if I were a millionaire, I'd be able to pay cash for a car, too!" No, you're not getting it. These people don't buy with cash because they're rich; they're rich because they buy cars with cash! Think about how much the average American spends on car payments over his lifetime. The average payment is around $464 a month right now. If you invest $464 in a good mutual fund every month from age thirty to age seventy, you'll end up with more than $5 million. Now, I love nice cars, but I've never seen one worth $5 million!

If you call my radio show, struggling to get out of debt, you can almost guarantee that the first words out of my mouth will be, "Sell the car!" If you want to take control of your money, you've got to amputate the out-of-control lifestyle. For most people, that starts with the car payment.

Myth: Leasing your car is what sophisticated, financial people do.

Truth: The car lease is the most expensive way to operate a motor vehicle, period.

Have you ever wondered why car dealers focus most of their advertising and sales techniques on leasing instead of buying? Let me clear it up for you: they make more money on a lease than anything else (with the exception of the repair center). Car leasing is a total sinkhole of financial waste. If a dealer sells you a car for cash, they make about $80 profit. That's not a great deal for them. If they sell you a car on payments, they do better; they'll make around $775 by selling the loan to another bank. If they can get you to lease it, however, their profit jumps up to more than $1,300 per car. So let's see . . . cash sales make them $80, and a lease makes them $1,300. Which one would they possibly prefer you to take? Duh.

A good friend of mine runs a luxury car lot. According to him, about 78 percent of the cars that drive off the lot are lease deals. That means three out of every four of his buyers take bad deals in order to look like something they're not. They're broke, and they're doing broke people stuff. You see, rich people ask, "How much?" Broke people ask, "How much down and how much per month?" When a rich person says she can afford it, she means she can *actually* afford the car. When a broke person says she can afford it, she means she can probably make the monthly payment as long as there are no emergencies and she doesn't lose her job. You'll never get rich as long as you do broke people stuff.

And don't talk to me about the tax advantages of leasing a car. You can write off mileage and depreciation on a car that you actually *own* and get the same tax advantages as a horrible lease.

Myth: I can get a good deal on a new car.

Truth: A new car loses 70 percent of its value in the first four years.[9] That's a bad deal regardless of the sticker price.

A new car is the largest purchase most of us make that actually goes *down* in value—and it goes down in value "like a rock." That's where Chevy got the line! Let's put the numbers in perspective. If you buy a brand-new $28,000 car, it's going to be worth $8,400 in four years. That means you're losing $408 every month in depreciation. If you think you can afford that hit, then try this: once a week on your drive to work, roll down the window and throw a hundred-dollar bill out. Can you afford that? I don't think so.

I talk about cars all the time on my radio show, in my other books, at our live events, and especially in our *Financial Peace University* class. It all comes down to this, though: there is no such thing as a good deal on a new car. The instant you drive it off the lot, you are immediately losing money, and you can't drive that car fast enough to catch up. Is it ever okay to buy a brand-new car? Sure, when you have a million dollars in the bank and can actually afford the financial hit of throwing tens of thousands of dollars away just for fun. Until then, do what most millionaires do: buy slightly used and pay with cash.

Myth: I'll take out a thirty-year mortgage and pay extra to pay it off early.

Truth: Life happens! Something else will always seem more important, so almost no one pays extra every month.

We'll cover all the different types of mortgage options in a later chapter, so we can attack them in detail then. For now, I'll just lay out my suggestion for mortgages as plainly as I can. Of course, my favorite mortgage is the "100% Down Plan," meaning you pay cash for your house. It's not as crazy as it sounds! But if you absolutely must take out a mortgage, never get more than a fifteen-year fixed-rate mortgage, and never get a payment that is more than 25 percent of your take-home pay.

Stay away from adjustable rates, balloons, ARMs, and all the other garbage options. And definitely stay away from a thirty-year loan! Let's break down some hard numbers. If you take a thirty-year loan on a $225,000 mortgage at 6 percent, your payment will be around $1,349. The same loan on a fifteen-year term will have a payment of about $1,899, or $550 more. These are the numbers most people look at when they're sitting at the finance table. But remember, rich people don't ask, "How much per month?" Instead, they ask, "How much?" So let's see "how much" this deal eventually costs.

In this example, if you took out the thirty-year mortgage, you'd end up paying $485,000 for that $225,000 loan. But if you take the fifteen-year, you'd end up paying just $341,000. That means for an extra $550 per month, you'd save yourself $143,000 *and* fifteen years of debt! And the thing about fifteen-year mortgages is that they *always* pay off in fifteen years—or less. If you get a thirty-year and think you'll pay it off like a fifteen-year, you're fooling yourself. Something else will also be more important or more urgent, and you'll never systematically pay it off early.

Myth: I need a credit card to rent a car or to make purchases online or by phone. Truth: A debit card will do all of that.

I run a big company with more than three hundred team members. We have groups traveling all over the country for business year-round. I've personally traveled all over the globe. We rent cars, book hotels, buy meals, and make purchases online every single day. And we do every bit of it with our debit cards.

I have two pieces of plastic in my wallet: one debit card for the business and one debit card for my personal account. That's it. If your debit card carries the Visa or MasterCard logo, then you have all the same protections with your debit card that you'd have with a credit card. The only difference is that your debit card won't allow you to rack up a pile of debt.

Myth: If I pay my credit card off every month, I'll enjoy the perks without the pain of overspending and debt.
Truth: When you pay with plastic instead of cash, you spend more.

We have an emotional, sometimes physical, response to spending actual, hard-earned dollars that we never feel when we swipe a piece of plastic. Carnegie Mellon did a study of the neurological impact of big purchases, and the results surprised a lot of people (not me). They hooked up a test group to MRI machines and monitored them as they went through different buying scenarios. They discovered they could predict when a person would or would not go through with a purchase based on their brainwave activity. When these people were faced with the prospect of handing over a fistful of actual cash, the pain centers in their brains lit up like Christmas trees! But when they used plastic instead of cash, they were much more likely to do the deal because there was hardly any pain registered at all. The bottom line: spending cash hurts![10]

McDonald's found this out in a more practical way several years ago: they started taking plastic. *Nightline* reported that when the fast-food chain started accepting credit cards as a form of payment, their average sale went from $4.75 to $7.[11] That's a 47 percent increase, and the only thing that changed was the method of payment! That's because it's a lot easier to add on a large fry and an apple pie when you aren't that concerned with how many dollar bills you have in your pocket.

JOIN THE CONVERSATION

You don't have to keep student loans—there is no such thing as GOOD debt.

—Dara

www.facebook.com/financialpeace

Myth: I'll make sure my teenager gets a credit card so he/she can learn to be responsible with money.

Truth: Teens are a huge target of credit card companies today.

This is one of the most devastating myths of all, and it is something the credit card companies have packaged and sold you with incredible effectiveness. Your teenager is the number-one target of credit card companies. Why? Because they've already given you all the cards they can! They're moving on to the next generation of debtors.

The problem is that our kids cannot handle the pressure of "easy" credit. Heck, most adults I know can't handle it, either! Some colleges are losing more students to credit card debt than to academic failure. In 2001, more young adults filed bankruptcy than graduated college![12] This is a huge, *huge* problem, and we are absolutely not helping our kids by putting credit cards in their hands. I wrote about this in my book *The Total Money Makeover:*

You are not teaching your sixteen-year-old child to spend responsibly when you give him a credit card any more than you are teaching gun responsibility by letting him sleep with a loaded automatic weapon with the safety off. In both cases, you as a parent are being stupid. People with common sense don't give sixteen-year-olds beer to teach them how to hold their liquor. By giving a teenager a credit card, the parent, the one with supposed credibility, introduces a financially harmful substance and endorses its use, which is dumb but unfortunately very normal in today's families. Parents must instead teach the teenager to just say no.[13]

Myth: The home equity loan is good for consolidation and is a substitute for an emergency fund.

Truth: You don't go into debt for emergencies.

This one is double dumb. First of all, it presumes you don't have an emergency fund, which means you can't cover any emergency at all with cash. Dumb. Second, it says that you should go deeper into debt in the face of a major emergency! Double dumb! If you're sitting in the middle of a major financial emergency, the last thing you want to do is dig a deeper hole *and* put your house at greater risk in the process!

Myth: Debt consolidation saves interest, and you get just one smaller payment.

Truth: Debt consolidation is a con. You can't borrow your way out of debt.

Consolidation typically saves little to no interest, because you'll throw your low-interest loans into the deal. The main problem, though, is that consolidation only treats the symptom (debt) without treating the cause (overspending). Most people who consolidate their debts into one payment attached to a home loan go right back into debt on the credit cards. Only then, they have a consolidation loan *and* a huge credit card bill. So they naturally end up worse than they started!

Besides, "smaller payments" is code for "more time in debt." The goal is to get out of debt—fast and forever. That doesn't happen with little-bitty, comfortable payments. If you want out of debt, you've got to do whatever it takes to throw huge payments at your debt every single month! There is no easy solution to debt. It takes time, discipline, and a heck of a lot of hard work! We'll talk about that after we cover this one last myth.

JOIN THE CONVERSATION

This lesson taught me that it's my money, not theirs, and I get to say who gets paid and who doesn't.

—Stewart

www.facebook.com/financialpeace

Myth: Debt is a tool and should be used to create prosperity.
Truth: The borrower is slave to the lender.

Back when I was getting out of debt, I really started to think about who taught me that debt was a tool. It was my old finance professors . . . who, by the way, were all broke. Something's definitely wrong with this picture, right? But that's the message I got in school: "Debt is a tool. Debt is like a fulcrum and lever. Debt is like a knife—it can help you or hurt you. Debt enables you to do things you'd never be able to do otherwise. Debt gives you the power of OPM—*other people's money*—and allows you to use it for your own ends." That is such a load of bull, but I bought it hook, line, and sinker. But not anymore.

I don't take advice from broke people anymore. I figured out a while back that if I want to win, I need to find some people who are winning and do what they're doing. If you want to get in shape, go spend time with some athletes. If you want to have a successful marriage, go spend time with a gray-haired couple who have been married sixty years and are still holding hands. And if you want to win with money, go find some people who are doing it right and do what they're doing. That's what I did.

Over the years, I have been blessed to spend a lot of time with some super successful men and women. The view of debt they've taught me is a lot different than what the broke finance professors taught. I have never met one millionaire who said, "Dave, the secret to my fortune is Discover cash-back bonuses" or "I'll tell you how I've been able to travel the world: free airline miles on my Visa." No, they all pretty much say the same thing: the most important key to building wealth is becoming and remaining debt-free.

Your largest wealth-building tool is your income. Over the course of your working lifetime, literally millions of dollars will pass through your hands. That's what you'll use to build wealth. It won't be lottery tickets or payday loans or American Excess. Your secret weapon is your income, but if every dollar of your income goes to an endless stack of payments every month, you're literally robbing yourself of millions of dollars in future wealth.

Proverbs 22:7 says it clearly, "The borrower is the slave of the lender." SLAVE. A slave can't go where he wants or do what he wants, because he is always working for somebody else. He can't make his own decisions, and he isn't free to become the person he wants to be. That's exactly what debt does to you. When you go into debt, you aren't using someone else's tools; you're submitting yourself to a new master. It doesn't get any clearer than that.

BEAT DEBT

Like I said before, these myths have been spread so loud and so long, it might feel totally weird to change your way of thinking now. That's fine with me. "Normal" in North America is *broke*. I don't want to be normal; I want to be *weird*! But I talk to people every day who have bought into the lies, who have run up their credit cards, taken out ridiculous mortgages on houses they weren't ready to buy, and who have more debt tied up in new cars than they make in a year. They did it for the same reason most of us have done it—because they didn't know any better. *That's just what people do. Debt is a tool to get us everything we need or want, right? Right?* Wrong.

Gazelle Intensity

If I've managed to convince you that debt really is dumb and that a debt-free life is *amazing*, then I want to share with you the secret to getting out of debt. There are a few steps out of debt that we'll talk about next, but there's one thing that is absolutely essential. No theories or principles or flowcharts or academic explanations will do anything to get you over the mountain of debt without this one fundamental ingredient. We call it "gazelle intensity."

Years ago, I was reading my way through the book of Proverbs. I came to Proverbs 6, which says, "My son, if you become surety for your friend [Bible talk for debt] . . . Give no sleep to your eyes, nor slumber to your eyelids. Deliver yourself like a gazelle from the hand of the hunter."[14] I wrote about this in my book *The Total Money Makeover*:

> I remember reading that Bible verse in my daily Bible study one day and thinking what a cute animal metaphor it was for getting out of debt. Then one day later that week I was surfing channels and hit the Discovery Channel. I noticed they were filming gazelles. The gazelles were peacefully gazelling around. Of course, you know the Discovery Channel wasn't just there for the gazelles. The next camera shot was of Mr. Cheetah sneaking up in the bushes looking for lunch in all the right places. Suddenly, one of the gazelles got a whiff of Mr. Cheetah and became very aware of his plan. The other gazelles noticed the alarm and soon also were on edge. They couldn't yet see the cheetah, so out of fear of running at him, they froze until he played his cards.
>
> Realizing he had been discovered, Mr. Cheetah decided to give it his best shot and leaped from the bushes. The gazelles all yelled, "Cheetah!" Well, not really, but they did run like crazy in fourteen different directions. The Discovery Channel that day reminded viewers that the cheetah is the fastest mammal on dry land; he can go from zero to forty-five miles per hour in four leaps. The show also proved that because the gazelle will outmaneuver the cheetah instead of outrunning him, the cheetah will tire quickly. As a matter of fact, the cheetah only gets his gazelle burger for lunch in one out of nineteen chases. The gazelle's primary hunter is the fastest mammal on dry ground, yet the gazelle wins almost every time. Likewise, the way out of debt is to outmaneuver the enemy and *run for your life*.[15]

They will chase you. They will hunt you. They will lure you in. They will try to make you comfortable. They will dangle all kinds of incentives in front of you. They will do anything and everything they can to corner you, trap you, and eat you alive! *This is how the Bible describes getting out debt*: If you want to live, you've got to RUN! You won't wander out of debt. You won't stroll out. You'll only get out if you set your eyes on the goal and attack your debt with gazelle intensity!

Steps Out of Debt

So with gazelle intensity as the background for everything else we'll talk about, there are five steps that will lead you out of debt and into a debt-free, stress-free way of life.

1. Quit borrowing more money!

You can't get out of a hole if you keep digging out the bottom. The first thing you have to do is stop the bleeding, which means you have to make the decision *today* to not borrow another dime. That means credit cards too. It's time for some plastic surgery, and all it requires is a pair of scissors. That's right, I'm actually telling you to cut up those cards and never look back! We call it a *plasectomy*, and it's the most life-changing procedure you'll ever have with your money. If you're currently in *Financial Peace University*, bring those cards to class and chop them up in front of everyone. You could be the one to start a whole wave of plasectomies in your group!

2. You must save money!

Getting the credit cards out of people's wallets is one of the toughest things I do. We've become so dependent on plastic that it scares some people to death to imagine not having one.

The credit card has replaced the emergency fund for most Americans, and that's one reason why so many people can't get ahead. That's why Baby Step 1 is a beginner emergency fund of $1,000. If you have that in the bank, guess what? You can pay to fix a flat tire. You don't need a credit card for that.

3. Prayer really works!

I'm not a preacher or theologian; I'm just a regular guy. But after years and years of doing this, I know for a fact that prayer changes things. You've got a Father in heaven who loves you like crazy, and He's rich! He wants to help you, to dress you up and love on you. I'm not saying God will make you a million-aire; I just want you to "call home" and talk to your heavenly Father about what's going on.

4. Sell something!

Sell so much stuff the kids think they're next! Name the dog "eBay" and call the cat "Craigslist"! Everything that is not tied down with the possible exception of your house may need to hit the classified ads *this week*. I challenge you to walk through your house, look at everything, and ask, "Do I want *this thing* more than I want to be out of debt?" That's a tough question, and you may find that your priorities have changed a whole lot since you originally bought that *thing* that you *could* turn into dollars.

I want you to have some nice stuff, but most Americans have garages and attics and rental storage units filled floor to ceiling with garbage they don't need. That's part of the reason why they're broke! One or two good garage sales and some online sales could clear out the clutter *and* get you out of debt. You could probably have your Baby Step 1 emergency fund in the bank in a few days just from the money you'd make on one garage sale this weekend!

5. Get to work!

My grandmother used to say, "There's a great place to go when you're broke: to work!" One of the main lessons I've tried to teach my kids from a young age is that money comes from work. Work creates income. If you need more money, it can be as simple as working more. Now, I don't want you to be a workaholic for the rest of your life, but if $8,000 is all that is standing between you and debt freedom, then I've got good news: You can be out of debt within a year just by throwing a few pizzas! We'll talk about a few different part-time jobs and home-based business ideas in the *Working in Your Strengths* chapter later.

THE DEBT SNOWBALL

We covered Baby Steps 1 and 3 in the *Super Saving* chapter. Now let's go back and fill in the gap with Baby Step 2. You'll remember that Baby Step 1 is $1,000 in the bank as a beginner emergency fund. With that money sitting in the bank as a buffer between you and life's little financial emergencies, it's time to take the next step.

Baby Step 2: Pay Off All Debt Using the Debt Snowball

The goal of the debt snowball is to get you out of debt while giving you quick wins and allowing you to build up huge momentum as you work through your list of debts. The plan is simple: List all of your debts (except your primary mortgage) from smallest to largest based on payoff balance, not interest rate. Then you'll work down the list and knock them out in that order. People sometimes say, "But Dave, doesn't it make more sense mathematically to pay off the highest interest rates first?" Maybe. But if you were doing math, you wouldn't have credit card debt, would you?

This is about behavior modification. You need some quick wins or you will lose steam and get discouraged. A gazelle needs a quick meal when it starts running! Knocking out a few small bills that have been buzzing around your head for months like mosquitoes gives you a boost. And every time you cross a debt off the list, you get more energy and momentum because you can see, maybe for the first time, that you're actually going somewhere! You start the plan with a few wins and all of a sudden, the emotional roller coaster of debt isn't a roller coaster anymore; it's a freight train that's heading downhill fast!

Focus on the first little debt, and attack it with gazelle intensity! Pay minimum payments on all your debts except for that one. With this one debt in your crosshairs, throw every dollar you can at it until it's gone and out of your life for good. Then cross it off the list and attack the next one. Every time you knock out a debt, you take the money you were throwing at it, along with any other cash you can squeeze out of the budget, and move on to the next one. So as you work down the list, you have more money to apply to each debt. That's why we call it a snowball; as the snowball rolls over, it collects more snow and gets bigger, so by the time it's halfway down the hill, it's an avalanche!

Use the Debt Snowball Form in the back of this book or download a copy from daveramsey.com. If you're in a *Financial Peace University* class, you can even use our online budgeting software to track your debt snowball and figure out your exact debt-free date.

What About Retirement and Savings?

While you're working your debt snowball, I suggest you temporarily stop all retirement savings, even a 401(k) that has an employer match. This makes a lot of people nervous, and I understand that. I'm a math nerd, and I know that getting a 100-percent match on your contributions is a sweet deal. That's why I want you to get out of debt as fast as possible, so you can get back to your investments and really do it with style without worrying about debt payments hanging over your head!

Most families going through our program are totally debt-free except for their house within eighteen months, so I'm only talking about unplugging your 401(k) for a year and a half or so. This will give you more money to use to get out of debt, and the motivation to get back to your long-term investing will add a little more fire to your get-out-of-debt-fast plan. Just imagine how much you'll be able to save and invest once you're free from all your debt payments every month! Unless you are in an extremely deep hole that will take years and years to climb out of, shutting down the 401(k) contributions for the short term is a good plan.

One more word on retirement savings: although I want you to stop contributing to your retirement account temporarily, I *do not* recommend cashing out your 401(k) or other retirement accounts and using that money to pay off debt. If you cash out a 401(k) early, you'll lose around 40 percent of your money in penalties and taxes. That is literally throwing half your money out the window, and it is a horrible, horrible idea. Don't do it, no matter how tempting it is, unless it is the only thing that will keep you from a bankruptcy or foreclosure.

Your Most Important Wealth-Building Tool

I'll say it again: Your most important wealth-building tool is your income. Forget luck and the lottery; it's your *income* that will build your wealth over the course of your working life. If your income is completely eaten up by payments every month, you'll be missing out on a lifetime of wealth-building opportunities. The debt snowball is probably the most important part of the whole process, because with it you'll draw a line in the sand, commit to getting—and staying—out of debt, and free up your income to build wealth like crazy!

WE DID IT!

We have been married for twenty-five years, and we've always seemed to live pretty well—even though we've really been on the edge of total financial disaster. We have owned our business for over seventeen years, and even opened another new business five years ago. Since then, we have racked up over $425,000 in debt not counting our house—$170,000 just in credit cards alone! Two years ago, our business was heading downward, but we were in denial about the economy and did not make the changes necessary to keep us afloat.

Needless to say, last year we were about to file bankruptcy. Instead, we decided to try to work things out with our creditors and stop using credit altogether. After all, we owed this money and did this to ourselves. In September, we joined a local *Financial Peace University* class. At one point, I admit that I wanted to quit because I thought that we were just in too deep for this to work for us, but my class coordinator, Susan, talked me into staying with it. Thank you, Susan!

Since we first started the class, we've knocked $30,000 off our debt. We still have a long way to go, but when we get all of this debt paid off, we just may set an FPU record! We may keep taking the class over and over again until we're debt-free. Take it from me: you are never in too deep for this class and material to help. I thank God for directing me to FPU!

FPU Graduate
St. Charles, MO

KEY POINTS

1. Debt is the most aggressively and successfully marketed product in history.
2. Visa has only existed as a brand name for thirty-five years.
3. The view that debt is "normal" is a relatively new concept in American history.
4. Most of the things we've heard and believed about debt are myths.
5. Debt is not a tool used to create prosperity.
6. The key to getting out of debt is attacking the debt snowball with gazelle intensity.

QUESTIONS FOR REFLECTION

1. How old were you when you got your first credit card? How did that make you feel at the time?
2. What would it feel like to have absolutely no debt hanging over you?
3. Add up how much of your income is currently going out in the form of payments every month (credit cards, home equity loans, mortgage, car loans, etc.). What could you do with that money if you actually got to *keep* it?
4. Have you ever believed (or spread) any of the myths covered in this chapter? Which ones especially got your attention? Why?
5. Why is gazelle intensity so important in getting out of debt?
6. What is your reaction to the phrase "The borrower is slave of the lender"? Have you ever felt *enslaved* because of debt?

5

CREDIT SHARKS IN SUITS

UNDERSTANDING CREDIT BUREAUS AND COLLECTION PRACTICES

One of the most revealing things we do in every *Financial Peace University* class is have the class members collect all the credit card offers that come in the mail during the thirteen weeks they're in FPU. Most of us see those in the mailbox and throw them away. It's almost a habit, right? It'd probably be easier if we just set a paper shredder outside next to the mailbox.

Not too long ago, one of our classes mailed in the stack of credit applications they received, and I'll be honest, even I was surprised at the amount of debt they were offered. In a period of just thirteen weeks, and in a group of just twelve families, the class as a whole was offered over $7.9 million in credit! Think about that for a minute. When you go out to get the mail tomorrow, just look down your street at the line of mailboxes. Can you imagine how much potential debt is sitting out there?

Credit is a big deal. We already talked about debt and the reasons why you should avoid it like your life depends on it, but the fact is, credit is a big part of our culture. We're bombarded with it every day. The credit industry gives us a million different opportunities to wreck our lives, so we've got to learn how to deal with this stuff—by avoiding it and by cleaning up the mess if we've already stepped in it.

WHY THIS CHAPTER IS FOR YOU

Before we get started, let me say something to those who don't think they need to read about credit bureaus and debt collectors. If you're reading this book, then you're already miles ahead of the "average" American. Remember, "normal" in North America is broke! If you're taking control of your money, you're totally weird. Maybe you're doing really, really well. Maybe you're out of debt, have a big, fat emergency fund, and will never have to suffer through a bill collector's horrible ranting on the phone. If that's you, then great! Congratulations! But this chapter is still for you.

Here's what we've found. As you take control of your money, as you get your financial act together, a strange phenomenon starts to happen. All of a sudden, people are going to start coming to you for help. These may be the same people who made fun of you for cutting up your credit cards at first. Over time, they see your life changing and they see you developing a peace about your money, and they realize that you can probably help them.

We see this all the time on our team. It's a joke around our place that if you tell someone you work for Dave Ramsey, you should expect to hear all about their money problems! One guy on our team was having blood drawn for a life insurance physical, and when the nurse saw "Dave Ramsey" on his paperwork, she started telling him all about her overspending at Christmas—while the needle was still in his arm!

Here's the deal. You've got hurting people all around you. If they see that you're doing well, they will see you as a safe place, someone they can go to for help. So even if you never have to personally deal with a crummy credit card collector, there's a good chance someone you know and love *will*. And if they come to you for help, you need to have some hope—and information—to give them.

CREDIT SCORES: FORSAKING THE ALMIGHTY FICO

There's a myth running wild out there that is setting up a lot of young adults for total failure. I can almost guarantee that you've heard it. In fact, go ahead and finish this sentence: "You need to take out a credit card or car loan to build up your . . ." If you said, "credit score," you win. If you ever bought into that lie, you lose.

Don't Buy the Lie

Hear me clearly on this: The credit score is NOT a measure of winning financially. It is 100 percent based on debt. The credit, or FICO, score is simply an "I love debt" rating. No part of the credit score calculation even *hints* at how much wealth you have.

We as a culture just take it for granted that a high FICO number means we're doing great! It doesn't. It just shows how much we enjoy being in debt. I'll prove it. Here's a breakdown of how your FICO score is calculated:

35%: Debt History
30%: Debt Levels
15%: Duration of the Debt
10%: Type of Debt
10%: New Debt[1]

So where does your income, savings account, retirement plan, real estate, and mutual fund portfolio factor in? Nowhere.

I told you, the score *only* reflects your affinity for debt. It has nothing to do with how much you make or how much you have.

Don't Mind Me. I'm Dead.

I got to thinking about this a while back, and I realized that I have not borrowed money in more than twenty years. I wondered what that meant for my credit score, so I went online to pull it. Here's what I got back:

> Our apologies, an error has occurred. We regret that we were unable to fill your score power order request because your credit report does not currently contain enough information to meet the minimum scoring criteria to calculate a FICO score.
>
> In order for a FICO score to be calculated, a report must contain at least one account which has been opened for six months or more, at least one account which has been updated in the past six months, and no indication of being deceased.

"No indication of being deceased!" Translation: In our debt-ridden, credit-addicted culture, you must be DEAD to not have a credit score!

Not a Measure of Winning

My wife and I have been following these Financial Peace principles for a long time now, so we have some wealth, but we still don't have a FICO score. You could inherit $10 million next week and it will not even change your FICO score by one point. You could go into work tomorrow and get a $1-million-a-year raise and it won't make a bit of difference to your FICO score. What kind of sense does this make? Don't sacrifice your wealth in the name of the almighty FICO. It's a lie, and it can ruin your life.

CREDIT BUREAUS: UNTANGLING THE PAPER TRAIL

I want to be clear as we discuss credit bureaus. First, like I said, the FICO score has nothing to do with wealth and success, so building a good credit score should not be a goal. But second, that doesn't mean I want you to intentionally go out of your way to trash your credit score. There's a big difference in having a *bad* credit history and having *no* credit history.

I want you to pay your bills, honor your debts, and act with integrity. If you do that, you won't wreck your FICO score all at once. Instead, it will just fade away into nothing as you tick away years and years of not borrowing any money.

JOIN THE CONVERSATION

I have a new confidence in dealing with creditors, and I no longer allow them to intimidate me. Knowledge is everything, and I now have more facts to know when they are lying or overstepping their legal limits.

—Christy

www.facebook.com/financialpeace

Cleaning Up a Mess

Account information stays on your credit report for seven years *from the date of last activity*. That "date of last activity" part is important. This means that you can't just stop paying your credit card bill and wait it out for seven years until it drops off your record. The collectors or credit card company can do inquiries on the account that can count as "activity," so they have ways of keeping that black mark on your record well beyond seven years. And every time there's activity, that seven-year clock starts over.

This is not a "get out of jail free" card. This system is designed to keep your most recent activity and behavior at the forefront and to allow old mistakes to go away over time. So, missing a few car payments while you were laid off four years ago isn't as important today as it was at the time. The older it gets, the less significant it gets until it eventually just disappears. The only exception to the seven-year rule is a Chapter 7 bankruptcy, which stays on the record for ten years.

The only information that can be legally removed from your credit bureau report is inaccurate information, so do not fall for credit clean-up scams. You cannot repair a bad credit report unless there are items on the report that are genuinely incorrect. This happens *all the time*. The National Association of State Public Interest Research found that 79 percent of credit reports contained some kind of error, and 25 percent of them were serious enough to result in the denial of credit.[2] About 30 percent of the credit reports contained accounts that had been closed by the consumer but still appeared as active on the report.[3] And if you have a mortgage, there's almost a one-in-four chance that your credit report has your mortgage listed *twice*.[4]

Correcting Report Inaccuracies

You've got to stay on top of this. Even if it's someone else's error, it's your responsibility to check the reports regularly and have any inaccuracies removed. Remember, this is your electronic reputation. This will impact your ability to do even basic things like get good car insurance. You need to personally check your credit report at least once a year. By law, you are entitled to a free copy of your credit report once a year from each of the three credit reporting agencies, Experian, TransUnion, and Equifax. So get a copy, check it closely, and pay attention to this stuff!

An updated version of the 1977 Federal Fair Debt Collections Practices Act requires a credit bureau to remove any and all inaccuracies within thirty days of notification. You notify them with a letter, where you point to the account and tell them there's a problem. You don't even have to spell out what the problem is. At that point, the credit bureau has the responsibility of correcting it, which means they'll have to go to Visa, MasterCard, or whoever is reporting the issue. If the credit bureau can't sort it out within thirty days, or if the lender drags their feet and doesn't reply to the credit bureau for thirty days, the entire item has to be removed from your report by law. But again, making that happen is your responsibility.

When you notify an agency of an inaccuracy, I recommend you do it with a physical paper letter, and that you send it return receipt requested. That way, you have an actual paper trail and you can prove that they received the letter on a certain date. That starts the clock. Without that, the agency can always say they never received your notice.

You may have to drag a credit bureau kicking and screaming into this, but you have the law on your side. Don't let them bully or ignore you. Once they have your letter, they have thirty days. If they don't fix it by then, you need to make it your new favorite hobby to beat on them until they fulfill their legal obligation to fix the inaccuracy. If they don't do what they're supposed to, your best course of action is to lodge a complaint with the Federal Trade Commission and your state's Consumer Affairs Division.

Identity Theft

One of the absolute worst things that can happen to your credit report is to have it completely trashed by identity theft. It's bad enough when your report has your own mistakes on it; it's a total nightmare when you have to untangle someone else's criminal activity from your record.

And don't miss that phrase—*criminal activity*. This is something I have to say over and over again to my radio show listeners who call in with an identity theft problem. Why? Because about half the people who call in about this issue have had their identities stolen by someone they know, either a friend or family member. Let me be crystal clear here: If your mother, for example, opens up a credit card in your name and runs up the bills, she has committed criminal fraud. She's a thief. It's not cute, funny, or her right as your mother.

In chapter 7, *Clause and Effect*, I'll talk about identity theft protection coverage and why I think it's a great idea for everyone. For now, though, let's take a look at some specific actions you need to take if your identity has been compromised.

JOIN THE CONVERSATION

I no longer allow collectors to intimidate me or threaten me with things they can't legally do. They have gotten to where they don't want to talk to me at all.

—Charlotte

www.facebook.com/financialpeace

1. Place a fraud victim alert on your credit bureau report. This is free and usually stays on your report for ninety days. This alerts people checking your report that you've had fraud activity on your account, and it prevents new accounts from easily being opened in your name. If you decide to open a new account or do some other action that depends on your credit report, you and the creditor

will have to jump through a few hoops to prove that it's actually you who is applying for a new account.

2. Get a police report. If someone has stolen your identity, you've become the victim of a crime. You *need* to get a police report—even if the thief is your mother, brother, or friend next door. If you know who the thief is, you have to be honest about it. It's an integrity issue. Once you have a police report attached to your credit report, your fraud victim alert can stay on there permanently.

3. Remember, this is theft. You owe nothing and should pay nothing. This was a little easier when we all paid by check. It was simple enough to check signatures and handwriting on paper checks. Now, however, in the age of online purchases and self-checkout registers, it can be tough to convince a creditor that you're not the one who made the purchase. Credit card companies especially will treat you like *you're* the criminal if you refuse to pay for charges someone else made with your card. Stick to your guns and don't let them bully you into paying a bill you're not responsible for.

4. Contact the fraud victim division of each creditor, and furnish documentation. Some companies have fantastic fraud victim divisions; other companies just assume that you're the criminal if you file a fraud claim. That's why documentation is so important. Gather up every little scrap of evidence you can to prove that you didn't make the charges, and work together with the creditors to resolve the matter.

5. Be persistent. Even though the policies and practices are making the identity theft cleanup process a little easier every year, it's still a huge headache. Just be patient and understand that this will take a while to sort out.

Whatever you do, don't just give up and pay the bills if you don't owe them. That will just make it harder to claim fraud victim status later if this happens again!

COLLECTION PRACTICES: WHEN SHARKS ATTACK

Now let's talk about collectors and collection practices. I realize that you may have never been on the receiving end of a collector's call, and hopefully, you never will be. I can tell you one thing, though: I *have* been on the receiving end, and I was shocked and disgusted by the venom and filth that came through the phone at my wife and me.

This is a major, heartbreaking problem for millions of families. Even if you never have to face it yourself, there's a good chance someone you love will have to deal with it. When that happens, you need to be able to offer some advice. With collections, as with most things in life, knowledge is power. If you have just a little bit of knowledge about how this process works and what collectors can and cannot say or do, you'll be way ahead of the game. You'll be empowered as you talk to them yourself or counsel your hurting loved ones who are being harassed.

Who's on the Phone?

Collectors have one—and only one—job, and that is to get your money. To do this, they'll do, say, or be anything they think might trigger a payment from you. Usually, they'll start with the friend technique. That is, they'll start softly, act like your buddy, and try to convince you that they're there to help you. This is a lie.

A bill collector is not your friend, pastor, counselor, financial advisor, or confidant. A bill collector is a trained salesperson or telemarketer. They are in *sales*, not support. They don't care about your situation or if your kids haven't had a meal in a week. They just want your money—and they're getting it. *SmartMoney* magazine's website reports that collection agencies are taking in more than $40 billion in debt payments per year.[5] The number of collectors has doubled since the early 1990s while the industry revenues have tripled.[6] Collections is definitely big business.

Despite the revenues, it's hard for collection companies to keep people on the job for very long. These are typically low-paid positions with extremely high turnover. *Business Week* has reported the turnover in some of the major collection agencies is as high as 85 percent a year.[7] It's not hard to understand why this is. How rewarding can your job be if you spend forty hours a week hammering away at people who are already hurting? No amount of money on earth could make that job worthwhile.

Remember, these are not professional people. When a collector calls, you are dealing with an idiot in a cubicle five hundred miles away. In eighteen states, you don't even need a license to start collecting.[8] Anyone with a phone and a computer can jump right in and start making calls. And yet, most people get so intimidated when talking to a collector that they allow this person to set the financial priorities for their family. It seems almost silly to consider the fact that a twenty-two-year-old loser yelling on the phone can talk a struggling single mom into sending her kids' food money to him.

All of that comes from the chief goal in their job training, which is to evoke strong emotion. If they can get you mad, sad, crying, or feeling guilty, they'll do it. They'll make you feel or think anything they need to in order to get your money. They don't care at all what the impact is on your family. That's probably why these companies have to shovel in a new batch of recruits every few months.

Spectrum of Collectors

I come down hard on collectors because I've seen firsthand how they can inflict harm on a hurting family. But I honestly don't have a problem with a professional collecting a legitimate bill. If you *owe* the money, and if you *have* the money, you should *pay* the money! But what I do have a problem with is the Gestapo tactics, threats, and intimidation that too often characterize the industry.

I sometimes get legitimate criticism from people for how I talk about collectors. Again, the whole issue just touches some deep part of my emotions and I react out of my experience. However, after working with families in collections for a couple of decades, I've found that there really are some quality, respectable pros in the industry. They fall into what I call a "spectrum of collectors" from the solid professionals to the grenade-throwing scumbags.

At the top of the pile are those people who collect on first mortgages. These are some of the classiest, most polite, and respectable men and women you'll ever deal with. They seldom violate federal law (which we'll talk about later), and they honestly will not bother you much. However, if you get behind on your mortgage and they do eventually call, get ready to duck—the bullet is already coming. These collectors don't fool around and they don't bluff. They'll generally be tough and firm, but fair. You have the best chance of working with this group.

The next best collector is usually with your small-town, local collection agency. This isn't a national chain or a publicly traded company. Instead, this is an agency owned by someone in the community, and they're collecting bills for local merchants. These collectors are generally your neighbors, and they don't want to get hit with tomatoes if you see them in the grocery store! We've dealt with a lot of local collectors, and I've generally found them to be fair and usually within the bounds of the laws governing collections.

As you move down the spectrum, things start to go bad fast. Next on the spectrum are the little storefront finance companies you see in strip malls and shopping centers in lower-income neighborhoods. These guys are generally punks, which you'll discover as soon as they sic their collection goons on you.

I was counseling a young lady several years ago, and she called me, crying, from a payphone. I asked what was going on, and she told me that she couldn't go home. The collector from the finance company was sitting in a lawn chair in the middle of her driveway, so she could not even pull into her own garage. This guy was trespassing. He was out of control, breaking the law left and right just to get her money. She was scared to death!

The bottom of the collections barrel, without a doubt, is credit card collectors. These are the worst of the worst. I have no hesitation at all in calling them scum. And these are the big guys, the household names we all know. They spend millions and millions of dollars on advertising to make us feel good about their brand, to cause us to have some kind of respect for them, but that all falls apart once you start dealing with their collections department.

Many years ago when Sharon and I were struggling to get out of debt, I owed a ton of money to *everybody*. One of the cards I had run up was the American Express. That's the "respectable" one, the one that claims to want to help you manage and organize your business, so they must run that whole company like a world-class organization, right? Wrong.

One afternoon, I was at work trying to drum up business to pay for all the money we owed, and Sharon called me, crying. A collector we had been dealing with called our home number, when he knew I wasn't home, because he wanted to get to my wife. They'll try any method, remember? So with me at work and Sharon at home trying to keep up with two little kids and worrying about bankruptcy, this guy calls up and goes through his usual line of bull. And then, he hit her with, "Mrs. Ramsey, why would you stay with a man who won't pay his bills?"

That comment, more than all the others we heard, is stuck deep in my emotions. That was a great picture of how these guys operate. A credit card collector would break up a marriage and create a broken home for young children if he thought it would trigger a payment. They'll do anything, so be ready for them.

Dealing with Collectors

I have never once suggested that you should skip out on paying a bill you legitimately owe. As hard as I am on collectors, I come down even harder on people who intentionally run up bills with no intention to pay. That is stealing. My goal here isn't to teach you how to scam your way out of your bills; I just want to empower you to act with integrity, courage, and confidence by knowing your rights under the law.

The first thing to remember when dealing with collectors is that you, not they, must set the priorities for your family. After teaching this material live one night, I had a young lady come up to me with tears in her eyes. She said, "Thank you so much for this. I've never heard this side of the discussion. You see, my father always told me to protect my credit score no matter what. So, I'm current with all my credit cards—but I haven't eaten in a week." She was serious. She had allowed the credit card industry, the fear of collectors, and the almighty FICO score to literally take the food off her plate. That's a bad plan.

You have to take care of necessities first. No matter how loud or long a collector screams at you, never again can you send them money before taking care of your family's basic needs. We talked about this in chapter 3. I called it the Four Walls: food, shelter, clothing, and (reasonable) transportation. Remember, if you have food in your belly, a roof over your head, clothes on your back, and a way to get to work tomorrow, you'll live to fight another day.

Your Rights Under the Law

In 1977, Congress passed a consumer law called the Federal Fair Debt Collection Practices Act (FFDCPA). Originally, this law just applied to collection agencies and not individual creditors. However, subsequent case law has broadened the Act to cover how individual creditors have to behave when collecting on a debt. So now, pretty much anyone officially collecting on a bill has to follow the guidelines outlined in the FFDCPA.

Of course, that doesn't mean they actually follow the law. Debt collectors break federal law on a daily—make that hourly or minutely—basis. But if you're aware of the laws, you can take steps to protect yourself and, even better, catch the collectors in the act of breaking federal law!

One guideline that is often ignored is the time frame within which a collector is allowed to call you. The act states clearly that collection calls can only be made between the hours of 8:00 a.m. and 9:00 p.m. local time. "Local time" means *your* time zone, not theirs. So if a collector is waking you up every morning at six or trying to catch you while you're making the kids' lunches at seven, they're breaking the law.

They do this all the time, and the good news is this is one of the easiest violations to record. If you're in an adversarial collection situation, I recommend you get an answering machine that has a one-button memo-recording feature. That is, have a way to easily record the conversation after the call has started. If you answer the phone in the middle of the night and a collector is on the other end of the line, hit the record button and say this:

> *Okay, please note that I am recording this call. For the record, you said that your name is John and you are calling from ACME Collections Agency in regards to a bill I owe. It is now 11:45 p.m. my time, which means you are in violation of the Federal Fair Debt Collection Practices Act by calling me after 9:00 p.m. For the purposes of this recording, would you please confirm this?*

My guess is the only sound you'll hear at that point is a dial tone. If "John" has an ounce of sense, he won't want his voice on tape acknowledging that he's breaking the law.

The act also allows you to demand that a creditor stop calling you at work, and I definitely recommend you do this. This is another emotion-based tactic they use, thinking that the embarrassment of being called at the office in front of co-workers will force you to pay. Don't play that game. Send them a letter, return receipt requested, directing them to stop the office calls. It's that simple. That way, when you're at work, you can work. And when you're at home, you can talk to them using the guidelines we're going over.

The act also gives you the right to demand that a creditor stop all contact except to notify you of lawsuit proceedings. While this is tempting for many, I very rarely recommend sending a cease-and-desist letter. It will often trigger a lawsuit you might have otherwise avoided with a steady stream of communication. I don't want you to ignore them; I just want you to control the conversation and force them to act in a civilized manner.

The "civilized manner" is the tricky part. A lot of collectors aren't capable of this, so you'll have to be assertive. Tell them that you're willing to have mature conversations with them on a regular basis, but not more often than every two weeks. Make them understand that if they try scare tactics, foul language, or demeaning and disrespectful actions, you will hang up on them. You may have to prove that to them once or twice until they get the message.

But if the situation is truly threatening or filled with harassment, then you may actually need to drop a cease-and-desist letter on them. Just make sure you have enough evidence of their bad behavior, because your next stop might be a courtroom.

The FFDCPA also prevents a collector or creditor from accessing a bank account or garnishing wages without proper, lengthy court action. The only exceptions to this rule are delinquent IRS and federally insured student loan debts. Collectors try this one all the time, screaming, "If you don't send us some money, we're going to file it with your workplace, and your next four paychecks will come straight to us!" That's a lie. They have absolutely no power to do that without a court order—and they won't have a court order without you knowing about it.

JOIN THE CONVERSATION

FICO? Only if it means "Finally, I'm Cash Only!"

—Joel

www.facebook.com/financialpeace

Getting Out of Collections: The Pro Rata Plan

Again, none of this is designed to teach you how to avoid paying your bills. Even if you know the law and hold their feet to the fire, if you never send them any money on legitimate debts, you're probably going to get sued. If you honestly don't have enough money to make all the minimum payments on your debts, you have to use the pro rata plan.

"Pro rata" means "fair share." With the pro rata plan, that's exactly what you're doing: you're sending every creditor their "fair share" of your disposable income. Figuring that out is fairly simple. First, write down your total income. Now subtract your necessity expenses (starting with the Four Walls). Your income minus your necessities equals your disposable income. That's how much money you have to send to your creditors.

Look at your debt and payments, and write down your total debt. Then look at all your bills and figure out the total of all your minimum payments. If the total of your minimum payments is greater than your disposable income, you don't have enough money to pay all your minimums. Instead of picking and choosing which bills you're going to pay each month, you'll use the pro rata plan to send all the creditors *something*, even if it's just $5.

Here's where the "fair share" comes in. Say that you have five outstanding debts, and the total payoff of all your debts is $2,000. In that mix, you owe Sears a $200 balance. What percent of your total debt does Sears represent? Divide $200 by $2,000, and you'll see that Sears represents 10 percent of your total debt. Since Sears is 10 percent of your problem, they'll get 10 percent of your available money this month. This may not be enough to cover the minimum payment on the account, but at least you'll be showing good faith in sending them *something*.

I recommend writing down your complete pro rata plan, outlining all your debts and income, and stapling that to a letter with your monthly payment to each creditor. Explain that you understand you're sending less than the minimum payment, but that you're on a plan and are attempting to do the honorable thing by all your creditors. They may yell and scream, and they may threaten to sue you. However, in all the years I've been doing this, I've found that if you keep sending them checks, they'll keep cashing them. Besides, this isn't your long-term plan. This is a temporary situation as you get extra jobs and fight your way out of debt with gazelle intensity!

You can download a copy of the pro rata form for free from our website. If you're in a *Financial Peace University* class, you can find the forms in the online resources for this lesson. Otherwise, you can find it at daveramsey.com.

Lawsuits

Eventually, if you aren't making payments and have cut no deals with collectors, you will get sued. This may seem like the worst thing in the world, and you may feel a lot of fear, guilt, and shame if you are sued for money you owe. However, in the grand scheme of life, this shouldn't be the worst thing that's ever happened to you. Don't let fear cloud the issue. Honestly, the whole process is fairly cut-and-dried.

Typically, lawsuits for under $10,000 are filed in General Sessions Court, which is essentially small-claims court. This is fairly informal, a lot like traffic court. If you're facing a General Sessions Court date, keep it in perspective. Obviously, you want to be respectful and dress appropriately, because this is a court of law, but don't be scared about it. I promise, it won't be like walking into an episode of *Law and Order*!

Before you are sued, you will be served by the local sheriff's department and typically given ten days' notice of the court date. The officer is not there to arrest you; he's just there to inform you that some gears are turning in the process. When Sharon and I went broke, it felt like the sheriff was knocking on our door every week! Near the end, we'd just invite him in for cookies!

In court—if the debt is valid—even if you fight, you will lose. The judge's only real question will be, "Do you owe the money?" If the answer is yes, then that's it. There's really nothing else to discuss. It doesn't matter whether or not you're broke. Judges aren't there to discuss your character or circumstances; they're just there to determine whether or not you owe the money.

Don't walk in thinking you will fight and win. Instead, I just want you to have an understanding of the process. After the verdict, you'll generally have thirty days before the judgment becomes final and garnishments or attachments begin. So they aren't going to drain your bank account *that day*. You have thirty more days to figure things out.

And anytime during that thirty days, you can work out a deal with the creditor or their attorney. In fact, this might be the best time of all to work a deal, because you won't be dealing with a brain-dead debt collector anymore. By the time it gets to this point, you'll be working directly with an attorney or a paralegal. That's a great time to work a deal with someone who will actually listen to you and try to reach an agreement that works for everyone.

If the time comes and you genuinely do not have the money to pay, you can file a slow-pay motion, sometimes called a "pauper's oath," which is a declaration that you don't have all the money, but you will pay what you can. That's when they'll discuss your pro rata plan, so it's always a good idea to have that ready. If they see you're doing everything you can to honor your agreements, it will go a long way with attorneys and judges working on your case.

PENNIES ON THE DOLLAR: CUTTING DEALS WITH CREDITORS

As we wrap up this chapter, I want to give you some practical tips for cutting deals with creditors. If you are a few months behind on your bills, it is possible to settle your debt for pennies on the dollar. That's perfectly legal and a great way to honor your debts to the best of your ability. However, there are some guidelines I want you to follow if you're ever in this situation.

1. Don't pay someone to settle your debts for you. The industry is filled with disreputable "credit counselors" who will convince you to intentionally stop paying your bills for a few months to try to force a creditor to take a settlement. That is just plain wrong and shows a complete lack of integrity. If you have the money, pay it. And if you want to work a deal, do it yourself. Don't pay someone else to do it for you.

2. Get it in writing. If you negotiate a deal on settling a debt, get it in writing before you send them any money. A lawyer friend of mine always says, "If it's not in writing, it didn't happen." Never trust a collector's word. Only trust what they'll put on paper.

3. Never give a collector electronic access to your bank account. If you're in any kind of adversarial situation with a collector, the *last* thing you want to do is hand them the keys to your bank account. If they tell you they'll take $500 on a $2,000 debt and you give them electronic access, they're going to hit you for the full $2,000. You can count on it. Make a deal, get it in writing, and then send a cashier's check along with a copy of the agreement by certified mail.

4. Save everything. Once you get a deal in writing, save a copy of it *forever*. Staple it to a copy of the cashier's check they cashed and the proof of certified mail delivery, and drop the whole file in a safe place. If this debt pops back up on your credit report in a few years, you'll need all this to prove that you're free from this debt.

The issue of collections is extremely sensitive and personal. I get that. I've been there, and I'll never forget the feeling I had standing in the courtroom, listening to creditors, lawyers, and judges talk about my inability to pay my debts. It was the most humbling experience of my life. But if you're in that situation, please realize that you don't have to stay there forever. The Baby Steps we're laying out in this book work for everyone, no matter where you are at the start of the journey. The process isn't always easy, fun, or fast, but it works.

WE DID IT!

I received a debt collection phone call on my work line. The woman claimed it was a $531 bill for lab work done two years ago and she needed to know how I was going to pay for it.

I asked for a contact number for the lab so I could file it with my insurance company. She said that no insurance company would let me file a claim two years later. She told me, "I am only calling you to figure out how you are going to pay for this."

I said, "I understand, but I am not going to pay you. I am going to file this with my insurance company."

She then yelled into the phone, "No insurance company will let you file a claim two years later! You just need to get this taken care of right now!"

I replied, "That may be true. However, I am going to get with my insurance company to see if it can be paid. Why should I trust you? You're a debt collector. Getting my money is your job. I will get with my insurance company and go from there."

She interrupted and said, "That won't work! You need to pay your bills or I am going to sue you!"

By this point, I was mad. My response was, "No, *you* aren't going to do anything. You are just a debt collector in a cube somewhere; you are not a lawyer."

She fired back: "Oh, does that make you feel better telling me that? Just pay your bills, and I won't have to call you!"

I laughed and said, "They couldn't pay me enough money to do your job. You must be very sad."

She hung up.

Whitney
Indianapolis, IN

KEY POINTS

1. The FICO score is not a measure of winning financially. It is an "I love debt" score.
2. It is your responsibility to check your credit report for errors regularly.
3. Bill collectors are not your friends or financial counselors. Their only job is to get your money by whatever means they can.
4. Never give a bill collector electronic access to your bank account or a postdated check, and always get any deals or settlement offers in writing before sending the payment.
5. If you are unable to pay the minimum payments on your debts, use the pro rata plan.

QUESTIONS FOR REFLECTION

1. What is your reaction to the statement, "The FICO score is not a measure of winning financially"? How is this contrary to what you have always believed or been taught?
2. Why do we say that the credit score is actually an "I love debt" score?
3. What are some practical ways you can defend yourself against identity theft? What do you need to remember if you become a victim?
4. In what way is emotion a collector's best weapon?
5. Why is it important to make the Four Walls (food, clothing, shelter, and transportation) a priority when dealing with bill collectors?

6

BUYER BEWARE

THE POWER OF MARKETING ON YOUR BUYING DECISIONS

I grew up in the real estate business, with builders and contractors and agents all through my family. So it didn't surprise anyone when I jumped right into the family business as soon as I graduated high school. When I was studying for the real estate license test at age eighteen, I remember coming across a Latin phrase that really stood out to me: *Caveat emptor*. That's Latin for "Let the buyer beware."

In real estate back then, sellers usually sold through agents, so the seller paid the agent's commission. "Buyer's agents" weren't that common, which meant that the buyer usually had no representation. Since the only agent in the deal was paid by the seller, we were taught to help the buyer understand that he had to watch out for himself. So, "let the buyer beware!"

The real estate business has changed a little since then, but the importance of becoming a wise, patient, and informed consumer has not. We are living in the most dramatically marketed-to society in history, and if we don't keep our eyes open as we go through life, we'll always be flat broke with a garage full of garbage and toys we don't need but couldn't resist. We've got to learn to open our eyes to the intense marketing that's going on all around us.

IDENTIFYING THE BATTLEGROUND

When you turn on the TV, listen to the radio, surf the web, or walk into the mall, you are stepping into battle—a battle for your dollars. Today, companies use every angle imaginable to aggressively compete for your money. Marketing is not an option for businesses that want to keep their doors open. Think about it. Between retail stores and online stores, you have thousands of different places to buy that *thing* you can't live without. Every one of those stores is fighting with all the others to get that thing in front of you in the most attractive, compelling way possible.

$10,000 per Second

In the great book *Affluenza*, researchers found that the average consumer is struck with more than 3,000 commercial messages a day, each one screaming for our attention.[1] Kids will see about one million commercials before they turn twenty, and over their lifetime, all the ads strung together would add up to two entire years of watching television commercials![2]

And this is big business. *Affluenza* reported that the typical thirty-second, national television commercial costs nearly $300,000 to produce—that's $10,000 *per second*![3] Here's the kicker. You know how much it costs to produce one episode of the average television show? About $300,000, roughly the same cost as a thirty-second ad. That comes to $83 per second for the actual TV program, compared to $10,000 per second for the advertisements during the commercial breaks. Is it any wonder why some people think the best thing on TV is commercials?

And these campaigns are working. I saw a study not too long ago that showed the average household in the U.S. has more television sets than people![4] Now, I'm not mad at these companies. They aren't doing anything wrong. I run a big company myself, and we do a lot of different types of advertising. But you need to be aware of what you're walking into whenever you hit the sofa with the remote in your hand.

JOIN THE CONVERSATION

A salesperson's job is to make sales, not make sure you get the best product for the best price. Your job is do your homework BEFORE you buy.

—Rebecca

www.facebook.com/financialpeace

Do You Smell Cookies?

Think you're really just window-shopping when you're walking around the mall? Think again. Stores are using all sorts of creative ways to slip past your buying defenses. For example, a lot of stores are attacking our wallets through our noses! *USA Today* reported that several companies have started pumping different scents through their stores to evoke certain emotions.[5] The Sony Style store, for example, pumps the subtle fragrances of vanilla and mandarin oranges into the store to make you feel relaxed so you'll let your guard down. Bloomingdale's uses a lot of different scents depending on which department you're in. If you're in the baby section, you may catch the faint whiff of baby powder. If you're in the swimwear area, you'll probably catch the smell of suntan lotion. This is designed to slip past our defenses and take the sales message straight into our brains without us ever even realizing it.

If you were to visit my office, one of the first things you'd notice when you walk in the front door is the smell of fresh-baked cookies at our coffee bar in the lobby. Now, we're not trying to put you into a cookie trance so you'll buy our stuff the moment you walk in, but we have found that it is a fantastic way to put people at ease and enable them to enjoy their visit from the moment they walk through the door. Besides, the cookies are free!

FOUR MARKETING TECHNIQUES TO GUARD AGAINST

Too many consumers just wander through life like Gomer Pyle on Valium. They stumble around, fall for all the marketing, and look up one day and say, "Shazam! I'm broke!" If you want to avoid that, you need to be on the lookout for four specific marketing techniques that businesses use. Of course, there are more than four ways for a product or service to get your attention, but these are four I've found people easily fall for.

Personal Selling

The first technique to be aware of is pretty obvious: personal selling. I love personal selling. I've been in sales all my life, and I grew up in a salesman's household. I just love buying something I want from an excellent salesperson. When it's done right, it's a fun, easy, and natural process that leads to a win-win sale (we'll talk about *win-win* in another chapter). When it's done wrong, though, it is horrible for everybody.

True pros have to know how to talk to customers, and they can't be shy about it. It's like author and salesman Judge Ziglar says, "Timid salesmen have skinny kids!" They have to sell like their lives depend on it—because it kind of does! And a good salesperson will never answer any question with a simple yes or no. If he knows what he's doing, the salesman will turn every question you ask into another question, and the answers to all of these questions are essentially filling out the order form.

Think about buying a car. If you ask, "Do you have this car in blue?" the sales guy who just says yes is going to be broke and unemployed in a month. Instead, he'd likely reply, "I think we do, but I'll have to check. But let me ask: if we do have it in blue, would you like the sport package or the luxury package? Oh, the luxury package. Great. Now, did you want the one with the moonroof, as well? Great."

They keep asking these questions, and as they do, you are telling them exactly what kind of car you want, you are visualizing every detail of the car, and they are actually leading you right up to the buying decision. It's subtle, but there's a definite process in place here.

Once you describe your dream car down to every detail, do you think they'd tell you, "Sorry, we don't have that car" and leave it at that? No way! They'll say something like, "Good news! We have that car in our computer system, and we can have it ready for you to check out first thing in the morning!" Translation: They don't have the car, but another local dealer does, so they're going to buy it from that dealer, ship it over to their lot, wash and wax it, and have it ready for you to fall in love with tomorrow.

Car dealers know that if you walk off the lot without a car, you probably won't be back. Most people purchase a car within forty-eight hours of taking a test drive, so even if you say you'll be back, they know you won't be. You've got the look in your eye, you're going to buy *something* from *someone*, and they will say or do practically anything to hang on to you.

Financing

In chapter 4, *Dumping Debt*, we talked about viewing debt as a product. Now let's look at it from another angle. When you see an ad for "0% Financing!" or "No Payments for Six Months!"

you are being marketed to using one of the most dangerous techniques out there—financing.

The main goal of financing is to keep you from asking, "How much?" Instead, they only want you to think about "How much down?" and "How much per month?" In most newspaper car ads, for example, you won't see an actual price listed anywhere. Instead, they just show you the monthly payment and maybe a "Zero Down" headline.

It is impossible to open a Sunday paper in any major market in the country without having dozens of these ads spill onto the floor. Have you ever thought about what it takes to put them there? Advertisers spend tens of thousands of dollars every week to get that furniture sales flyer into your hands every Sunday. Do you think they'd go to all that trouble and spend all that money just to give you "free money" through their "generous" financing? Forget it. They only do it because they know the financing options will get you into the store, and once you're there, they'll make a fortune off your "free" financing.

One offer you'll see all the time is "90-Days-Same-as-Cash." Trust me: NO form of financing, even one billed as "same-as-cash," is the same as cash. In fact, I have a good friend who is a finance manager at one of these stores, and he told me that 88 percent of that store's same-as-cash contracts convert to payments, which are usually at 24 percent interest. And that interest goes all the way back to the day you bought the item, so at the end of ninety days, you immediately get hit with three months' worth of back interest.

Furniture stores, car dealers, and all other retailers are not in the business of giving you free money. They put these offers out there because they know—they KNOW—most people will naively take them up on them and then make some tiny little mistake that will turn a huge profit. They have this stuff down to a science, so please don't walk into a store with the idea that you'll beat them at their own game!

JOIN THE CONVERSATION

"Let the buyer beware" means I am responsible for my own foolish purchases.

—Julie

www.facebook.com/financialpeace

Media Advertising

We may not always see financing as a marketing tool, but there's no denying the advertising punch of the old standards: television, radio, Internet, and other media. The goal with these is to put a brand or product in your face in the most clever way possible, as memorably as possible, and of course, as many times as possible.

I've been doing radio for twenty years, which means I have done a ton of radio commercials. I use them for our own products, and I sell ads to our sponsors. Radio is usually a captive audience. If you have someone stuck in traffic at 5:45 every evening, hearing you talk about the same product over and over and over again, there's a good chance they'll remember your name.

Bottom line: repetition works. You could probably sit there and quote ten different product slogans from memory in under a minute. And you can probably finish Clara Peller's famous catchphrase for Wendy's restaurant chain: "Where's the . . ." even though she passed away almost twenty-five years ago! These things get stuck in our brains, and twenty-five years later, we find ourselves passing a Wendy's and whispering to ourselves, "Where's the beef?" And suddenly, the car heads straight toward the drive-thru.

Product Positioning

When you walk into a store and see a display for soda right near the entrance, do you think the store manager just *happened* to set up the posters and life-size cardboard standees right there? Not a chance. Everything you see in the store is laid out according to a well-researched marketing plan that outlines product positioning. The whole experience, from brand recognition, to the colors they use, to the shelf position, to the product packaging, is all managed down to the last detail.

The first element here is brand recognition. When you walk in and see that soda display, if the product's marketing team has done a good job, you should immediately connect that brand with something you've seen or heard in the past. Actually seeing the display in the store is very rarely your *first* exposure to a product.

For example, several years ago, those of us familiar with marketing knew about the ketchup wars going on between Heinz and Hunt's. Both were large, national brands, and both were competing against the cost-cutter generic brands that the grocery stores were pushing. The big brands put a lot of money into advertising, trying to convince us that their ketchup was "thick and rich," compared to the store brands that were "thin and runny." So, when you saw a bottle of Heinz on the shelf next to Brand X, your gut reaction would be to grab the "thick and rich" ketchup. Even if you paid more for it, you reached for the known brand because they had planted that seed in your mind through their advertising. The only problem is that "thick and rich" was usually produced in the same factory as "thin and runny"! The only real difference? The label.

Also tied to product positioning is color. The colors these companies use on their labels aren't an accident. They don't go with their own in-house designer's gut feeling of what looks good. They have this down to a science.

In my early years as a real estate agent, I worked for a company that had the ugliest yard signs I had ever seen. When we had a house on the market, we stuck these bright orange "For Sale" signs in the yard that were about the same color as orange traffic cones. I thought they were horrible at first, and then I realized what was going on. You see, if you're targeting buyers who are driving down a neighborhood street, you can't use a sign that's dark like a tree or green like grass. Those signs just blend in and won't get any attention. You need a color that pops, something that is different than anything else in the yard, or no one will ever see it. It's true in yard signs, and it's true with items lined up on a grocery-store shelf. If no one sees the product, no one buys the product. Color is important.

Of course, shelf position is also a big deal. Most stores can't put their product wherever the stock clerk or store manager wants to. For example, I write books, so we work with a lot of publishers and bookstores. If I want my books on a display table near the front door or on an end-cap at the end of the Finance shelf, I have to pay for that. It's not random. The whole store is mapped out and the most valuable product-positioning spots cost the most money.

Think about the cereal aisle at your local grocery store. Are the name-brand, cartoon-character, sugary cereal boxes at *your* eye level or your *child's* eye level? They're not targeting you; they're after your kids' attention! They know if your children get excited about the bunny rabbit on the box right in front of them, there's a much better chance of that box landing in your cart. That's why the shredded wheat and oat bran are usually up top and the Fruity Pebbles are in the middle or near the bottom. There are no accidents in shelf positioning.

JOIN THE CONVERSATION

Don't believe everything the salesman says. If it sounds too good to be true, it probably is!

—Jessica

www.facebook.com/financialpeace

BIG MONEY: MAKING SIGNIFICANT PURCHASES

All of these marketing tactics prepare us to make purchases. Sometimes, it's just a pack of gum or a soda at the checkout line. Other times, it's a big-screen TV or a car. Whether it's a big or small purchase, we have to remember that we're the targets of intentional, directed, and well-thought-out marketing plans. Of course, we don't *feel* it as much when it's a soda on a hot summer day as we do when we're walking onto a car lot ready to buy. The size of the item raises the stakes—and our blood pressure.

Every family should come up with their own definition of a significant purchase. These days, I could go out and spend a few thousand dollars without breaking a sweat, but there was a time when a $20 shirt was a pretty significant purchase for us! Usually, though, most families will define "significant purchase" as something in the neighborhood of $300.

Emotions of Purchasing

Our bodies go through physiological changes when we make a significant purchase. Our heart rate picks up. We get a little sweat on the upper lip. Our palms get clammy. Our eyes dilate a little bit. Endorphins and adrenaline start pumping, and our senses are heightened. It's a rush!

All this starts happening, and all of a sudden, our brains get a little foggy. It gets harder to think rationally, and the salesperson senses that and pounces. That's how you may have woken up one morning with a brand-new car sitting in your driveway, even though you swore you were "just looking" when you hit the car lot the day before! When we make these big purchases without being fully prepared, we are setting ourselves up for a serious case of buyer's remorse.

In my home-selling days, the company I was working for got into a string of several contract reversals. That is, we'd sell a home, and then the buyer would freak out and back out of the deal within seventy-two hours. This became such an issue that the home office sent some sales trainers in to teach us how to prepare for this in the early part of the sales process.

We started walking buyers through this emotional aspect, telling them all about buyer's remorse and preparing them for the range of emotions they'd likely feel once they signed the papers. We told them that they'd probably wake up the morning after signing the papers and have a mild panic attack, and if that happened, it was perfectly normal. It was just because they spent a lot of money, but that in itself didn't mean it was a mistake or that the deal was bad. It was just a physiological effect of a big purchase.

Just by talking to people about this and helping them understand what was going to happen, it cut our contract loss to practically zero. We didn't lie or manipulate people at all; we just took the time to help them understand what was happening so that they didn't confuse the natural anxiety with a bad deal.

The Spoiled, Red-Faced Kid

When our children were little, one thing we absolutely did not allow was uncontrolled, angry, temper fits. You'd get your little tail tanned at our house for doing that. If you really wanted a spanking, you'd try it at the grocery store. One day, my youngest got his little motor running in the cereal aisle and I could tell he was going somewhere. Before I could do anything, both his sisters grabbed him by the arms and said, "Listen, you *really* don't want to do that." They knew what was coming, and they knew it wouldn't end well for him.

You know what I've discovered? Every one of us has a little, spoiled, red-faced, grocery store kid living inside of us. His name is Immaturity, and he wakes up when we're shopping. At the electronics store, he wants a big-screen TV. At the outdoors store, he wants a bass boat. At the car lot, he wants a convertible. At the furniture store, he wants a new leather sofa. If we let that kid make our financial decisions, we'll always be broke. Children do what feels good; adults devise a plan and follow it.

JOIN THE CONVERSATION

Research what you're going to buy, and ask yourself, "Do I need this or will it sit in the closet?"

—Beth

www.facebook.com/financialpeace

POWER OVER PURCHASE

Does all this mean that I don't want you to ever spend money or get anything nice for yourself? Not at all. I have a beautiful home filled with many wonderful things my family enjoys. I don't want you to live in a cave, collect lint, and only come out on triple-coupon Tuesday! But I do want you to think about this stuff and make sure your spending is done according to plan, and that your purchases line up with your financial condition.

It is easy to overspend. That's what the financing industry is all about. The only reason "90-days-same-as-cash" is so popular is because most shoppers *don't have* the cash in their hands on the day they buy! They're spending money they don't have, and that way of life will always keep you broke. Because we can always spend more than we make, we must develop power over purchase. Here are five guidelines that, if followed every time, will guarantee wise buying decisions:

1. Wait overnight. Remember, when you're on the edge of a big purchase, your body starts going haywire. When that happens, step away, go home, and sleep on it. That gives you time to cool down and get some perspective. Trust me—that thing will still be available tomorrow. And if it's not, then maybe that's God's way of saying you didn't need it after all.

2. Consider your buying motives. Why are you making this purchase? Is it something you need or want, or are you buying it to make someone else happy or to please the kids? No amount of stuff will ever give you contentment or fulfillment. If I buy a new ski boat, I do it because I know my family and I want it and will enjoy

it, not because I believe *that thing* will make me happy. It won't. Money can buy fun, but it can't buy happiness.

And even if the item is a "want" and not a "need," it could be a perfectly reasonable purchase. There is absolutely nothing wrong with buying some "wants," as long as they fit within your overall financial plan and you understand your motives.

3. Don't buy what you don't understand. This is especially true with financial products like investments and insurance. We'll cover those areas in other chapters. For now, just don't buy any gadgets or gizmos because they're "cool" or someone said you should get one. Buy what you need and get yourself some wants, but *use what you buy.* You don't need a NASA-caliber computer to surf the web and play solitaire. If you don't understand what it is or how to use it, don't buy it.

4. Consider the opportunity cost. Your money is finite—it has limits. If you spend it on one thing, you can't spend it on another. That is, if I have $10,000 in the bank and use that money to buy a car, then that $10,000 is gone. So, I can't buy a $10,000 car *and* put the same $10,000 into a mutual fund. That's opportunity cost. Before you make a significant purchase, ask yourself what else you could do with that money that might be a better idea. You'll likely think of a dozen things *after* you buy the item, anyway, so you might as well ask yourself the question up front!

5. Talk to your spouse. Proverbs 31:10–11 is a prescription for wise financial decisions for those of us who are married: "Who can find a virtuous wife? For her worth is far above rubies. The heart of her husband safely trusts

her; so he will have no lack of gain."[6] Every single time I have made a financial decision that Sharon disagreed with, it cost me money—*lots* of money. She was right. I don't even argue with her anymore. If she has one of those "feeeeeelings," then that's it. I don't do the deal.

Ladies, this goes for you too. If you're married, then you and your spouse are one. If you run off and make a huge purchase solo, then you're only operating with half your brain. The result is rarely a blessing. This one step alone would have saved countless people from bankruptcy—not to mention divorce. And if you're single, check in with your accountability partner that we talked about in chapter 2, *Relating with Money*. The point here is to get outside of your own head, say these things out loud, and give others permission to tell you if the deal is a bad idea.

I want you to have fun with your purchases, but I don't want you to be a victim of clever marketing and impulse buying. Be aware of how, when, and where you're being marketed to. Look past the glitz and glamour and really see every product for what it is and what its benefits are for you and your family. When you figure out what things you need and want, make a plan and buy with confidence. Then you'll enjoy your stuff without remorse.

Caveat emptor!

WE DID IT!

My wife and I took *Financial Peace University* at our church last year and loved it. The best part for us (besides getting DEBT FREE!) was the discipline of using cash for purchases. We had been saving for months in our "SOFA" envelope. We'd been window-shopping a lot, so we knew exactly what we wanted. I called the store and told the sales guy which sectional we wanted, and I told him I expected a great deal because I was paying cash. He said he'd work some numbers and call me back.

I missed his return call, and in his voicemail he admitted that his "best price" was a few hundred more than I told him we'd spend. Flexing our "walk-away power," I didn't call him back. He called again the next day. And the next. I still didn't return his calls. Finally, he left me a message saying that his "manager" had approved an even better price. This time, I called back. We agreed on the price and I made him repeat it back to me *twice* just to make sure we were clear. We were ready to buy!

When I went to the store to pay, I noticed they had tacked on a random $100 "service fee" to our agreed-upon price. I told him I didn't have it, and he replied, "Come on, man. Yes you do!" I opened my envelope, counted out exactly what we had agreed on, and said, "This is what I have, and that's it." Knowing I was about to walk out of the store with my money, he finally agreed. They even threw in delivery and a warranty!

What did I learn through this? First, cash is king. Second, knowing exactly what you're willing to spend and *only* bringing that much money to the store saves you from the pressure of overspending—and the pressure of pushy salespeople! Thanks, Dave!

**David and Holly
Atlanta, GA**

KEY POINTS

1. Companies have detailed plans for marketing their products and competing for your money.
2. By learning the common marketing methods, you can guard yourself against unwise purchases and impulse buying.
3. Always wait overnight before making a major purchase.
4. Discuss major purchases with your spouse (if married) or with an accountability partner (if single).
5. Never buy anything you do not understand—including products, services, or investments.

QUESTIONS FOR REFLECTION

1. How do marketers use emotion to compel you to purchase their goods?
2. How can waiting overnight before making a purchase change your behavior? How would this have helped you avoid debt in the past?
3. How would you define a "major purchase"? Why is it so important for married couples to agree on major purchases?
4. What can singles do to guard themselves against impulsive buying decisions?
5. What steps can you take to guarantee that you will always *enjoy* your purchases?

7

CLAUSE AND EFFECT

THE ROLE OF INSURANCE IN YOUR FINANCIAL PLAN

One September day several years ago, I was holed up in my office, trying to meet a deadline. I had Do Not Disturb signs plastered all over because I had to stay focused to get a book finished. So when my assistant walked in to tell me there was someone there to meet me, I'll be honest . . . I wasn't thrilled.

But my assistant knows me pretty well, and I trust her, so when she told me it was important, I believed her. I got up, huffed a little bit as I walked across the lobby, and opened the door to our reception area. I worked up a smile as I reached out my hand to the young guy in front of me. "Hi. I'm Dave."

This tall, skinny guy in a wool ski cap shook my hand and said, "Dave, it's great to meet you. My name's Steve. Steve Maness. My wife and I just wanted to come by to say, 'Thank you.' You changed our lives."

Now, I hear that from people fairly regularly, and it's always an encouragement, so I thanked him and said something like, "Well, thanks. I'm glad you're winning!"

He said, "No, you don't understand." Then he pulled that ski cap off and I'm pretty sure my jaw hit the floor. He had a huge scar running front to back across his shaved head. "I'm twenty-eight years old, and I've got brain cancer. The docs say I'm not going to make it." I *don't* hear that very often.

I'm sure I stammered around because he said, "No, no. It's okay. Because of the stuff you teach, we paid off $46,000 in twelve months, and now we're debt-free. We have a big emergency fund. We've got great health insurance that covers 100 percent after the first $5,000, and I took out a $400,000 term life insurance policy on myself before all this started. Because we listened to you and did the details like you say, my twenty-three-year-old wife, Sandy, is going to be okay when I'm gone."

I just didn't know what to say. This kid was a superstar, and he had more faith and joy than anyone I'd ever met. We became friends that day, and we stayed in touch regularly after that. A while later, I asked Steve to write his story, which we featured in my book *The Total Money Makeover*. He said:

> I can't imagine worrying about making payments on $46,000 in debt and worrying about coming up with the cash to cover our part of an 80/20 insurance plan. Or wishing I'd taken the time to set up term insurance to take care of my wife. Thanks to Dave, Sandy and I can stand side by side and fight this fight. With God's help, we will win.[1]

Well, Steve is winning right now—in heaven. He died shortly after writing that testimony for us. Sadly, he passed away just three days before the birth of his son. I can't imagine what Sandy went through, losing her husband and becoming a mom in the same week. But she and their son are doing just fine now, thanks to Steve. He did the important things, even though they weren't fun or exciting, because he wanted to take care of his family "just in case." That's what a real man does.

Wake Up!

I tell this story as a wake-up call. I get to have a lot of fun on the radio, in my books, and in our FPU classes, but insurance is one area where even I start to yawn a little bit. But I cannot say it often enough, loud enough, or long enough: get this stuff taken care of! If you don't have health insurance, life insurance, and a will in place, do not go to bed until it is done! It is *that* important. Just ask Sandy.

Now that I have your attention, let's take a look at this stuff. There are a lot of traps and gimmicks in the insurance world, so I'm going to walk you through exactly what you need—and a few things you absolutely *don't*. You ready? Good, because I'm serving up meat and potatoes in this chapter!

Insurance Basics

Nobody really *likes* spending money on insurance. It's pretty much the only thing we pay for—and over time spend a lot of money on—and hope we never have to use. But when the time comes that something major and unexpected happens, we all of a sudden *love* insurance—as long as we have the right kind.

There are seven key areas of insurance that you need to understand and get—immediately—if you don't have them. They are:

1. Homeowner's or Renter's
2. Auto
3. Health
4. Disability
5. Long-Term Care (if sixty or over)
6. Identity Theft
7. Life

The primary purpose of each one of these is the same: to transfer risk. That's what insurance does. Its sole job is to transfer the risk of financial loss *from* you *to* the insurance company. Picture it like a big umbrella over your financial life. Without it, you'll be caught out in the rain!

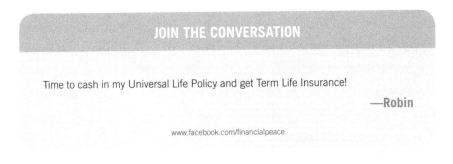

JOIN THE CONVERSATION

Time to cash in my Universal Life Policy and get Term Life Insurance!

—Robin

www.facebook.com/financialpeace

HOMEOWNER'S, RENTER'S, AND AUTO INSURANCE

We can handle these three together, because they're pretty similar. The main job of these is to cover loss or damage to your property (house, apartment, or car), and to protect you from liability. Homeowner's and auto insurance can get expensive, though. Car insurance, especially, goes way up or down depending on your driving record, how many accidents you've had, how old (or young) you are, and several other factors.

Figuring Your Deductible

The best way to keep premiums down is to get a higher-than-normal deductible. A deductible is what you have to pay out of pocket before the insurance company kicks in any money. So if you're flat broke, neck-deep in debt, and have two nickels in your savings account, you'd probably opt for a cheap, $250 or even $100 deductible, right? Big mistake! That's going to cost you a ton of money. Not only will you have higher premiums, but you'll be more likely to make a lot of small claims instead of just handling minor issues out of pocket. And when you file more claims, the insurance company raises your premiums even more at renewal.

I recommend a $1,000 deductible. Now, $1,000 is a lot of money. I know that. But remember, we're on a plan here. If you're following the Baby Steps, you know that Baby Step 3 is a fully funded emergency fund with three to six months' worth of expenses set aside for a rainy day. So if you've got $10,000 or $15,000 sitting in the bank just for emergencies, do you think you could cover a $1,000 deductible if you had a fender bender? Of course you could! See how all this stuff starts to work together? An emergency fund doesn't just give you peace of mind; it also saves you money on insurance because you can afford a higher deductible!

Before you run to your agent and start raising all your deductibles, though, take a minute to do the math to see if it makes financial sense to assume more risk. That's what we call a break-even analysis. For example, if you've got a $250 deductible and you raise it to $1,000 on your car insurance, you're raising your risk by $750. So if you have a wreck, it will cost you $1,000 out of pocket instead of $250.

Before you do that, you want to know if that deal makes sense in the long run. If your premiums go down by $75 a year as a result of taking on $750 more risk, then you'd have to go ten years without having a wreck. Make sense? Your risk ($750) breaks even with your savings ($75/year) at the ten-year mark. So in this case, that's not a great deal because it's pretty tough to go ten years between accidents.

However, if instead of $75, you end up saving $750 a year on your premiums by going with the higher deductible, then you just need to go one year without an accident to break even.

That's a no-brainer. I'd make that switch in a nanosecond, because I don't have wrecks every year.

Liability and Collision

Always carry good liability coverage on your home and car. Liability covers property damage and medical bills if you're at fault in a car wreck or if someone gets hurt on your property. Liability is one of the best deals in the insurance world, but most people still don't have enough coverage on their homes and cars. Never, *never* cut corners here. Always take *at least* $500,000 in liability. It's a difference of only pennies a month, but this one change could save you from bankruptcy if you're at fault in a major accident.

If you drive an older car, you could save some money by dropping your collision coverage. That's the insurance that pays to fix your own car. This isn't as true as it used to be, though, because collision rates have dropped a good bit over the years. Do a break-even analysis like we did earlier to see how many years you'd need to go without a wreck for it to make sense. For example, if you have a $4,000 car and dropping collision would save you $800 a year, you'd need to go five years without a wreck to break even. Depending on your driving record, that could be a tough call. Just remember, if you drop collision coverage and you have a wreck that's your fault, you won't get a penny to replace your own car. So don't do it unless you have enough cash on hand to buy another one!

Renter's Coverage

Renter's insurance, sometimes called "contents insurance," covers the stuff you own inside an apartment or other living space you don't own. A lot of renters just assume that if the building burns down, the apartment or landlord's insurance will cover their belongings, as well. It doesn't. Say you're renting a house. If the house burns down—taking all your stuff with it—the landlord's insurance will pay to rebuild the house. It covers *the landlord's* losses, not yours. Your stuff is your responsibility.

This actually happened to me once. One of my rental properties burned down, and I will never forget the conversation I had with the young family who lived there. They had just lost everything. They were *devastated*. And they looked up at me and asked, "When will we get the insurance check to replace all of our stuff?" Telling them that *my landlord's* policy didn't cover any of their belongings was one of the worst conversations of my life. They were crushed, but they hadn't planned ahead and didn't have a renter's policy in place. It broke my heart, but there was nothing I could do.

Renter's coverage is dirt-cheap. If you're currently renting, take care of this *today*! There's no excuse for not having this in place before you go to bed tonight!

Umbrella Policies

Once you build up some assets, an umbrella liability policy will be a really good idea. An umbrella policy picks up where your homeowner's or car insurance liability leaves off. So if you have a half million dollars in auto liability and someone sues you for a million, your insurance company will pay out the $500,000 in coverage—and that's it. The other $500,000 would have to come from you. If you can't pay it, you're sunk.

But an umbrella policy is fairly affordable and provides another layer of protection beyond the basic liability. It attaches to your liability and builds from there. So, if you have an umbrella policy for $1 million and basic car liability for $500,000, you'd have a total of $1.5 million in liability protection. If you're starting to build up some wealth in your retirement accounts, making good money, have a paid-for home or at least some good equity, and have other quality assets, you really need an umbrella policy. It's too good a deal to pass up, and skipping this one could cost you all the wealth and assets you've built up from a lifetime of hard work!

HEALTH INSURANCE

I think it's ridiculous that I even have to say this, but the number of uninsured people I talk to every week causes me to say it anyway: You absolutely *have* to have health insurance! Only 59 percent of people have health insurance furnished at work.[2] That means the rest of us have to pay all or part of it ourselves. How do we save money on health coverage? The same way we save in other areas of insurance: we raise the deductible and/or your coinsurance amount.

Deductibles and Copay

I've paid for my own health insurance for practically my entire adult life, so I'm pretty familiar with how much it costs, how to save money here and there, and how much the price can skyrocket year over year. One thing I've always done to keep costs down is to have a high deductible. Just like with your home or car insurance, a high deductible means you take on more risk, but in return, you get a lower premium. None of us who pay for our own insurance have a measly little $250 deductible! Most of us have a $1,000 or higher deductible, which is no problem if you have a big emergency fund.

On a standard PPO plan, you're probably used to what we call 80/20 coverage. That means after you pay the deductible, the insurance company will cover 80 percent of the costs and you'll pay 20 percent. That 80/20 has become the standard, but it is possible to change it. Many companies will give you a 70/30 policy, meaning you'll be responsible for 30 percent. Since you're taking on more risk, you'll get a lower premium. Again, if you have a good emergency fund, you should be able to cover a little more risk in order to get a lower rate. That's a good option if you have it with your plan.

Another money-saving option is to raise your stop-loss amount. That's the maximum out-of-pocket amount you have to pay if you have a ton of medical bills. If you've got a $20,000 emergency fund, then technically you could afford a $20,000 stop-loss hit, meaning you pay up to $20,000 out of pocket before the insurance company starts covering 100 percent. So raising the stop-loss amount is good, but *do not* reduce the maximum pay. That refers to the insurance company's maximum out-of-pocket expenses. If you start chemo or need a triple bypass, the bills start to get astronomical. Do not put a cap on what the insurance will pay; otherwise, you could be recovering from cancer with a $1 million hospital bill that you're responsible for.

Health Savings Accounts

The best health insurance deal on the market today is the Health Savings Account, or HSA. This isn't for everyone, but if it works for your family, it's one of the best deals the insurance companies and government give you. Basically, the HSA is a tax-sheltered savings account for medical expenses with a high-deductible insurance policy. So, you've got a quality insurance plan in place, but you're on the hook for a large deductible (usually over $5,000) every year. Plus, you have a savings account that grows *tax free* for medical expenses, so it's kind of like a government match on your healthcare savings!

I had my insurance guy put some quotes together for me as an example. A thirty-year-old couple with two young kids in my area could get a traditional 80/20 PPO with a $500 deductible for $640/month. That's a big premium to pay every month! That same family could get an HSA for just $316/month but with a $5,650 deductible. Whoa, that's a big deductible! That means every medical expense up to $5,650 is an out-of-pocket expense. Once they hit that mark, the HSA pays 100 percent, but until then, you better believe the family would watch every medical expense like a hawk.

In that example, the cost of the HSA would be over $300 less than the PPO. The family can then put that $300 in the savings account of the HSA, where it will grow without taxes. They can pull that money out for any medical expense, from doctor's bills to Band-Aids, and any unused money in the account just rolls over and continues to grow tax-deferred. In a sense, you're growing a new emergency fund in the HSA just for health expenses, and the government is letting you write off the contributions! It's a great deal!

So, what does that do to how this family "shops" for medical care? It makes them wise, thrifty consumers. When someone else is paying the bills, we don't really shop around or second-guess every test or idea the doctors have, do we? But when we start paying for those $10 aspirins in the hospital, we get very, very careful about how, where, and when we spend our medical dollars.

To figure out if an HSA would work for your family, you need to do a break-even analysis like we did with car insurance. In our example, the family saves more than $300 per month on premiums, which would round up to about $4,000 a year. However, they're taking on $5,000 more risk in the form of a higher deductible. That means they'd need to go a little over a year without many major healthcare costs. If you have a healthy family and don't spend much time in the doctor's office, this makes sense. But if you have some chronic illness in the family, it probably won't, because you could end up paying that full deductible every year. Also, not every HSA plan pays 100 percent after the deductible, so be sure you know exactly what you're getting into when you go insurance shopping.

DISABILITY INSURANCE

Disability insurance is designed to replace income that is lost due to a short-term or permanent disability. It basically provides an income for you and your family if you have an accident or health condition that prevents you from working. We don't like to think about that, but there's a good chance you could depend on some kind of disability protection during your working lifetime. In fact, if you are under age thirty-five, you have a one in three chance of becoming disabled for at least six months during the course of your career.[3] This insurance is an essential part of your financial plan, but it is probably the most underinsured area in the industry. Most people don't overlook medical, auto, and life insurance, but they do overlook disability.

I had been going on and on about this at a live event once. Later, while I was doing a book signing, a guy in his late twenties came up to me and thanked me for driving home the point about disability insurance. He said, "Dave, this stuff absolutely saved my family's life. You're looking at a twenty-eight-year-old man who is making $60,000 a year and is on permanent disability." At that young age, he had developed a disease that would just continue to get worse, and he had been declared permanently disabled; he'd *never* be able to go back to work. He was making $100,000 a year in his job before this started, but because he got 60 percent disability coverage, his family has an ongoing $60,000 income while he fights through the health problems. You think he's glad he committed a few bucks to disability insurance?

Try to buy disability coverage that pays if you cannot perform the job that you were educated or trained to do. This is called occupational, or "own-occ," disability. It can get a little pricey, so you may only be able to get a couple of years' worth of coverage. But that will give you enough time to transition into another line of work, go back to school, or get training in another field so you can get back to work.

For example, I'm a radio guy. If I lost my voice due to an accident or illness, then I wouldn't be able to do my radio show very well, would I? If I had two years of own-occ coverage, the insurance company would provide an income for me for two years. Then, they'd tell me to get a job! That's because permanent disability is different from occupational disability. If I'm permanently disabled, then I can't work at all, and that's just the way it is. If I'm occupationally disabled, it just means I can't do *that* job anymore.

How Long and How Much?

Stay away from short-term disability that covers less than five years. If you're following the Baby Steps, you already have a short-term disability plan. That's called the *emergency fund*! If you have six months' worth of expenses in the bank just for emergencies, you'll be able to pay your bills while you recover from a short-term problem.

Long-term disability is the only thing I personally own. That covers anything over five years. The pricing of long-term disability is all over the place, though. If you go out and try to buy it as an individual, you may get some sticker shock. And it's not really based on your age or health at all; it's more based on what you do, what kind of job you have. If you're a construction worker, for example, it's probably going to be more expensive than if you sat at a desk all day. Why? Because it's a lot easier to get hurt on a construction site than at your desk! Since the chances of a disabling accident are great, it costs more.

The best way to get long-term disability insurance is through your workplace. A lot of companies just pay for it for all their employees as a benefit. That's actually what I do for my team. But even if the company doesn't pay the bill, you could still buy it yourself through your company and get a great group rate. If you have that option, take it. This is the one time I'll tell you not to even bother shopping around; I promise, your group rate at work will be the cheapest option you'll find. If they don't offer it at work or if you're self-employed, you may still be eligible for a group rate through a trade organization. Talk to your insurance agent and see what options you have, because you need this!

I recommend buying disability coverage in the 60–65 percent range. That means if you become disabled, the insurance will pay that percentage of your regular income. I personally like 65 percent, because that's about how much of your salary you actually bring home after taxes, Social Security, and other deductions that come out of your pay. So, if you make $100,000, a 65-percent plan would provide a $65,000 income for your family. There is a cut-off point, though, so if you're making a million dollars a year, you're not going to find an insurance company that will pay you that forever! The goal of disability insurance is to pay your bills and keep food on the table, not to make you rich!

LONG-TERM CARE INSURANCE

Long-term care insurance is for nursing home, assisted living facilities, and in-home care. Statistically speaking, long-term care coverage is pretty much a complete waste of money—*until* you turn sixty. Then, something dramatic happens. Long-term care coverage goes from being a waste to being an essential part of your insurance plan. You don't need it when you're fifty-nine, but you need to be on the phone setting it up the day you turn sixty.

With the average life expectancy going up, adults are living longer than ever, and the cost of giving our seniors the treatment and care they need—and deserve—can break them or *whoever* is paying the bills. According to the American Association of Homes and Services for the Aging (AAHSA), 69 percent of those turning age sixty-five today will need some form of long-term care.[4] However, Kaiser Health News reports that only 10 percent of seniors have long-term care insurance in place.[5] Don't miss that. *Seven out of ten* will need some form of long-term care, but only *one out of ten* plan for it in their insurance coverage! That means six out of ten seniors will one day pay long-term care expenses out of pocket—either *their* pockets or their adult kids' pockets. That's a bad plan.

Boomers Stuck in the Middle

Based on my experience and the people I talk to every day, I think the biggest expense facing baby boomers nowadays is not their children's college bills, but their parents' elder care. That's why some have started calling boomers the "sandwich generation." They're stuck between taking care of their kids in college and their parents in the nursing home. Without proper coverage to pay the care facility, these boomers are in for a rocky time, which can ultimately destroy their own nest egg for retirement.

Studies show that the last six months of your life are often the most expensive, possibly more expensive than any previous *decade* of your life. Our own research has found that seniors who are admitted to the hospital for a serious medical emergency stay there for an average of sixty days.[6] That's *two months* of round-the-clock hospital care! And if you're thinking about moving your folks' assets around to try to get them to look broke so they'll qualify for Medicaid, let me set the record straight. Sadly, this is a common practice, but it is considered fraud and it is ILLEGAL. It is immoral, unethical, and you could go to jail for trying it. If the investigators even get a whiff of something fishy, they have the power to dig back through five years of records in some cases to get to the truth. Don't become a criminal just because you and your parents failed to plan ahead!

The Powdered Butt Syndrome

This can be a tough conversation to have with an aging parent. I get that. It is an incredibly stressful and sensitive experience when a grown man or woman has to help "parent" Mom and

Dad. And honestly, your folks may not want to hear it. Isn't it funny how you could be the worldwide leading expert in your field but your parents *still* won't take your advice on something? I call this the "powdered butt syndrome." That is, once someone's powdered your butt, they don't want your advice on sex or money! Even Jesus had a hard time getting things done in His own hometown:

> Jesus told them, "A prophet has little honor in his hometown, among his relatives, on the streets he played in as a child." Jesus wasn't able to do much of anything there—he laid hands on a few sick people and healed them, that's all. He couldn't get over their stubbornness.[7]

If Jesus had a hard time getting His point across to His family, you better believe it's even harder for you and me! But it is a conversation you *must* have with them. The stakes are just too high on this one. I've seen too many families work their entire lifetimes to set up sizable retirement incomes, only to lose every dime of it on a few years of long-term care. Don't run a fabulous marathon and stumble in the last mile. Plan ahead and finish strong.

IDENTITY THEFT PROTECTION INSURANCE

The fastest growing white-collar crime in North America today is identity theft. Some studies report that as many as one in three Americans have their identities stolen, and that number grows each year.[8] And if it happens to you, you can expect to spend up to 600 hours cleaning up the mess![9] Basically, if someone rips off your identity, getting everything ironed out will be your full-time, forty-hour-a-week job for the next ten to fifteen weeks. Personally, I don't have time for that, so I better have some quality ID theft protection in place.

When you start looking around, you'll find a ton of bad policies and bad information. Do some research and check the reviews of the company you're dealing with. One "leading" provider can't stay out of fraud lawsuits long enough to get anything done! Also, a lot of places just offer basic credit report monitoring. Do *not* fall for this! That's something you can do yourself. In fact, you should be checking your credit report at least once a year, anyway. We covered that in chapter 5, *Credit Sharks in Suits*.

So look for coverage that actually provides restoration services if your identity gets hacked. That means *someone else* will spend the time it takes to clean up the mess so you won't have to. Remember, insurance is all about transferring risk, right? In this case, you're paying someone to take on the risk of cleaning up the aftermath of your stolen identity. This is someone who is ready, willing, and able to go to battle with the banks and creditors that will start coming after you to collect bad debts that you genuinely do not owe. And beyond that, these are people that do this for a living. They know who to call and what to do a lot better than you and I do.

LIFE INSURANCE (AND WILLS)

We started this chapter talking about my friend Steve Maness. This guy was a superstar for a lot of reasons, but one of the very best things he did in his entire life was to get some good, quality term life insurance. Now, this was a young man in his twenties. His wife was even younger than he was, and they had no kids at the time. How many couples like that do you know who haven't even thought about life insurance? When you're twenty-five, you feel bulletproof, like you have all the time in the world. But Steve didn't. When he got that policy, he didn't know he was going to get sick. He didn't know that his wife would become a widow in her midtwenties. He didn't know that he would have a son that would need to be taken care of financially. He just knew that wise, loving people get life insurance so their families will be okay.

If you wait until you get sick, you've waited too long. Remember, insurance is all about risk. It's easy and fairly inexpensive to get life insurance when you're young and healthy, but if you wait until after you've been diagnosed with some serious health problem, you're probably out of luck. You'll either be denied coverage or you'll end up paying astronomical premiums on a subpar policy. So if you don't have life insurance in place, make the call TODAY! You never know what could happen tomorrow.

Two Types of Life Insurance

Life insurance has one job: it replaces your income when you die. If you have a family and you earn an income, that income will go away when you die. Life insurance steps in and pays a benefit that, when invested properly, can replace your income for life. Your family will still miss you, but they won't miss you *and* wonder how to pay the light bill after your funeral.

There are two main types of insurance on the market today: term and cash value. I have a very strong opinion about which one you should get, and that has brought me an endless stream of hate mail from insurance people for decades. That's fine with me. You send me all the hate mail you want. I've got a great shredder in my office that loves the attention.

Term insurance is for a specified time period. If you get a five-year term policy, you are insured for a five-year term. That's why they call it "term." Term is easy to understand, cheaper than other options, and has no savings plan attached to it. It has one job and one job only: it replaces your income when you die. If you buy a $400,000 term policy for a twenty-year term, and you die within that twenty-year period, your family will get $400,000. It's pretty simple.

Cash value insurance plans usually aren't for a specified term; they're for life. They are a *lot* more expensive, because you're not just paying for the insurance; you're also funding a savings account inside the insurance policy. We'll talk about that later. You might hear cash value insurance called "permanent insurance," because there's no term attached to it. That really plays into what I think is the most common myth about life insurance in general, which is that the need for life insurance is a permanent situation. It's not. If you do the things we teach, you'll ultimately become *self-insured* because you'll be out of debt with a full emergency fund and a whole lot of money in investments.

I want to be crystal clear here: Cash value life insurance is total garbage. (Cue the hate mail.) It is a horrible, horrible product, but it makes the insurance companies the most money, which means insurance salespeople get the best commissions on this trash. The agents and the companies make a whole lot more money on cash value policies than they do on term policies, so which one do you think they push more? Don't fall for it!

Insurance Is a Lousy Investment

Some agents will try to win you over by talking about how cash value is really an investment. They may say something like, "Term is like renting, but cash value is like owning." Here's the

truth: you never want to use an insurance plan as an investment. Insurance is for insurance. It *costs* you money because
you're transferring risk. Keep your investments separate and
you'll always come out ahead.

First of all, the returns on cash value insurance as an investment are historically low. The lifetime average of the stock
market is around 12 percent, so you'd think that any investment, even inside a cash value plan, would be somewhere
around that. Think again. The different types of cash value policies grow at different rates, but generally they come in between
2 and 7 percent. Some products, like variable life, may average
better, but then the insurance company hits you with all sorts
of fees, so your net yield hits somewhere around 7–8 percent.

But here's the kicker for me. Let's say Joe gets a $125,000 cash
value policy at thirty years old. He'll pay somewhere around $140
per month for that if he's in good health and doesn't smoke. Part
of that $140 goes to pay for the insurance, and the rest goes into
that "great" savings account someone sold him. After forty years
of paying way too much for his insurance, Joe's built up around
$65,000 in cash value by age seventy. So, he has $125,000 in
insurance *and* $65,000 in cash value. At that point, Joe dies. How
much will the insurance company pay out to his wife? She'll get
$125,000. Can you guess what happens to the $65,000 he's built
up by overpaying for his insurance for forty years? The insurance
company keeps it! Good-bye, Joe! Thanks for playing!

If Joe had gone with term instead, he could have gotten a
$400,000 twenty-year policy (more than three times as much
coverage) for about $11 a month. That's about $130 less every
month. If he were to invest that $130 into a good mutual fund
at 12 percent starting at age thirty, it would grow to around
$133,000 by age fifty when the term expires, and to more than

$1.5 million by age seventy! And if Joe dies at that point, guess what? His wife still has that $1.5 million! That's why it's always better to keep your insurance and investments separate. You don't want to faithfully invest your whole life and leave all that money to an insurance company, do you? I sure don't.

JOIN THE CONVERSATION

I learned I don't need to buy the extra insurance on things like electronics from the store. I always felt so responsible when I opted to do so. Now, I put that money in my account and I've become my own replacement plan. About 99.9 percent of the time I don't need it, and I can use it for something MUCH better!

—Diana

www.facebook.com/financialpeace

How Much Coverage?

You need to get coverage equal to ten times your income. So, if you're working and making $40,000 a year, you need $400,000. The ten-times rule of thumb is not an arbitrary number. Remember, life insurance is designed to replace your income. If your surviving spouse invests that $400,000 in good mutual funds at an average 10–12 percent return, he or she could peel off $40,000 a year from that investment to replace your income without ever cutting into the principal.

Also, all you stay-at-home moms need term coverage too! Even if Mom's not an "income earner," she does bring financial value to the family. Just think of all the things she does around the house that Dad would be responsible for if something happens to her. She may not be earning an income, but if she were gone, Dad would have to pay Mary Poppins—or at least a pricey childcare service—to take care of the kids. So figure out how much a nanny or other childcare would cost per year, multiply that by ten, and get that much in term coverage on Mom.

Last Word on Life Insurance

If you currently have a cash value life insurance policy, you need to get rid of it immediately. You're throwing money away every month. Before you do that, though, be sure to get a good term policy in place. Once your new term policy is active, drop the cash value and don't look back. And don't even bother arguing with the agent who has sold or is trying to sell you this mess. You don't owe them an explanation! Just say no and move on.

TWO FINAL WAYS TO SAY, "I LOVE YOU"

I've got some bad news for you. The death rate for human beings is 100 percent. You *are* going to die someday! None of us know when that's going to happen, but that doesn't mean it should catch us totally unprepared. There are two things we can do to make sure our loved ones are taken care of after we're gone.

The Legacy Drawer

If you were to die today, would your spouse or other family members know where all your important papers, life insurance policies, bank account information, computer passwords, and final instructions are? In my years doing the radio show, I have talked to countless mourning spouses who have no idea how to put their hands on this information. On top of the crushing loss of their husband or wife, they are immediately thrown into a financial nightmare because they don't know what to do or how to access the accounts or where the final instructions are. It's a total disaster.

After talking to those spouses, I decided I was absolutely not going to leave my wife in that position if something happens to me. So I dedicated some time to creating what I call our "legacy drawer." There is one drawer in our home where I have neatly organized everything Sharon will need to put her hands on when I'm gone. It outlines where our life insurance plans are, where all of our retirement and bank accounts are, and what all our account passwords are. It has a contact list of our lawyer, tax attorney, accountant, insurance agents, and other relevant people on our financial team. It has a copy of our will and final instructions. It may or may not even have a love note in there to comfort my wife after I'm gone!

The goal of the legacy drawer is to take all of the questions, confusion, and guesswork out of the ordeal. I encourage you to get all this stuff together as a family and make sure those you'll leave behind know exactly where your legacy drawer is and how to access it. Sure, it will take several hours to pull all this together and make all the copies, but it's an investment your loved ones will treasure. It's an act of love that will enable you to take care of your family's needs after you're gone. Don't skip this.

Your Will: The Last Gift You'll Ever Give

Before we close this chapter, I want to mention one more thing. This may be one of the most important things you'll ever hear me say, so get ready, here it is: *you need a will!* The financial planners and counselors I work with tell me that up to 70 percent of Americans do not have wills in place. This makes me sick! If you absolutely, positively *hate* your family, then go ahead and die without a will. But if you like them even a little bit, put one in place today!

If you die without a will, you are going to tie up your heirs for years. This is your final, possibly greatest gift to them because it lays out exactly what you want to happen with all your assets. If you die without a will, the state gets to decide what happens to your stuff, your kids, and your financial legacy. I'd rather make those decisions myself instead of letting the government sort it out. I don't care if you're single or married, young or old, kids or no kids; YOU NEED A WILL!

JOIN THE CONVERSATION

We purchased renter's insurance immediately after taking this lesson. We simply never thought about what we would do if something caused us to lose everything we owned while renting.

—Katie

www.facebook.com/financialpeace

INSURANCE RECAP

This chapter is all about doing the details. Insurance isn't all that exciting—unless you fail to get this stuff done and then wind up with an exciting stack of bills after an exciting emergency! We covered a lot of ground here, so let's do a quick recap.

1. Homeowner's, renter's, and auto: Save money by raising the deductible. Carry adequate liability. On older cars, you may consider saving money by dropping your collision coverage (as long as you can afford to buy a replacement car out of pocket). Umbrella policies are a good idea once you have some assets to provide an extra layer of protection.

2. Health: Save money by raising the deductible and stop-loss amount. Never accept a maximum payout limit from the insurance company. Check into the Health Savings Account to see if it's a good fit for your family.

3. Disability: This replaces your income if a disability prevents you from working. Own-occ coverage provides an income for a specified period, giving you time to learn a new trade if a disability prevents you from continuing your current occupation. Stay away from short-term policies (five years or less).

4. Long-term care: Buy it the day you turn sixty years old. You may need to have this conversation with your aging parents, especially if you'll be responsible for their elder care.

5. Identity theft protection: Don't buy a policy that only provides credit report monitoring; you can do that on your own. Only buy those that provide clean-up services. That's the risk you really want to transfer to professionals.

6. Life insurance: Only buy term life insurance. Never mix investments with your insurance. Get ten times your income, and don't forget the stay-at-home mom. Insurance is not a permanent need, so a good term policy will give you time to become self-insured.

WE DID IT!

My husband and I are both fifty-six years old, and we are totally debt-free! However, we still wanted to take *Financial Peace University* to learn how to honor God with our money and learn more about investing and retirement. The week we had the class on insurance was very eye-opening for us!

When we were in our twenties, we took out two whole life insurance policies—$25,000 on each of us. We paid for those plus two other term insurance policies, which totaled almost $250 per month. We made some phone calls and checked into Zander Insurance at Dave's recommendation. We realized we were underinsured and that we'd been paying way too much! We got an additional $125,000 in term life insurance and we're now saving $120 per month on our premiums. And the BEST part is we cashed in our whole life policies, which gave us more than enough to fund our full six-month emergency fund!

We have more coverage, less monthly expense, and now a fully funded emergency fund. Thank you, Dave Ramsey!

Cindy and Gary
Arvada, CO

KEY POINTS

1. Insurance is a crucial part of any financial plan.
2. The purpose of insurance is to transfer risk from you to the insurance company.
3. An emergency fund will allow you to carry higher deductibles, which in turn lower your premiums.
4. You should always keep your insurance and your investments separate. Never use an insurance product as a wealth-building tool.
5. Disability insurance is one of the most underinsured areas, but it is actually one of the most important. Get it today!

QUESTIONS FOR REFLECTION

1. Have you ever allowed financial stress to prevent you from getting adequate insurance coverage in the key areas discussed in this chapter? Why is that so risky for your long-term success?
2. How does having a full emergency fund of three to six months of expenses change your approach to insurance?
3. What are some strategies for lowering premiums?
4. Why is cash value insurance such a bad deal?
5. Is life insurance a permanent need? What does it mean to be self-insured?
6. Do you have adequate coverage in each of the areas discussed in this chapter? What action steps do you need to take immediately to fill any gaps in your insurance plan?

8

THAT'S NOT GOOD ENOUGH!

HOW TO BUY ONLY BIG, BIG BARGAINS

I spend a lot of time in my books, live events, and radio show telling people how to save money, invest money, make their money go further, and give more money away, but that's only part of the puzzle. The truth is, sometimes you've just got to spend some money! I mean, even you savers are really spenders part of the time, right? Otherwise, you wouldn't have clothes on your back or food in the fridge. We're all *consumers*, even the cheapest, most penny-pinching folks in the bunch!

And here's the truth: I *love* buying things when I know I'm getting a good deal. It's just fun all the way around. If I can work a deal where everyone wins, where I get what I want and the salesperson gets what he wants, it's one of the best feelings in the world to me. I'm happy; he's happy. I have what I want; he has my money, which is what he wants. We both feel good about it, and neither one of us walks away regretting the deal. When those pieces come together, it's magic—and it's true at home and in business.

So in this chapter, I'm going to teach you my absolute favorite phrase in negotiating: *That's not good enough!* Those four little words have saved me more money than I can count over the years!

NEGOTIATING GOOD DEALS IS NOT IMMORAL

One of the funny things I've noticed almost every time I've taught this material is that some people think negotiating for a better deal is a form of abuse. I've had people walk up to me and say, "Goodness gracious, I could never do those things. If I try to get someone to give me a better deal, I'd be taking money out of their pocket. I don't want to save money by hurting someone else. That'd be taking advantage of them!"

Think Globally

That whole way of thinking is totally foreign to me. In my house growing up, my whole family were world-class bargain hunters. We called it "horse trading." We were always looking for a better price on the things we wanted. And you know what? That's exactly what almost every other culture in the world does! Practically everywhere outside the U.S., negotiation is a way of life. If you've ever gone overseas, you've seen it. In fact, some cultures will even get *offended* if you don't engage in some back-and-forth dealing!

But not us. Here in America, Joe and Suzie hop in their fleeced—ahem, sorry, "leased"—car, use a credit card to fill up the tank, pull onto the bond-financed highway, and head to the shopping mall where they'll pay 120 percent of retail on an 18 percent store card, and still think they got a good deal just because it was sitting on a shelf with "SALE" written over it! Most people don't even think about this stuff. They pay the sticker price and figure that's just what everyone else does, never even thinking about asking for a better deal.

I had a good friend who spent some time as a missionary in another country. We think she may have been on the mission field a little too long, if you know what I mean. She was there for about three years, and when she got home, she almost got into fights with the retail clerks at department stores, haggling over prices. She would yell in their faces, "Better price! Better price!" because that's what she'd been doing at all the markets and with merchants for the past three years.

JOIN THE CONVERSATION

I learned to have patience when looking for a good deal. There is always another "one" tomorrow.

—**Richard**

www.facebook.com/financialpeace

Ground Rules for Big Bargains

We'll start with a fundamental point: it's okay to want a better deal. It's not immoral to want to save more of your hard-earned money. You're not hurting the other party by asking for a deal as long as you follow some basic principles of negotiating.

First of all, you should feel good about a deal only if you have in no way misrepresented the truth. Don't tell half-truths or complete lies just to save a buck. That's wrong, immoral, and if you do this, you should be ashamed of yourself! We're not looking for ways to con people out of their goods, services, or money. The goal here is to create an environment where *everybody* gets what they want.

Second, you must never set out to harm the other party. Negotiating deals is not, and should not be, focused on inflicting pain or hardship on someone else. If you're using a negotiation as a way to "get" somebody, back off. You're coming at this from the wrong spirit, and you don't deserve the deal.

Third, you've got to set out to create a true win-win deal. Again, the point is to set up a situation where everyone wins. If you've done a good job talking through all the parts of the deal and following the steps we're about to lay out, everyone should walk away feeling fantastic about doing business together.

JOIN THE CONVERSATION

I get a good deal when I take cash, do my homework, and walk away! Salespeople need to sell it worse than I need to buy it!

—DeCole

www.facebook.com/financialpeace

THE THREE KEYS TO OPENING THE DOOR TO BIG BARGAINS

None of what I'm about to outline is revolutionary, and it's only the rare person who walks up to me and says, "You know, I've *never* heard this before!" So the problem obviously is not that we don't know what to do; it's that we're just not doing it. My goal in this chapter is to help you do it! To do that, we're going to look at three keys to unlocking the door to huge bargains.

The First Key: Negotiate Everything

The first key to opening the door to big bargains is learning to negotiate everything—yes, *everything*! Just start with the assumption that you can get anything at a discount. Assume that the sticker or sales tag says, "Price starting at:" before the actual listed price. It's the starting point. It's not the final price. Get it into your head that everything in every store in every city in the world is negotiable. You just have to ask. You have to make it a way of life.

I am amazed at the number of people who shell out huge amounts of money for things and never even think to ask if they can have a better price. And I'm not just talking about cars, computers, and Sea-Doos here. What about asking your plumber for a discount? Or your landscaper? Or your doctor? MSN Money reported a while back that fewer than one in five consumers had ever asked for a lower price from their doctor, dentist, hospital, or pharmacy.[1] That amazes me—only one in five people asked for a deal! But guess what? Of those who actually bothered to ask, HALF of them got a better price![2]

If you really grasp what a win-win deal looks like, it will become perfectly natural and comfortable to ask for the deal every time. The best example of a win-win deal that I've ever seen, and one I've used countless times onstage and even in *Financial Peace Revisited*, is taken from Roger Fisher and William Ury's outstanding book *Getting to Yes:*

> There were once two elderly ladies who had one orange between them which they were negotiating for. After a lengthy discussion these two ladies could not come up with a solution except to split the difference, so they cut the orange in half, each taking one half. One lady proceeded to peel the orange and use the peel for baking a cake, while the other peeled her half and ate the fruit.[3]

In *Financial Peace Revisited,* I explained the story this way:

> If the two had spent time, through good communication, finding out what the other's needs were for the orange, they both could

have had the whole orange, and neither would have been the lesser. The point of the story is that if you bring creativity and communication to your purchases, you can make excellent buys and help people in the process.[4]

The bottom line of the win-win deal is that, with a little bit of communication, both parties can walk away with 100 percent of what they want. It doesn't have to be 50/50. Both parties can have it all.

JOIN THE CONVERSATION

To get a good bargain, you have to walk away, walk away, walk away. I looked at 119 houses before I found the (little and very economical) one I bought. Then we negotiated to knock 20 percent off of that price. It was a nail-biter, but worth it for the bottom line.

—Deena

www.facebook.com/financialpeace

The Lucky Seven: Basic Rules of Negotiating

Getting a great deal doesn't happen by accident, and it doesn't always happen *just because* you bothered to ask. Sure, that's where you have to start, but if the guy on the receiving end doesn't bite, does that mean you're out of luck? No way! Remember, this is a *negotiation,* and that means it's a conversation of back-and-forth give-and-take. Over the years, both in my personal life and in my business deals, I've come up with seven guidelines that can help you make the most of every single negotiation. If you follow "The Lucky Seven," I promise you'll get some fantastic deals.

1. Always tell the absolute truth.

If you're selling a car and the transmission has been slipping, that should be one of the first things you tell a prospective buyer. Don't hold your breath while he's taking a test drive and hope that it doesn't slip while he's checking it out. No amount of money is worth your integrity.

If you want to be poor, do poor people stuff. If you want to be rich, do ricn people stuff. And most rich people don't cheat and swindle when dealing. In fact, Thomas Stanley, in his groundbreaking study of millionaires, titled *The Millionaire Mind*, interviewed dozens of deca-millionaires—men and women worth more than $10 million—and through his analysis came up with thirty-eight character qualities shared among America's ultrarich. You know what character quality was at the top of the list? Integrity. The single most common characteristic of the top one-quarter of 1 percent of the wealthiest people in the country is fanatical, off-the-chart levels of integrity. So always tell the truth when you're negotiating.

This works the other way, too. If you're trying work a deal and realize the other person is flat-out lying to you, get out of there. Not too long ago, my wife and I were shopping in a major, national-chain appliance store. We picked out what we needed, the salesperson and I went back and forth on price (yes, I do still haggle for deals in big chain stores), and we were close to wrapping up the deal. Near the end, the guy turned to me and says, "Well, of course you want the extended warranty."

I laughed a little and said, "No, I don't buy extended warranties."

He came back with, "But you need it. I tell you what, even Dave Ramsey buys extended warranties." Now, I've been teaching people *not* to buy extended warranties for decades. I say it a few times a week to more than four million listeners on my radio show. This store was close to my home and my office, and I thought this guy knew who I was and was just joking around. He didn't, and he wasn't.

I said, "I can assure you, Dave Ramsey does *not* buy extended warranties."

This got the guy hot under the collar. He got all defensive and said, "He does, too! He was in this very store the other day and bought a television with an extended warranty! I can show you the paperwork!"

At this point, my face was changing colors, and I was doing my best to bite my tongue. I take my personal integrity so seriously that I start to lose my mind a little bit when people spread complete lies about me. This guy was in my face telling all about what "Dave Ramsey" does, so I reached for my back pocket. He was going on and on, and finally I just put my driver's license in front of his face and said, "DAVE RAMSEY DOES NOT BUY EXTENDED WARRANTIES!"

At that point, all the blood immediately left his face. He said something like, "Oh, I'm *so* sorry. Listen, Dave, we can get you a deal today. We can take care of you right now." By that point, I was on my feet and heading to the door. We went down the street and ended up paying a little more at another store, because I absolutely refuse to do business with liars. Life's too short to work with people you can't trust and who have no integrity.

2. Use the power of cash.

It's getting less and less common to see cash when you're shopping, isn't it? Go to any mall, grocery store, or retail place and you'll see rows of customers lined up with their plastic already in their hands. But if you walk into a store fanning yourself with a handful of $100 bills, I promise you'll get some attention. That's because actual cash is emotional. It triggers a response in people. In chapter 4, *Dumping Debt*, we said that spending cash hurts because it makes you realize you're spending *real* money. You don't get that with plastic. It works the other direction too. If you're trying to make a purchase and have a fistful of bills, it definitely catches the eye of the person you're dealing with.

Cash also shows the seller that this deal could happen immediately. If he wants to sell his car today, your cash will look a lot more attractive than someone coming with a check or someone else who has to go to the bank to get a loan before they can buy. The seller knows that if he nods his head and shakes your hand, it's a lock. The deal is done. You have the car and he has his cash *immediately*. That's pretty compelling for most people, especially private sellers.

3. Understand and use "walk away" power.

Even if you work these steps throughout the whole process, there's still one area where you can get destroyed in a deal: the closing table. A lot of salespeople, especially those selling big-ticket items, will humor you throughout the process until it's time to wrap up the purchase. Then they'll change something at the last minute. By then, they figure you're so emotionally tied to the product that you won't be able to back out. Usually, they're right.

Do not get married to a purchase before you buy it. Sellers can smell desperation, and if they see that you are already imagining lounging by the pool in the deck chairs they're selling, there's no chance you're going to get a deal. Why would they deal? They already know you'll pay full price. Play it casual throughout the whole process, and always be willing to walk away at any point in the negotiation if you simply cannot get the deal you want or need. If you just say, "Well, we can't do that" and start walking away, nine times out of ten the salesperson will follow you to the door, yelling out lower offers!

4. Shut up! Don't talk too much.

If you're trying to buy something, it's not your job to come up with a good price. Make the seller work for it a little bit. If he says the price is $5,000, just stand there and look at him without saying a word. Silence is powerful, and most people can't stand sitting in awkward silence.

I drove past a car lot one Saturday just goofing off, and I decided to pull in to check out a little Jeep that had caught my eye. I didn't really need it, but it would have been a fun little car to drive around. Plus, I had some time to kill and thought I'd test some of these ideas on a car salesman. So I'm standing out there, looking at this Jeep, and of course the sales guy pops out of the office and starts talking immediately. I consciously chose to not say anything because I wanted to see what this guy would talk himself into if I just stood there quietly. I mean, I wasn't a total jerk; I acknowledged his existence, but I stuck to nonverbal communication.

He said, "The sticker price is $5,500, but I could get it down to $4,500 for you." I just stood there and nodded. I walked over and looked at one of the wheels, and he said, "You know, I have a good friend at the tire store next door. I could throw on a new set of tires at no cost, too." I didn't say a word. I walked around the front of the car and stared at the hood. My silence was killing him. He said, "Okay, I can tell you're a man who knows his cars, and you can tell this car has been hit."

I had no idea! All I did was stand there silent, and this guy went from $5,500 to practically giving me the car with new tires and admitting it had been in an accident! I don't think you should be rude or disrespectful to people, but you are probably talking too much in your deal negotiations. Try shutting up, and see what happens.

5. "That's not good enough!"

This has been a magic phrase in many, many of my negotiations. Most people don't like conflict, so this little phrase can make a huge difference when you're trying to work a deal. This is especially powerful if you pair it with shutting up. When the person trying to make the sale gives the price, just look him in the eye, say, "That's not good enough," and then shut up. At that point, it's up to him to change the deal.

In those situations, what do we do? Most of the time, we start going back and forth on price, right? I'll say $200, you'll come back with $100, and then we'll "compromise" by going with $150. Hasn't that happened to you before? But if we'll just make the other guy start chopping at the price himself, you can come out ahead. His first price cut could be lower than where you would even start!

6. Good guy, bad guy.

We see the "good guy, bad guy" technique in cop shows all the time on television, but you should be aware that it is a staple of the sales industry. It's called "position selling," meaning the salesperson tries to "position" himself between you, the buyer, and "the bad guy," which is usually some mean old sales manager in the back office. If you've ever had a salesperson "go check with the manager" about a deal you're asking for, chances are the manager isn't even there! The sales guy may just run to the back room, have a few sips of coffee, and then come back to you, looking all beat up and saying, "Man, my boss was not happy about me asking him for this, but this is what he said we can do . . . "

Now, this technique can be used by buyers, but I don't recommend it. Some people try to position themselves between the sales guy and the mean, tightwad spouse at home in order to get a deal. Remember, if there's no integrity in the deal, it's not a good deal. I just want you to be aware of this one when you see it being used on you.

7. "If I" take-away technique.

This one can be fun, because you never know what you get out of it. You use this one near the end of the deal, after you've pretty much figured out that the price has gotten as low as it can go. That's when you say, "Okay, if I take the car for that price, you've got to throw in new wipers and floor mats." Or, "If I take the house for that price, you'll have to cover the closing costs." The point is to agree to the price, but then throw something else into the deal.

A good friend of mine used this one all the time while doing real estate deals. He'd walk through the house and had a special knack for finding that one thing in the house that didn't quite fit, the one point of pride in an otherwise average house. The process went something like this. Say he was looking at a little dump of a house, but the owner had a bass boat on a trailer in the driveway. He'd say, "I see that you're standing firm at the $100,000 price for the house. I can do that, but if I pay that much, you're going to have to throw in the bass boat."

The seller would likely respond, "What? I can't do that. That boat is my baby!"

So my friend would reply, "Okay, but if you keep the bass boat, you'll have to throw in something else or we'll have to come down on price." See what he did? He put the boat in the deal, and when the buyer didn't agree, my friend carried on *as though he had ever had the boat*! Basically, he was saying, "If you take the boat from me, what are you going to give me for it?"

"The Lucky Seven" rules can get you incredible deals on the stuff you buy every day, but they only work if you actually use them. Have some fun with them! I've found that some of the best deals happen when we stop taking everything so seriously and just enjoy the process!

The Second Key: Practice Patience

The first key to unlocking incredible deals is learning to negotiate everything. The second key is to have patience. I'll be honest; this is the hardest part for me. I can do it as a matter of personal discipline, but it's not my nature to be patient. My wife can wait days, weeks, months, and even years to get back around to buying something she wants. Not me. Once I decide I want something, I want it right now and I'm tired of messing around.

Our collective, consumer lack of patience always makes headlines whenever a hot new gadget comes out, doesn't it? Now, I've got nothing against Apple; I own some Apple products myself, and I'm incredibly impressed at their ability to market their products and create demand in the marketplace. However, I'm always blown away when I see the long lines of people outside their stores for hours or even days before the release of the next new "i" gadget. Why would someone wait in line for six hours to buy something when they could just walk into the store with no lines the next day to buy it? It's because we have a deep-rooted "I need it NOW" mind-set around certain products.

This lack of patience can get rather extreme. Not too long ago, Apple released their latest gizmo. It went out of stock pretty quickly, and online orders had shipping dates of three to four weeks. This drove a lot of people so crazy that they immediately hit eBay and paid enormous premiums—up to 150 percent of retail—on the darn things! Why would someone pay 50 percent *more* for an item they could have at a much better price just a few weeks later? They had no patience. That's definitely not the way to get good deals. Take a breath, put this stuff in perspective, and make wise decisions.

JOIN THE CONVERSATION

Ask for a cash discount! Even at the car repair shop, we got $100 off. You just have to ask!

—Jennifer

www.facebook.com/financialpeace

The Third Key: Know Where to Look

The third key to unlocking great deals is pretty basic: you have to know where to find them. Finding great buys is like a treasure hunt. It's a skill that will get better the more you sniff out bargains. But remember, most really, really good deals won't be found underneath a giant banner that says, "SALE!" Retail sales are usually a crock. Don't fall for a "lower" price that's still not a *good* price. We covered some of those sales and marketing techniques in chapter 6, *Buyer Beware*, so go back and review those points and see how they relate to the bargain-buying principles we're laying out here.

When it comes to specific places to find great deals, I can give you a few ideas, but remember: the trick is to be a little creative. Get to know your local area, farmers' markets, mom-and-pop shops, as well as great places online to find bargains. There really isn't a "one-size-fits-all" spot to find good deals, so you'll have to learn the basics and then apply them to your own location.

1. Individuals and garage sales.

One of the best sources of deals is simply buying from individuals. Private sellers aren't trying to make a sale for profit; they're just trying to get some money out of the stuff they don't need or want anymore. If you're trying to buy a used car, for example, a car dealer has a certain amount he simply can't take. He would have paid some amount of money for the car, and he can't sell it for less than he paid for it. He'd be losing money on all his deals, and he can't stay in business doing that. A private seller is more flexible, though.

Besides, an individual may have other motives besides money. I once had two bikes sitting in my garage for a year. They kept falling over and scratching up my car. I was *over* these bikes. I put them outside with a sign that said, "Two bikes, $10." A lady walked up and offered me five bucks, and I took it. It wasn't about the money; I just wanted those bikes out of my garage. Win-win.

2. Estate sales, public auctions, and repo lots.

You'll find some terrific deals at estate sales and auctions, but you have to be careful. Those things are so exciting and fun that it is easy to get carried away. I've seen people get excited and end up paying *more than retail* for things! The best defense to this is basic preparation. Get the auction listings ahead of time, make a note of the things you're interested in, and go into deep research mode. Before bidding in an auction, you should know exactly what you're bidding on, how much it is worth, and how much you are willing to pay. Then do not go past that line, no matter how much fun you're having or how swept up you are in the spirit of friendly competition. The same goes for online auctions too!

3. Couponing and refunding.

My wife was once a grade-A coupon queen. Sharon made a game out of coupon shopping, saving us literally hundreds and hundreds of dollars every year. The trick with coupons, though, is to only use them on the items you need to buy, anyway. There's a huge marketing element to coupons, and the manufacturers put them out there to get you to buy their stuff. If you need it, then coupons are a great way to save some money. If you don't, then you're spending money you don't need to spend on stuff you don't need to buy. Be careful!

4. Flea markets.

One of the best places to hone your bargain-buying skills is at the local flea market. Usually, this is a great mix of individuals and small businesspeople, so you can really work some great deals without beating your head against the retail-chain sales zombies. Pretty much everyone at a flea market table is empowered and willing to make a deal, so get in there and see what you can do!

5. Foreclosures.

You can get an incredible deal on a house with a foreclosure, but be careful. This is not for amateurs! If you don't know what you're doing, this is a great way to lose all your money and end up with a total dump of a house. Be very careful here and don't buy one until you've worked several times alongside someone who really knows what she's doing. But if you're prepared, then go for it. This is another fantastic way to work a win-win, because if you do a deal on a foreclosure before the auction, then the seller actually gets to avoid having a foreclosure on his record *and* you get a great deal on a house. Everybody wins!

6. Pawnshops.

Every time I recommend pawnshops as a place to get a good deal, people always say, "Everything in there is stolen!" No, no, no. You watch too much TV. In the real world, everything that comes into a pawnshop is checked out with the police department. These places are highly regulated and a great place to find deals, especially on music and video games. I shop in them myself occasionally. Just don't *sell* anything to a pawnshop. It may be quick and simple, but you can always get a better price selling it to an individual.

7. Conventions.

This is one of my favorite ways to get a good deal, mainly because no one ever thinks of it. In my business, we've been to plenty of conventions and trade shows, and they all end pretty much the same way: with vendors virtually *giving* all their stuff away because they don't want to pack it up and take it back home! If there's a cookware convention in town, I guarantee you all those vendors do not want to ship a ton of pots and pans back home. Just hang around until near the end of the show, walk up to a vendor's display area, and ask, "Hey, what are you going to do with those leftovers?" You may need a wheelbarrow to get the freebies to your car!

8. Trading goods and services.

Another way to find good deals is to create them yourself by trading something of value, goods, or just your time. That's called bartering, and it's a fantastic way to get some stuff if you don't have the cash on hand to buy it. Back when I was just starting out on radio, I was still getting my financial life back on track and we didn't have a lot of money sitting around. So,

I bartered with local retailers and gave them radio ads in return for their products and services. If you have young kids, you and your friends could all trade babysitting nights, so you get free babysitting just by trading some of your own time. My kids used to give "gift certificates" for babysitting or yard work to neighbors for Christmas. Those are all great ideas, and they are absolutely win-win scenarios. Get creative and figure out what you have or what you could do in exchange for someone else's stuff or services.

JOIN THE CONVERSATION

I used the "That's not good enough." with my cable provider and they didn't beat the other offer, so I walked away. Now they are paying me about $1,600 to come back! That's a deal in any book!

—Mark

www.facebook.com/financialpeace

None of this information should have surprised you. You've probably heard most of this before, and you've most likely *done* some of this stuff before. That's great! Now, kick it up a notch. Don't just do these things sometimes; do them *all the time!*

Never settle for retail! Assume there's a deal in there somewhere, and go get it!

WE DID IT!

I took the *Financial Peace University* class last summer and it has really changed the way I view money and the way I live my life. Since starting the class, I've been using a monthly budget and the envelope system, and I feel like I'm finally in control of my money and know where it's going every month!

When the economy crashed, I was making just enough to get by. Living on a budget was the key that kept me from over-spending. Before taking this class, I didn't even know what an investment was! I learned about the different types of insurances, how to bargain, fight credit sharks, save money, and even how to invest. I may not have been able to utilize all of that information immediately in my life, but I'm starting to be able to use more and more as I get older and enter into different opportunities.

I used to think it was rude to bargain, but not anymore! I have bargained for everything from a dining room table (which I got for $300 instead of $500 just because I asked), a washer and dryer, and even $150 per month off my rent! I didn't know that was even an option before!

I am so glad I'm "getting this" at age twenty-four instead of waiting until my thirties or forties. Because of FPU, I have a future and security! Thanks, Dave!

Aidan
Nashville, TN

KEY POINTS

1. Don't be afraid to ask for a deal and negotiate.
2. Don't get "married" to a purchase too early. A good deal often depends on your ability to walk away.
3. Always use the power of cash. It has an emotional impact on the buyer *and* the seller.
4. Get creative. Sometimes, you can get great deals by trading something of value or your services.

QUESTIONS FOR REFLECTION

1. Why do most people avoid negotiating for deals?
2. Are you personally comfortable asking for a better deal on your purchases?
3. What is a win-win deal? Have you ever negotiated one?
4. Why is integrity so important in the area of bargain hunting?
5. What are the seven rules of negotiating?
6. How could a cash envelope system help you in buying situations?

9

THE PINNACLE POINT

UNDERSTANDING INVESTMENTS

When I was a kid growing up in Tennessee, one of my favorite things to do was to go out with my buddies and ride bicycles. Now, my bike didn't have all the fancy gears and options that you see on bikes today. My bike had one gear. And it didn't have a little engine to help it get moving. All it had was two little stumpy legs to get it moving. And those little legs had to work hard to keep this thing going, because in Tennessee, we don't have many flat stretches of land. You pretty much have two options: up or down.

I remember a million times as a kid, I'd be riding along and all of a sudden the road in front of me would just start going straight up. Sometimes it was too steep to pedal straight up, so I'd start steering right and left, swooping side to side to keep my momentum going. You've been there, right? I'd fight and fight to get up that hill and then . . . there it was. After all that struggling to get to the top of the hill, there was a moment where the hill leveled off for a second, just before the downhill ride of my life began.

That's a great place to be, and I'm not just talking about bicycles. It's that point where all the hard work and struggle is behind you, and all the fun is in front of you. That's the Pinnacle Point, and as fun as it was on my bike as a kid, it's even more fun in my financial life as an adult. In your money, the Pinnacle Point is the point when your savings and investments—after years and years of dedication and hard work—make more money for you in a year than you make for yourself. It's when your investments produce a higher return than your work. That's the best downhill ride you'll ever have.

JOIN THE CONVERSATION

I never thought investing was an option for me. I just figured I would live paycheck to paycheck for the rest of my life. Now I see a better future!

—Megan

www.facebook.com/financialpeace

THE TIME IS RIGHT NOW

This is one of my favorite topics, and it's one of my favorite lessons in our *Financial Peace University* class. But every time I start talking about investments or we get to this lesson in FPU, we always hear the same few objections, so let's get them out of the way.

"Oh, Dave, Investing Is So BORING!"

Every time I teach on investing, I can immediately spot the Nerds and the Free Spirits in the room. The Nerds perk up, pull out their pencils, and start to run the numbers in the margins of their notebooks. The Free Spirits? Well, they go to their happy places. I can see all the Free Spirits in the room start to float out of their bodies. Their eyes glaze over, and all of a sudden, they are running through a wheat field or singing in the rain in their minds. They just totally check out.

So here's my suggestion for those of you who find this stuff boring. When I say "investing," picture a vacation home in the French countryside. Or picture a ski trip with your whole family in a beautiful chalet that you've rented for a month. Or picture your spouse being home with you to laugh and play, and to just enjoy life. That's what investing is all about. It's not about the dollars; it's about the kind of life you want to live later on. What you do today will determine that.

"I'm on Baby Step 1! I Can't Even Think About Investing Right Now!"

I know you may just now be getting started with this whole process, and that's okay. Wherever you are in the Baby Steps, I'm on your team. But even if investing is a few years off, you need to learn some basics so you'll know what to do next as you knock out the Baby Steps.

I love to ski. In the snow, on the water, I don't care where. I just like moving fast and having two long planks strapped to my feet. If you've ever been on skis, you know the first thing they tell you is that your whole body will go wherever you're looking. If you're looking straight ahead, you'll go straight ahead. If you look to the right, you'll drift right. If you look down, don't forget to tuck and roll, because you're about to hit the ground or water. That's true with your money too. I promise, if you do the things we teach, you're going to get out of debt and save up a full emergency fund faster than you ever thought possible. And when you do, it'll be time to invest for wealth building. So let's get your eyes on that goal, okay?

"Long-Term Investing Is Too Slow! I Want a Fast Return on My Money!"

The only people who get rich from get-rich-quick schemes are the people selling them. They play on your emotions, set you up for a quick return, take your money, and then leave you high and dry. And the truth is, risky investments have become a playground for people with gambling problems. Hoping to turn $100 into $1,000 overnight isn't investing; it's gambling. You've heard me say before that the stuff I teach isn't always easy and it isn't a quick fix, but it absolutely works every time.

KISS YOUR INVESTING

Back when I was just starting to sell houses, one of my biggest problems was that I talked too much. Hard to believe, right? More times than I'd like to remember, I just talked and talked and talked, and I ended up talking myself out of a sale. The reason is that I was flooding buyers with information—more information than they wanted or even needed! I went on and on about all these features, contract issues, upgrades, neighborhood stats, and everything else I could think to say. Fortunately, I finally figured out how to shut up, but not before a lot of good people missed out on some good houses, just because I was overcomplicating the whole process.

Investing gets like that. Sometimes "financial people" come in and start talking about all the options and tricks and strategies, and our eyes glaze over. As a result, we either sign whatever they put in front of us, letting them make all our financial decisions, or we just decide it's not worth it and we walk away. Either way, we lose.

That's why I always recommend the KISS strategy for investing: "Keep It Simple, Stupid." No, this does not mean that you are stupid if you make simple investments! Just the opposite. I'm saying that people get in trouble when they overcomplicate things. I've met with a lot of really, really rich people over the years—multimillionaires and even several *multibillionaires*—and most of them have a simple, even *boring*, investment plan. They do the same few, simple things over and over again, over a long period of time. Why? Because it works.

But a lot of people truly believe that investing has to be complicated, or that there's some trick to it—as if there's one big secret to investing, and those people who figure it out get to be rich. But nothing will send you to the poorhouse faster than stupid, long-shot, high-risk investments. It's like that old joke: What's the most common last words for a redneck? "Hey, y'all. Watch this!" (Don't be offended; I'm a redneck myself.) In investing, I think the most famous last words would be, "Don't worry. I know what I'm doing!"

"Financial People"

Too often, we play these games because "financial people" have sat across the table and talked down to us like we're children. That drives me crazy! A financial advisor is usually an invaluable part of your team, as long as he remembers what his primary job is: to teach you how to make your own decisions. You need someone with the heart of a teacher who will sit down with you and teach you this stuff, so that you can then make your own decisions about how, where, and how much to invest. You should never buy any financial product or service if you can't explain to someone else how it works. That level of education is what you're paying your advisor for!

There are two words you should say to financial and insurance people who talk down to you or won't (or can't) teach you how their products work: "YOU'RE FIRED!" Remember, these people work for you. If they aren't doing the job you're paying them for, cut them loose. And if you need help, be sure to check out our list of Endorsed Local Providers (ELP) in your area. We've handpicked excellent men and women all over the country to help you make your own investing decisions. You can learn more about that at daveramsey.com or, if you're in an FPU class, in the online resources for this lesson.

FANCY TERMS: $10 WORDS FOR $3 CONCEPTS

Whenever I write, one of my guiding principles is that I don't use "$10 words," or words that sound too highbrow or stuffy. There are a few investing terms, though, that might fall into that category, so I'm going to take a minute to lay them out for you.

Diversification: Spreading the Love

Diversification is one of those terms that financial people throw around just to sound impressive. Let me take the wind out of their sails by clearing this up. Diversification just means "to spread around." It's a real simple idea. Basically, don't bet the family farm on a one-horse race. This is a financial principle you may have learned in Sunday school, even if you didn't realize it at the time. Ecclesiastes 11:2 says, "Give portions to seven, yes to eight, for you do not know what disaster may come upon the land."[1]

Grandma said it, too, didn't she? She always said, "Don't put all your eggs in one basket." The problem is, if you put all your eggs in one basket, something bad might happen to the basket. If it does, then you lose all your eggs. In recent years, we've had a lot of bad things happen to a lot of baskets. We've seen Katrina, 9/11, political drama, massive unemployment, and even a full-blown recession slam into a lot of single baskets, breaking a lot of eggs. But those who spread out their investments over several different options were better protected. If you spread them out over a wide area, you won't lose the whole thing when something goes wrong in one part of it.

The bottom line is that diversification lowers risk. So basically, what we're saying is that investments are like manure. Left in one pile, it starts to stink. But when you spread it around, it grows things. I bet your financial guy never laid it out like that!

Risk Return Ratio

With virtually all investments, as the risk goes up, so does the hopeful return. That is, if I don't take much of a risk, I'm not going to make as much money. All investing requires some degree of risk; there really is no sure thing. In my book *Financial Peace Revisited*, I explain it this way:

> The lion at the zoo is a pitiful sight—the king of beasts is eating processed food. You can see deep down in his soulful eyes that he misses the thrill of the hunt. Any of you who want a guarantee on your money need to understand that you are paying the same price as the lion.[2]

The only real method to totally guarantee you won't lose your money is to put it in a cookie jar, but your return will be equal to your risk: zero. Actually, the cookie jar can't even offer a foolproof guarantee if the house is robbed or burns down.

Besides, earning zero return is the same as moving backward once you factor in inflation, which we'll cover in a minute.

When you lay out investment options, you start to see a progression of risk. You start with the cookie jar—no risk, no return. One step up from that is a savings account, which is fantastic for your emergency fund but a joke for your investing. Your money will be fairly safe, but you'll be lucky to make 2 percent on it. A step up from that would be a certificate of deposit (CD), which is not much better than a savings account. A little more risk leads you to a mutual fund. A little more risk gets into single stocks. A few steps later and you hit day trading, which totally drops you off a cliff risk-wise.

I don't recommend single stocks or day trading, or Vegas, for that matter, because the risk is just too high. But I also don't recommend cookie jars or CDs for long-term (more than five years) investing. The sweet spot, which we'll talk about later, is mutual funds. That's a great balance of reasonable risk and excellent returns.

Inflation

Something that should be handled alongside risk return ratio is inflation. This is something that is too often left out of risk calculations. When we talked about the cookie jar, we said that it was basically no risk, no return. But that's not really true. With inflation working against us, if we left $100 in a cookie jar for a year, we'd still have $100 a year later, but that $100 would be worth less.

Inflation has averaged around 4.2 percent over the last seventy years, according to the Consumer Price Index (CPI). So, if your money is not earning at least a 4.2 percent return, you're actually losing money every year. In fact, once you factor in taxes on your growth, you really need your investments to make around 6 percent just to stay ahead of inflation. So if you stick with cookie jars, savings accounts, and CDs as your long-term investing strategy, your money will be relatively safe, but inflation will tackle you from behind. You've got to see 6 percent as your break-even point; so a little risk is going to be vital to your long-term plan.

Liquidity

Liquidity is a funny word, but again, the concept is simple. It just means availability. If you have a liquid investment, then you have quick and easy access to your money. The cookie jar is totally liquid, because you can walk over and get your cash out whenever you want. A savings account is about the same, and a CD is fairly liquid even though there's a short time frame attached. Pretty much the least liquid investment is one that a lot of Americans own, which is real estate. If you're a home-owner, your house is likely your greatest investment, but it is not liquid at all. If an emergency came up, you'd have a tough time liquidating your house by tomorrow.

TYPES OF INVESTING

We can already see the ground rules for investing. We're going to keep it simple. We're going to find investments that show a good, reliable balance between risk and return. We're going to listen to advisors but make our own decisions. We're going to stay away from gimmicks and get-rich-quick schemes. We're going to keep our investments diversified. And of course, we're going to stay ahead of inflation. Before we do any of that, though, we're going to make sure it's time for us to start investing. Investing is Baby Step 4, so before you start saving up for retirement, you are debt-free except the house, and you have three to six months of expenses saved up in an emergency fund. If you've done that, then it's time to start investing. So let's look at some of the most common types of investing, or investing "vehicles."

CD: The Certificate of Depression

A CD is a certificate of deposit, typically at a bank. This is just a savings account. That's it. I always crack up when people tell me they have solid investment strategy, and then tell me all their money is in CDs. It's a *savings account*. The word "certificate" does not make it sophisticated; the certificate is basically a receipt showing that you made a deposit at a bank. Whoopee! My kids had savings accounts when they were six years old! That's barely a step up from a piggy bank!

A CD will give you a higher rate of return than a standard savings account because you'll be required to leave your money alone until the CD matures. You may get a five-year CD, which means you deposit the money for a guaranteed rate of return— about 5 percent in most cases—and you can't take the money back out until it matures at the end of the five years. If you do, you pay all sorts of fees and penalties. Even without the fees, though, the CD gives you a lousy rate of return. Remember, 5 percent isn't even enough to keep up with inflation once you factor in taxes. At the end of the day, a CD requires you to tie up your money for a few years, but then it gives you practically nothing in exchange. I don't own a single CD. I just don't see a need for them.

Money Markets

But what if you want to get *some* return on a pile of money you don't need *today*, but you know you'll need in a few years? This is like when you're saving up for a house or a car over three to five years. I use money market accounts for that. This is essentially a checking account that you open up with a mutual fund company. These are low-risk, and they offer about the same rates as you'd get with a six-month CD. However, your money isn't tied up and you have check-writing privileges (with no penalty) in case you need to access the account sooner than you thought. Just keep in mind that money markets are for *savings*; this is not an investment. That's why money markets with a mutual fund company make a great place to put your emergency fund. It keeps the money liquid while still giving you at least a little return.

Single Stocks

Single stock purchases give you a tiny piece of a company. The company issues a number of shares to sell to shareholders, and those shareholders jointly "own" the company. That's what it means when a company "goes public." They go from being privately held to being publicly owned through the issuance of stocks. The value of the shares is tied to the value of the company. If the company's value skyrockets, the value of each share—each individual piece of ownership—also goes up. That's good if you get in and out at the right time.

For example, let's say you were an Apple Computer fan in the early 1990s. The company was having some trouble back then, and the stock hit the low twenties per share around 1993. But for some reason, you had a good feeling about where the company was going, so you bought one thousand shares at $23 each.[3] By 2011, that $23,000 investment would have been worth somewhere around $350,000. Not bad, right?

But here's the reality: For every Apple, IBM, or Google, there are hundreds of publicly traded companies in bankruptcy, and it is impossible to know what the future holds for individual businesses. Can you say, "Enron"? The collapse of that one company completely obliterated $74 billion of wealth in the four years leading up to Enron's eventual collapse.[4] More than twenty thousand former employees were thrown into years and years of legal battles and lawsuits just to get back a piece of the money they lost in company stock.

Why? Because they had put all their eggs in one basket, and that basket fell apart. The same could be true for any business, at any point in time. That's why diversification is so important, and single stocks are the most UN-diversified investment you can make. Stay away!

Bonds

A bond is a debt instrument by which a company owes you money. Instead of buying a piece of ownership, as with a stock, you're pretty much loaning a company (or the government, in the case of government bonds) some money. That means instead of becoming an owner, you become a creditor. Like I said in *Financial Peace Revisited*: "When you purchase a bond, the company that issued it becomes your debtor. The income is usually fixed, but again, the value or price of the bond will go up or down according to the performance of the company and prevailing interest rates."[5]

I personally do not like bonds for several reasons. First, it's based on debt, and it's no secret what I think about debt—borrowing *or* lending. Second, bonds are high-risk because the company's ability to repay your investment is tied to their performance. So in that sense, it's like a single stock and has no diversification. And last, the performance of bond-based portfolios is generally pretty weak. This is another one I just stay away from.

Mutual Funds: The Alphabet Soup of Investing

Now we come to one of my favorite vehicles for long-term investing, the mutual fund. I *love* mutual funds. They have excellent returns, and they have built-in diversification that keeps me from having all my eggs in one basket. The problem is, a lot of people are scared off because they don't understand what a mutual fund is. Heck, I graduated college with a finance degree and I still had trouble understanding it! It's really not that complicated, though, once you strip out all the highbrow financial lingo. Let's take a look.

Picture a big bowl in the center of a table. You and your ten best friends are sitting around the table. Everyone puts a dollar in the bowl. That bowl is a mutual fund. You and your friends have all contributed, so you have *mutually funded* the bowl. It is a *mutual* fund. Get it?

So, what's in the bowl? It contains little pieces of stock in a whole bunch of companies. Picture it like a bowl of alphabet soup. If you look in there, you might see an *I* floating around, which could be IBM. You could see a *W*, which might be Wal-Mart. There's an *A* and an *M*, so that could be Apple and Microsoft. Just imagine several companies floating around together in the bowl you and your friends funded.

A professional portfolio manager manages the fund, making sure that only the best investments are in the bowl. And this guy isn't flying solo. He's got a huge team of Nerds working for him—the best, brightest, nerdiest Nerds in the world! If the fund includes tech stocks, he'll have a Tech Nerd. If it includes restaurants, he'll have a Restaurant Nerd. These specialists spend all day, every day, learning every detail about these companies and industries. They pass that information to the fund manager, and the manager uses it to keep the fund filled with the best of the best investments. That crack team of Nerds can do a lot better job than any average bubba sitting at home, picking stocks using a dartboard and dumb luck!

What the fund does depends on the goal, or the *fund objective*. If our fund is a growth stock fund, the fund manager will by growth stocks. If it's a bond fund, the manager will buy bonds. If it's an international stock fund, the manager will buy—can you guess?—international stocks. You're getting it!

Diversification is fantastic in mutual funds. Let's say I wanted to invest in some good ol' American companies. If I were using single stocks, I could put $20,000 in Ford, for example. But what happens if Ford implodes? I lose all my money!

We talked about that with single stocks. That's just too much risk. But instead of going all-in with Ford, I could get a mutual fund that has a little Ford in it, along with up to two hundred other great American companies. So if Ford's value goes way up, I still benefit because I have a little Ford in my mutual fund. But if Ford goes bankrupt, I won't feel that much of a loss because it's just one small part of my fund. The other two hundred companies in the fund can protect me from a loss because they're all in there together.

Now, is there some risk involved with mutual funds? Sure. There are no guarantees. But remember what we said about inflation? If you just park your money in a "safe" CD, you're already behind the curve, because inflation will take your legs out from under you. Besides, if you are invested in mutual funds containing the best and brightest two hundred companies in the country and they *all* fail at the same time, you've got bigger problems than your mutual fund. That would mean the entire U.S. economy has fallen apart, the stock market would be worth zero, and the FDIC would have collapsed—so your "safe" bank savings would be worthless too!

Mutual Fund Diversification

Like I said, there are different kinds of mutual funds, and they all have built-in diversification. But I still recommend you diversify a little further by spreading your investments out over four different kinds of mutual funds. I tell people to put 25 percent in each of these four types: growth, growth and income, aggressive growth, and international.

Growth stock mutual funds are sometimes called mid-cap or equity funds. Mid-cap refers to the fund's capitalization, or money. So, a mid-cap fund is a medium-sized company. These are companies that are still in the growth stage; that's why it's called a *growth* stock fund.

Growth and income mutual funds are the calmest funds of the bunch. These are sometimes called large-cap funds, because they include large, well-established companies. These funds usually don't have wildly fluctuating values. That's good and bad; they won't shoot up as much when the market's up, but they also won't fall as much when the market's down. These are basically slow-moving, lumbering dinosaurs.

JOIN THE CONVERSATION

We have a road map for all our financial goals. For the first time, I feel safe and secure in our finances. Best of all, I'm living a thriftier life and am happier for it!

—Stephanie

www.facebook.com/financialpeace

Aggressive growth mutual funds are the exciting wild child of mutual funds. They represent small companies (so they're often called small-cap funds), and these are active, emerging, exciting companies. This is the roller coaster of mutual funds. There will be really high highs, and probably some really low lows. I had one back in the 1990s that had a 105 percent rate of return one year, then lost it all the next year. You absolutely don't want to put all your money here, but you need some aggressive funds in your plan.

International mutual funds are sometimes called overseas funds, and they represent companies outside the United States. I recommend putting a fourth of your investments in international funds for two reasons. First, you get to participate in the growth of some foreign products that you probably already enjoy; and second, it adds another layer of diversification just in case something weird and unexpected happens to the U.S. stock market.

Picking Mutual Funds

Always look at the track record of mutual funds before you buy one. And make sure that it has a good track record over at least five years, preferably ten or more. My favorites are the ones that have been around over twenty years and have proved themselves to be quality, reliable investments. I have some mutual funds that are over fifty years old! Those may be harder to find, but they give you an excellent track record. Whatever you do, don't buy a fund that's less than five years old. These are babies! If you can't see a track record of at least five years, keep looking. If it's a fund that really interests you for some reason, just make a note of it and check it a few years later.

I personally like to find funds with a good track record averaging at least 12 percent. But every time I say that, I get a million e-mails from people saying, "BUT DAVE, you can't get 12 percent on your investments! Are you crazy?" No, I'm not crazy. I use 12 percent because that's the historical average annual return of the S&P 500, which gauges the performance of the five hundred largest, most stable companies in the stock exchange. The average annual return from 1926, the year of the S&P's inception, through 2010 is 11.84 percent. Just keep in mind that's the eighty-year *average*.

Sure, within that time frame there are up years and some down years. I'm not that interested in the performance of any individual years or even any short-term time spans, but just for fun, let's take a look at a few. From 1991 to 2010, the S&P's average was 10.66 percent. From 1986 to 2010, it was 11.28 percent. In 2009, the market's annual return was 26.46 percent. In 2010, it was 8 percent. See, this thing is up and down all the time, so 12 percent isn't really a magic number. But based on the history of the market, it's a reasonable expectation for your long-term investments.

Bottom line: Mutual funds make excellent long-term investments, but don't bother with them unless you can leave that money alone for *at least* five years. This is where you park your money for the long haul, looking toward retirement.

JOIN THE CONVERSATION

It's not *how much* you invest but *that* you invest! Sometimes we put it off, thinking investing requires a lot of money. Ben and Arthur gave me a new perspective.

—Kim

www.facebook.com/financialpeace

Rental Real Estate

Real estate can be a lot of fun, especially for old real estate guys like me. However, this is the least liquid investment you can make. You know what they call houses that sell fast? Cheap. Don't mess around with real estate until you are out of debt, have a full emergency fund, have maxed out your 401(k) and Roth IRA options, have paid off your own house, and have some wealth built up. Only *then* are you ready.

And, of course, don't even think about real estate as an investment until you can pay cash for the houses. Never, never, *never* borrow money for an "investment." The risk is enormous.

I've seen literally thousands of so-called investors lose their shirts in real estate because they bought houses when they were broke. If you start playing with rental real estate without any money, you will crash. I promise. That is *exactly* how I went broke and ended up in bankruptcy court myself. I know what I'm talking about here.

Annuities

I personally don't use annuities very much, but they're out there and they do have a place in some people's investing strategy, so let's take a quick look. There are two types of annuities: fixed and variable. Fixed annuities are terrible. They're basically a savings account with an insurance company, and they pay somewhere around 5 percent. They're really not that different from a CD you'd get from your local bank. By now, you know that a 5 percent rate of return isn't worth your time, so we'll pass on those.

Variable annuities are the only ones I like. These are essentially mutual funds inside an annuity. The annuity provides some protection against taxes for the mutual funds inside, so if you've already maxed out your other tax-favored plans, like a 401(k) and Roth IRA (we'll talk about these in chapter 10, *From Fruition to Tuition*), then a variable annuity might make sense. There are fees involved, but in exchange for the fees, you don't have to worry about taxes on the investment. Plus, some variable annuities offer a guarantee on your principal. So if you put $100,000 in the investment and the value drops below that level, you'll still be able to get your $100,000 back out of it. They're not for everyone, but if you're further along in your investing, you may want to look into some quality variable annuities. Just don't buy an annuity with an investment that is *already* tax-protected. If the investment is already safe from taxes, the added fees of an annuity just don't make sense.

All That Glitters Is NOT Gold

I just might be the only talk radio host in the country that does not endorse gold! The reason is simple: gold is a horrible investment! Here's the deal: Gold value has been rising since September 11, 2001. People started buying it more not because it's a good investment, but because of some false belief that if the economy totally collapses, gold will hold its value. If that were true, then gold coins would have become the dominant currency in New Orleans during the Katrina disaster! That's a great picture of a mini economic breakdown. If you had been there at the time, I bet you would have gotten a lot more for a bottle of water than for a gold coin!

But let's look at the numbers. Gold was worth $21 an ounce in 1833, up to $275 per ounce by 2001, and then shot up to about $1,345 by 2010. Even including the crazy growth gold experienced in the first decade of this century, the 177-year track record for gold is just 2.38 percent. Would you look at a mutual fund with a 2 percent rate of return over the past 177 years? No way! Besides, if gold was *ever* a good investment, it doesn't make much sense to buy it at its 177-year high! You always want to buy low and sell high. Gold gives you the chance to do the opposite. That's a bad plan.

THE TORTOISE WINS

I have been blessed throughout my career to have had the chance to sit down and talk with a lot of wildly successful, super-wealthy men and women. I love those opportunities, and

I always pull out a pen and some paper, because I want to hear from them how they got where they are. I believe you'll stop growing the instant you stop learning, so I'm always looking for some new insight.

One day, I was talking to a really, really rich guy—I mean *billionaire* rich. We were having lunch, and I gave him my standard billionaire question: "What can I do today that will get me closer to where you are in your business and in your wealth building?"

He leaned back and said, "Okay, here's two things. First, I've never met anyone who wins at money who doesn't give generously. You've got to keep a giving spirit if you want to win long term." *Hey, that's no problem. Giving is one of my favorite things in the world! Check.*

"Second," he said, "I want you to read a book. This is my favorite book. I read it several times a year. I read it to my children, and now I read it to my grandchildren over and over. It will change your life, your money, and your business forever." Now, I'm a huge reader, so I was pretty excited at this point. *This mega-billionaire is about to tell me the book that changed his life. Let's go!*

"Dave, have you ever read *The Tortoise and the Hare?*" *Huh? A children's book? An old fairy tale? What does this have to do with building wealth?* I just sat there for a second, trying to decide if he was kidding or not. He wasn't.

He leaned in and said, "Dave, we live in a world full of hares. Everyone's racing around doing all kinds of crazy stuff. They're running ahead and falling back, running ahead and falling back. They're going back and forth, side to side, and all in circles. But the tortoise just keeps moving forward, slow and steady. And you know what? Every time I read the book, the tortoise wins."

That phrase has been stuck in my head for years: "Every time I read the book, the tortoise wins." It's not about fancy options. It's not about jumping on every new and exciting investment that comes down the pike. True, reliable, long-term wealth building is surprisingly simple—and even a little boring. It's a matter of doing just a couple of things over and over and over again, over a long period of time. Eventually, over time, when it counts . . . the tortoise wins.

WE DID IT!

When I was fifteen years old, my parents sent me through *Financial Peace University* to help me start learning about finances. At sixteen, my grandparents and I bought my first car together, and I have paid for every tank of gas since then. I'm now twenty years old and a totally self-supporting college student, paying for my own groceries, car insurance, cell phone—not to mention $35,000 a year in college expenses!

I worked like crazy my senior year of high school to apply for as many scholarships as possible. I save every paycheck. I pick up every penny on the ground. When I was sixteen, I received an inheritance that ended up being about $38,000, and I put that money straight into investments—I never even touched it! I also have about $10,000 in a long-term mutual fund. Even if I never put another dollar in, I'll be a millionaire when I'm 65. I'll take it!

Not only did your class teach me how to be smart with money so that I can live like no one else someday, it also taught me how to own my financial destiny and be completely self-supporting. I will NEVER have to ask my parents for money! Thank you, Dave!

Felicia
Nashville, TN

KEY POINTS

1. Diversification is crucial in investing. It simply means "to spread around" or, as Grandma would say, "Don't put all your eggs in one basket!"
2. Most millionaires have a simple, repeatable investment strategy. There's no need to overcomplicate your investments.
3. Mutual funds are the best choice for long-term investing.
4. Diversify your mutual fund investments evenly across four types: growth, growth and income, aggressive growth, and international.
5. Only work with investment professionals who have the hearts of a teacher.

QUESTIONS FOR REFLECTION

1. Why are so many people intimidated by investing? Are you?
2. How does a mutual fund work?
3. Why is it dangerous to invest with borrowed money?
4. What role does diversification play in long-term investing? Why is this important?
5. Why is it important to make your own educated, well-informed investing decisions, rather than simply surrendering your decisions to an advisor?
6. What makes CDs and bonds poor choices for long-term wealth building?

10

FROM FRUITION TO TUITION

PLANNING FOR RETIREMENT AND COLLEGE

There is a phrase that I want you to remember. This is a phrase that will subtly creep into your life, knock over your financial plan, and absolutely steal your chances at winning with money. It's just three little words, but it has the power to wreck everything you ever want to accomplish. That little phrase is, "Right now, today."

"Right now, today, I'm thinking about what kind of car I'm going to buy."

"Right now, today, I'm planning my next big vacation."

"Right now, today, I'm sick of watching TV on a screen the size of a postage stamp."

"Right now, today, I really want steak and lobster instead of rice and beans."

"Right now, today" can steal your whole life if you're not careful. If all you ever think about is right now, today, you'll never win over the long haul. In the previous chapter, we talked about the pinnacle point, that point in the future when your investments start making more money for you than you earn at your job in a year. That's a fantastic place to be, but you won't get there overnight. It takes a long time, and it takes a whole lot of discipline to reach that point.

Children do what feels good. Adults devise a plan and follow it. That's called *maturity*, and one definition of maturity is learning to delay pleasure. A shiny red convertible may be fun right now, today; but is it worth the $4 million extra you could have at retirement by avoiding car payments your whole life? Wise, mature consumers think about stuff like that—not to rob themselves of any fun, but to make sure their fun fits in their overall plan. I want you to have some fun stuff; I just don't want your stuff to have you!

So in this chapter, we're going to take what we learned about investments in the mutual fund chapter and turn it into practical steps for how to develop a wealth-building plan for retirement. Plus, we'll take a look at how to plan for the kids' college tuitions without breaking the bank and without feeding the student loan monster that's going crazy across the country!

BUILDING WEALTH FOR RETIREMENT

Even though I teach on this topic a lot, it's one of those things I almost dread talking about. I've seen a lot of people teach retirement planning in such a dry and boring way that you'd almost rather stay broke your whole life than listen to them go on for another hour! I'm just not one of those overly technical, detailed, boring money guys. I actually *enjoy* money! I like playing with it. I like having fun with it. I like giving it away. I like helping people get out of debt so *they* can do those things, too. That means I'm the guy that has to get in there, blow the dust off the retirement-planning discussion, and show you what this stuff means in real life.

The sad truth is, most Americans haven't figured it out yet. In fact, a recent survey found that 53 percent of all workers have less than $25,000 in a retirement plan. When asked how they made their long-term financial planning decisions, 44 percent said they "guess."[1] They guess! They put a blindfold on and played "Pin the Tail on the 401(k)"! That's a bad plan. This stuff is too important to ignore *or* leave to chance.

You see, if you want to win with money, you've got to pay attention to these things. If you get out of debt and start building some wealth without learning a little bit about what all these letters and initials mean, here's what will happen: You will spend the next few decades building up a gigantic pile of money for yourself. And then, when you're ready to crack that nest egg open and enjoy your wealth, the government will come in and take all of your money in the form of taxes! That means a big part of winning with money is figuring out how to shelter your money from taxes—legally, honestly, and with integrity.

Stick to the Plan

At this point in the Baby Steps, you're out of debt and have a full emergency fund of three to six months' worth of expenses. I've told you not to start investing until that is done, which is something I sometimes get a lot of push back on. "But Dave! I get a match on my 401(k)! Isn't it a waste to not take that match even if I have some debt and no savings?" No, it's not a waste. You're not being sophisticated; you're doing the steps out of order, and it will eventually bite you in the back end.

If you don't have an emergency fund, but you do have a 401(k), guess what will happen in an emergency? Your 401(k) will *become* your emergency fund! You'll get stuck in a crisis— remember those "unexpected" emergencies?—and you'll go to the one place you have some money. The problem is, the fees and taxes for cashing out your 401(k) early will cost you about 40 percent of your money.

That means if you bring $10,000 home, they will charge you a 10 percent penalty plus your tax rate. That's a 40 percent hit for most people. In other words, you're going to turn your $10,000 into $6,000 immediately. I can't figure out how people can flush 40 percent of their money down the toilet and then scratch their heads wondering why their financial plan isn't working! It's because they went out of order and went straight to investing without taking care of the protection that an emergency fund gives them.

JOIN THE CONVERSATION

My husband was smart enough to start the college savings when the girls were first born. Today, we feel far more comfortable about sending them, while others are concerned about how to pay for it in this economy. It pays to start saving early!

—Lorraine

www.facebook.com/financialpeace

So stick to the plan. Once you're debt-free except for your house and have a full Baby Step 3 emergency fund, you're ready to take the next step:

Baby Step 4: Invest 15 percent of your household income into Roth IRAs and pretax retirement plans.

This is the step that takes you to the pinnacle point, where we all want to get!

Why 15 Percent?

When I first started doing financial counseling, the Baby Steps weren't set in stone yet. In fact, I used to teach people to go right into the debt snowball before putting *anything* in savings. Then I found that those families needed some kind of buffer as they got out of debt, so I went back and tweaked it to provide a $1,000 beginner emergency fund in the plan. Another thing I've tweaked over the years is the recommendation for how much you should put into retirement as you work the Baby Steps. I explained it this way in *The Total Money Makeover*:

> Gazelle intensity in the previous steps has allowed you to be able to focus on growing a sizable nest egg. The tens of thousands of people we have met have helped me develop the 15 percent rule. The rule is simple: Invest 15 percent of before-tax gross income annually toward retirement. Why not more? You need some of your income left to do the next two steps: college saving and paying off your home early. Why not less? Some people want to invest less or none so they can get a child through school or pay off the home super-fast. I don't recommend that because those kids' college degrees won't feed you at retirement. I don't recommend paying off the house first because I have counseled too many seventy-five-year-olds with a paid-for house and no money. They end up selling the family home or mortgaging it to eat. Bad plan.[2]

We've found that 15 percent is just the right amount for most people to build a sizable retirement while still enjoying their lives "right now, today." The key is to do these things in order. And by the way, I'm talking about 15 percent of your *income*, not your *take-home pay*, and this 15 percent does not include any matching you may get on a 401(k). If you get a company match, that's great—but it's just extra. You're still responsible for your own 15 percent.

PROTECTING YOUR MONEY FROM TAXES

I absolutely love my country, but the truth is, the federal government is not exactly well-known for their ability to handle money. That means I'd rather not depend on them to take care of me at retirement in the form of Social Insecurity, and I'd rather not give them half (or more!) of the wealth I build up over my lifetime in the form of taxes. I do my duty as a citizen, and I never try to break or even bend the laws in the name of money. However, there are a ton of legal, ethical ways to protect your money from taxes, and as a wise consumer, I'm going to take advantage of them.

When it comes to retirement savings, you should always save with tax-favored dollars. We used to say you should save with "pretax" dollars, but new investing plans have popped up over the past several years that actually work better with after-tax dollars. We'll see that when we look at the Roth IRA and Roth 401(k). "Tax favored" simply means that the plan is a *qualified plan* or that it receives special tax treatment. This is something like a 401(k), 403(b), or an IRA. The thing to remember when we're talking about these plans is that the plan only refers to the *tax treatment*, not the *kind of investment* itself.

A lot of people get tripped up here, so let's look at it this way: The plan is like a coat that wraps around your investment to keep it "warm" from the cold of taxes. So if you have a 401(k) that's invested in mutual funds, the mutual fund is the investment and the 401(k) is the coat. The 401(k) is not the thing that is making money; instead, the 401(k) is the protective wrapper that helps shield the investment from excessive taxes. Make sense? Good! Now let's look at the most common qualified plans that you'll probably be working with.

Individual Retirement Arrangement (IRA)

One of the most popular qualified plans is the good old IRA. I know you saw the word "arrangement" in the subheading above and thought I made a mistake, but I didn't. The truth is, banks have done such a fabulous job selling IRAs that most people think it stands for "Individual Retirement *Account*," but it's actually "Individual Retirement *Arrangement*." And that makes sense, because the qualified plans we're talking about are tax arrangements, not actual investments, right?

The key phrase with IRA eligibility is "earned income." Anyone with an earned income is eligible, even children. If your child does a diaper commercial at six months old and receives compensation under his name, then you can open an IRA for him. Otherwise, Junior will have to wait until he gets a job. That also means that seniors living on Social Security or others living on disability benefits with no other earned income are not eligible. The only real exception to this rule is a nonworking spouse. For example, if Dad is working full-time and Mom is at home with the kids and has no earned income, she can still have an IRA in her name as part of her husband's earned income.

The IRA has a maximum annual contribution of $5,000 per person. So, if you're married, you can max out at $5,000 and your spouse can max out at $5,000. That's the current figure as of this book's printing, but it can change anytime. Be sure to double-check this with your advisor when you're ready to start maxing out your retirement savings! If you're in a *Financial*

Peace University class, you can always check the online resources for this lesson to get the most up-to-date information.

Remember, the IRA is just the tax treatment on your investment. The actual investment could be anything, like mutual funds or even real estate. I personally think mutual funds are the best way to go, but you do have some options with an IRA.

Roth IRA

There is a phrase you don't often hear in the world of investments, but it's one of the sweetest things I've ever heard: "tax-free growth." The Taxpayer Relief Act of 1997 contained a section written by Senator William Roth of Delaware that provided a new tax arrangement that has become known as the Roth IRA. That little word "Roth" is a big deal. It can save you millions and millions of dollars at retirement, because the investment grows *tax-free*. No taxes. None. Ever. That's a great deal in investing!

Here's how it works. In a regular 401(k), for example, you get to invest pretax dollars. That is, the money you put into the investment has no taxes taken out up front. Then, years later at retirement, you're taxed as you pull the money out. It's a great deal on the front end because it allows you to invest more money, but the taxes on the growth can bite you when you take the money out. If you have $4 million in your 401(k) at retirement, you can pretty much assume that the government will take about 25 percent of that—$1 million—in taxes.

The Roth IRA is different. With a Roth, you invest after-tax dollars. In this situation, you get paid at work, your income is taxed like normal, you bring the money home, and then you put it into a Roth IRA. As that investment grows, it grows tax-free. So if you have $4 million sitting in a Roth IRA at retirement, you get to keep the whole $4 million! That means that in our example, "Roth" is a $1-million-worth word!

I love the Roth IRA for several reasons. First of all, it gives you more flexibility. After the account has been open for five years, you can take out withdrawals up to your contributions with no penalties. Of course, I don't really recommend tapping into your retirement account early, but if you have a huge emergency, you'll at least have a fallback once your emergency fund is depleted.

You can also take up to $10,000 out for a first-time home purchase, but I strongly advise against that option. Once you hit age fifty-nine and a half, you can make tax-free, penalty-free withdrawals of up to 100 percent. You can even access the account with no penalties if you have a disabling event and can't work.

The Roth IRA is my favorite way to invest. I'm personally not eligible because there are income limits in the Roth requirements, but if I could, I would max this thing out every year. We'll see what role it plays in your overall investment strategy when I give my recommendation on how to fund your Baby Step 4, 15-percent investments.

Simplified Employee Pension Plan (SEP)

If you're self-employed or own your own small business, you might want to take a look at the SEP, or Simplified Employee Pension plan. This is nicknamed the SEP IRA because it essentially acts like a big IRA for small business owners. The SEP allows you to deduct up to 15 percent of your net profit and put it into the SEP pretax. Annual contributions max out at $49,000 per year as of this book's printing, but that's still a huge chunk of money.

Say, for example, you are self-employed and you make $100,000 net profit on your business. With a SEP, you could put up to 15 percent—or $15,000—into the plan. That blows the doors off the $5,000 max you'd get on a regular IRA, so it's worth looking at. There's a catch, though. If you have employees that have been with you three of the last five years, you have to give them the same percentage deduction that you take. With a required employer match on top of that, this can get *really* expensive if you have several employees in the plan. Be careful not to let the SEP get away from you if you try it out. Work with your financial advisor to make sure this one works for you, and keep a close eye on it as you add more employees.

JOIN THE CONVERSATION

Put your own oxygen mask on first! Take care of yourself; kids can work their way through college if they need to.

—Marla

www.facebook.com/financialpeace

401(k) and Roth 401(k) Plans

The days of working for one company for forty years and retiring on the company pension are gone. Our grandparents and maybe our parents may have enjoyed company-funded retirement pensions, but not us. Now, the only money we'll have at retirement is the money we've saved for ourselves.

Over the past twenty years or so, the self-funded 401(k) has largely replaced the traditional pension plan, and I'm okay with that. The pension was nice, but it had some serious risk attached to it. A pension is an asset of the company; so if the company goes broke, guess what happens to grandpa's pension? It's gone. If I have a 401(k), though, it's *my* money. It's not even on the company's books and never shows up on its balance sheet. It's all mine, and it is totally portable. If I leave a company, I can take my 401(k) with me. However, you can't move your 401(k) while you're still with the company. As long as you're an employee, your 401(k) has to stay put. When you leave, though, you can roll it over into an IRA, which we'll talk about later.

This is such a better way to go than the old pension! But there's a downside. With a pension plan, the employer does all the saving and the money's just there for the employee at retirement. With a 401(k), if I don't put any money in it over my working lifetime, how much is there when I retire? Nothing. Even if your employer gives a company match on your contributions, you still have to put *something* in there. A 100-percent match on zero dollars is still zero! So, the burden is on me to do my own retirement planning.

Several companies have started offering a new option, the Roth 401(k). This puts two of my favorite plans—the Roth IRA and the 401(k)—together in one awesome plan. I love this thing; we put it in place at my company the instant it became available. Anytime I can put the phrase "tax-free growth" into my investment strategy, I'm doing it!

Here's how the Roth 401(k) works: Just like a Roth IRA, you invest after-tax dollars into the Roth 401(k), but it comes out of your paycheck automatically on payday just like a regular 401(k). It grows just like a Roth IRA, and you pay zero taxes on it when you withdraw the funds at retirement. So on that end, you get all the benefits of a regular Roth IRA, but you can do it *in addition to* a Roth IRA *and* you may get a company match on top of your contributions. Even better, the Roth 401(k) doesn't have income limits attached to it, so you can use a Roth 401(k) even if you don't meet the income limits for a normal Roth IRA. This thing is awesome!

There's one thing worth noting about a company match on a Roth 401(k), though. The matching funds from your employer *do not* grow tax free. The company matches with pretax dollars, so you'll have to pay taxes on that part of it when you withdraw the money, kind of like it was a regular 401(k). So, in a sense, the Roth 401(k) with a match is like two separate pieces growing alongside each other. You have the Roth part that's growing tax free, and then you have the matching piece that's growing without taxes until you take the money out.

403(b) and 457 Plans

You'll find the 401(k) mainly in corporations. If you work for a nonprofit, hospital, church, school, or somewhere similar, you'll probably have a 403(b) instead of a 401(k). The 403(b) works almost exactly like the 401(k) in that you make pretax contributions and you pay the taxes when you take the money out. One benefit of the 403(b) over the 401(k) is that you can move the money out of the 403(b) into an IRA while you're still working at the company. That gives you a little more freedom.

The downside of the 403(b), though, is that there are a lot of horrible investment options inside the 403(b). Remember, the 403(b) is just the tax treatment; it's not an actual investment. The investment is what's *inside* the 403(b), and we've found that those investments in particular have a lot of crummy track records. Always be sure your 403(b) funds are going into good mutual funds and not into weak annuities. Insurance companies especially love to pitch "whole teacher accounts" or "whole hospital accounts" because these are big moneymakers for them. But what's great for the insurance company selling the annuity isn't that great for you. Stick with mutual funds as much as possible!

The 457 plan is typically found in a municipality and offers a deferred-compensation investment option. With a 457, you're basically deferring—or putting off—part of your compensation. Instead of taking that $1,000 home now, you're putting it into an investment, and it will act pretty much like a 401(k). The only real difference is that funds going into a 457 can only be deferred compensation. Personally, I don't like the 457 plans. This is the last thing I'd do. The biggest problem is that rolling your funds out of a 457 can be a major headache, and in some cases, you can't roll the funds out of a 457 at all. In that case, your money is just stuck there, and since all you're doing is deferring your compensation, you could end up with a huge tax bill. The 457 is better than nothing, but you've got to be really careful here. Always talk to an investment professional to make sure you know what you're getting into.

"But My Mean Old Company Doesn't Match!"

I often hear people say something like, "My mean old company doesn't match, so I'm not putting any money into my 401(k)." Oh, that's a great plan. You get back at them by staying broke your whole life. That'll show 'em. You should be contributing to your 401(k) whether your company provides a match or not. Even if they don't, this gives you an opportunity to invest pre-tax dollars, which effectively means you're able to invest more, which means the investment will earn more, which means you'll still have more money than if you did this thing on your own. It's a win-win-win.

Here's how that works. If I earn $1,000 at work, it looks a lot more like $700 by the time I bring it home because the government is going to take its share in the form of taxes. But if you put $1,000 into your 401(k), guess who gave you a match? Congress. They were getting ready to take $300 of your money (in taxes), but they didn't take it. So, you were able to put all $1,000 into the 401(k). You get to earn a return on that extra $300 all the way until retirement. Then, you and the government will split the growth when you pay the taxes on the withdrawal.

Remember Ben and Arthur from chapter 1, *Super Saving?* They taught us that compound interest is a big deal in investing. Whether you get a company match or not, the 401(k) gives you an opportunity to invest money the government would have otherwise taken. You get free use of that money until retirement, so you get to enjoy all the benefits of compound interest on that extra money for a while. It's a fabulous deal.

Take Your Money With You

You should always—*always*—roll your company-sponsored retirement plan into an IRA when you leave the company. The 401(k) is great as long as you're with the company, but once you're gone, you can roll that money out into a regular IRA, which gives you more options. If you're in a 401(k) plan, you probably have ten to twenty mutual funds to choose from. Once you roll that into an IRA, though, you'll have your pick of around eight thousand funds. The field gets a lot bigger, so you have a better chance of finding some outstanding funds to invest in within the IRA.

But one word of warning: Do not bring the money home; make it a direct transfer into an IRA! I cannot stress this enough.

If you cash out the retirement plan, the plan provider will temporarily hold about 20 percent of it. At that point, you'll have sixty days to put that money into an IRA before penalties and taxes are due. So, if you have $100,000 in your 401(k) and cash it out, they'll hold 20 percent and cut you a check for $80,000. However, you have sixty days to put $100,000 into an IRA or you're going to get hit with a big tax bill. That's a $20,000 problem because you brought the money home!

When you leave a company, ask for a direct transfer form for your 401(k). That will essentially send your money straight from your 401(k) into an IRA without the money ever passing through you or your bank account. You want to move the money without touching it! If you do it this way, there is no withholding required, nothing taken out for taxes, and no tax impact later on.

Roll Over Into a Roth IRA?

Of course, when you do a rollover, you have the option of rolling the funds into a Roth IRA to take advantage of the tax-free growth. That's an attractive option to consider, but there are some serious conditions to keep in mind. The main thing to remember is that rolling a 401(k) into a Roth will instantly create a big tax bill. Remember, all the money you put into that 401(k) was pretax, which means you haven't paid any taxes on that money yet. A Roth, though, is funded with after-tax dollars. So, if you move funds from a pretax 401(k) into an after-tax Roth IRA, those taxes will be due immediately.

For example, if you had $100,000 in a 401(k) and rolled it into a Roth, you'll have a $25,000 tax bill coming. If you pay the taxes out of the investment, you'll only have $75,000 to put into the Roth, which means you've totally blown off $25,000. Bad plan. I want you to experience the benefit of tax-free growth in a Roth, but not if doing the deal eats up a huge chunk of your investment. So, I've come up with three guidelines for rolling a 401(k) into a Roth IRA. You should only do this if you meet all three of these conditions:

1. You will have saved more than $700,000 by age sixty-five. If you have that much in your retirement account, you'll be at the top tax bracket at retirement, so you will get the biggest benefit from having primarily tax-free retirement dollars.

2. You pay the taxes due out of pocket, and not from the investment funds. Do not crack open the nest egg to pay the taxes that will be due from the rollover. Only do the rollover if you can pay the taxes off to the side without cutting into the retirement account. In the example above, that means you'd need to have $25,000 lying around to pay the tax bill, which effectively means you'd be adding $25,000 to your investment (because you'd be freeing yourself of later taxes on the growth).

3. You understand that all taxes will become due on the rollover amount. Again, you have to go into this knowing that the rollover will instantly trigger a big tax bill. I keep saying it over and over because I don't want you to be shocked after the deal is done!

If you can meet all three of these conditions, then rolling over into a Roth IRA can be a great way to maximize your old 401(k).

Federal Thrift Savings Plan

If you're in the military or a government employee, you likely have the Thrift Savings Plan (TSP) available to you. The TSP gives you several options, and like everything else, some of the options are great and some are stinkers. Here's a quick rundown of what I suggest for those of you in a TSP:

1. Put 60 percent into the C Fund. This is a common stock fund, which works a lot like the growth stock mutual fund we discussed in chapter 9, *The Pinnacle Point*. This is a great, stable fund that grows at around 8–12 percent. This should make up the bulk of your TSP.
2. Put 20 percent into the S Fund. This is made up of small companies in emerging markets, much like the aggressive growth stock funds we've discussed. The recent average growth on these funds is pretty good, and it gives you a little excitement in the mix.
3. Put 20 percent into the I Fund. This is your international component, just like the international funds we've already discussed in chapter 9. It gives you a little piece of overseas companies to add more diversification to your investments.

There are other TSP funds available, but I recommend staying away from them. The F Fund and L Fund are especially lousy, even though they're often pitched pretty heavily. Just stick with the 60-20-20 breakdown above and you should be fine.

Borrowing Against Your Retirement Account

Earlier I said that if you start doing your retirement investing before you have a full emergency fund, your 401(k) will eventually *become* your emergency fund. That's largely due to retirement loans, one of the worst things you could do with your money. These things are terrible, and they're eating away at the average American's retirement savings.

All kinds of "financial people" have talked about what a great idea retirement loans are. Their reasoning is that it's better to pull your own money out of your own account than use a credit card at 18 percent interest. They'll say something like, "It's wiser to borrow from yourself and pay yourself back at 6 percent interest than borrow from a bank and pay them 18 percent." Part of that is true. In a standard retirement loan, you take money out and then repay the loan with 5–6 percent interest, so it is basically paying yourself back the interest. What these goobers fail to consider, though, is that this is still costing you big-time. When you borrow money from your retirement plan, you are unplugging that amount from a mutual fund earning 12 percent or more. So while that chunk of cash is missing, you're missing out on that growth, and you won't make up that ground by paying yourself 5–6 percent.

JOIN THE CONVERSATION

I'm in my forties and only have a 401(k). My takeaway is that I am WAY behind and need to get busy saving.

—Michelle

www.facebook.com/financialpeace

But that's not the biggest risk. The really risky thing about retirement loans is what happens when you leave your job. You *are* going to leave your job someday, and you don't know when. You could find a better job and quit. Your spouse could get a great job in another state, which means you'd quit. You could get fired. You could get laid off. You could die (which, of course, means you'd be leaving your job). Any of this could happen. And as soon as you leave your job, the whole 401(k) loan is due right then.

If you leave your job with an outstanding 401(k) loan, you'll have sixty days to repay it in full before you lose about 40 percent of your money to taxes and penalties. Think about that. If you're in that situation, you're already broke because you borrowed against your retirement. Now, on top of that, you're out of work *or* your family is reeling from your death. Is that a good time to have a huge, urgent financial crisis to deal with? That's exactly what will happen when you or your heirs have to scramble to repay a 401(k) loan.

JOIN THE CONVERSATION

College is not a right, and I shouldn't feel like a bad parent if I can't afford to pay for all of my kids' tuition. If they work hard and pick a school wisely, they can still get a college education without debt.

—Sarah

www.facebook.com/financialpeace

I have talked to thousands and thousands of people who have fallen for this trap. They went into it thinking that a retirement loan was the best way to make a home improvement or get out of debt, but then life happened and they got stuck in a major crisis. What they thought was a wise move turned out to be one of the worst financial decisions of their lives. This is too risky! Don't do it! But if you follow the Baby Steps and build up a full emergency fund before getting into retirement planning, this won't be an issue.

Over the past few years, we've even seen the introduction of the 401(k) debit card, which gives you instant, immediate, no-strings-attached access to your retirement funds at any time! No cash for that taco dinner? No problem! You can just use your retirement funds to pay for dinner! What a horrible idea!

Your retirement funds are just that—funds for your retirement. This is all the money you're going to have when you're older and no longer working. You can't afford to waste your future income by nickel-and-diming your investments today. Put your investment money aside and don't touch it!

FUNDING YOUR 15 PERCENT

Okay, that covers the alphabet soup of retirement options. We talked about the IRA, Roth, SEP, 401(k), 403(b), 457, TSP, and anything else that could likely be an option for most people. That's a huge mess of letters and numbers, isn't it? No wonder people go cross-eyed when this topic comes up! I rarely go into this much detail on these things, but I think it is important to have a basic understanding of how all these things work so that you can make your own investing decisions. Remember, you can't outsource your financial planning to anyone else. This is *your* money, so it needs to be under *your* direction.

So with all that under our belt, let's turn all that information into an easy, practical suggestion for funding your retirement. Just as a reminder, here's where we are in the Baby Steps:

Baby Step 4: Invest 15 percent of your household income into Roth IRAs and pretax retirement plans.

What do we do with that 15 percent of our income? I suggest the following three steps:

1. Use your 401(k) or other company plan up to the match (if there is one).
2. Above the 401(k) match, fund a Roth IRA.

3. Complete 15 percent of your income by going back to your 401(k) or other company plans.

Let's break that down a little bit.

Step 1: Matching 401(k) or Other Company Plan

If your company offers a match on a company plan, take it. It's free money; that's a no-brainer. But only take it up to the match amount. For example, if your company offers a 3 percent match, the first 3 percent of your 15 percent will go into your 401(k). That way, you're maxing out the match amount from your company.

Step 2: Above the Company Match, Fund a Roth IRA

After you've taken advantage of the company match, move over to a Roth IRA. If your employer does not offer a match on a company plan, then you will start with the Roth and skip the 401(k) for now. As of 2011, the maximum contribution for the Roth IRA is $5,000. For married couples filing jointly, each spouse can have his or her own Roth IRA and take each one up to $5,000 per year.

Step 3: Complete 15 Percent of Your Income by Going Back to Your 401(k) or Other Company Plan

Doing the first two steps will pretty much get most families to the 15 percent mark, but if you've taken the 401(k) match and maxed out a Roth IRA and still have not hit 15 percent, then you'll go back and add more to your 401(k) or other company-sponsored plan.

A Real-World Example

Let's see how this plays out in a real-world example. Joe and Suzie have a household income of $100,000. Joe works full-time and Suzie is an awesome stay-at-home mom. They went through *Financial Peace University*, so they are now out of debt and have a full emergency fund of three to six months' worth of expenses. Now they're ready to start investing for retirement. The household income is $100,000, so 15 percent of that is $15,000. How are they going to invest that 15 percent?

Joe's company offers a 401(k) with a 3 percent match, so they'll start there. They'll invest 3 percent of his income to take full advantage of the match. That means so far, they've invested $3,000 of their income.

Next, Joe and Suzie will each open up a Roth IRA. The Roth maxes out at $5,000 each, so combined, the couple has $10,000 in Roth contributions. This plus the 401(k) contribution comes to $13,000, which means they still have not hit 15 percent of their income yet, right?

So, to get to 15 percent, they will go back to Joe's 401(k) and increase their contribution above the match. They have $2,000 left to get to 15 percent, so they add that to the 401(k) contributions and that's it!

Just Imagine . . .

If you're sitting there reading this right now and you're in your late twenties, I just made you a millionaire. Think about it. If a young couple really got this message in their twenties and took a few years to get out of debt and save up a full emergency fund, they could start investing 15 percent of their income from age thirty on. Even if they only had a household income of $40,000, they could be looking at more than $5 million at age seventy just by faithfully investing 15 percent every month— *and that's if they never got a raise!*

I've said it before: there's no excuse for anyone to retire broke in America! These opportunities are available to everyone, no matter when you get started! All it takes is some discipline and attention to a few simple concepts, and anyone can become a millionaire, totally change their family tree, and leave an incredible legacy of generous giving. So go do it!

COLLEGE FUNDING

Okay, at this point, you are out of debt, you have a full emergency fund of three to six months' worth of expenses, and you are contributing 15 percent of your income into tax-favored retirement accounts. Just breathe that in for a minute. Do you realize that if you've done those few things, you have done far more than most American families? Remember, 70 percent of the households in the country can't even afford to miss a single paycheck without being in a financial bind.[3] But not you! You're charging ahead into some serious wealth. Now it's time to take care of the kiddos' college fund:

Baby Step 5: Save for your children's college using tax-favored plans

If you don't have kids or if your children are already grown and gone, you can skip Baby Step 5. Otherwise, let's tackle some of the issues surrounding college funding and expenses.

"But My Baby Should Come First!"

College funding is one of the biggest areas of pushback I get from the families we work with. When I lay out the Baby Steps to some parents, they are shocked and appalled that I would suggest they make their retirement planning a priority over their children's college fund. It's like they'd prefer to send Junior to an Ivy League school for four years, even if it meant eating Alpo every night when they retire. I just don't get that. I talked about it in my book *The Total Money Makeover*:

> I have done financial counseling for parents who I was afraid would need years of therapy if they didn't provide their children the most expensive school, free for the taking. I am sure that as we start this Baby Step, we need to examine our culture's value system on the college issue. We have sold our young people so hard and so long on college that we have begun to accept some myths about college degrees. College degrees do not ensure jobs. College degrees certainly don't ensure success. College degrees do not ensure wealth. College degrees only prove that someone has successfully passed a series of tests. We all know college-educated people who are broke and unemployed. They are very disillusioned because they thought they had bought a ticket and yet were denied a seat on the train to success.
>
> If you are sending your kids to college because you want them to be guaranteed a job, success, or wealth, you will be dramatically let down. In some cases, the letdown won't take long because as soon as they graduate they will move back in with you.[4]

The degree of guilt and shame in the name of college that I've witnessed in some families is just plain crazy. I've sat with single moms who work two jobs and are barely keeping food on the table for their kids who weep because they can't afford a college fund. This overwhelming guilt just washes over them because they feel like a failure as a parent. I always look these hardworking moms in the eye and tell them that their children should rise up and call them blessed for their hard work and sacrifice. Please don't be confused about this. I know you want to bless your kids, but you've got to take care of yourself too. Private school tuition is not worth wrecking your retirement.

College Is a Privilege

Early on, I made it clear to my kids that I expected them to go to college. There was never a doubt in their minds about whether or not they were going to go. I love school, and I believe that a good education is vital in today's marketplace, but no child *deserves* a free ride at the school of his choice. College is just like anything else we spend money on: You don't deserve it unless you can pay for it. It's not a right for anyone; it's a privilege.

And let's not forget that college students are little adults. You know what adults do for money? They work. There are always pizzas that need throwing. There are always boxes that need stacking. There are always yards that need cutting. It's not child abuse to make your kid work while he or she is in school. Some of the greatest success stories in the country are about men and women who worked hard to put themselves through college. We've already seen in other chapters how much more you value something if you work hard to earn the money for it. Education is no different.

But if you are able to save money toward your child's education, then by all means do it! I'm not saying you shouldn't help your kids through school; I'm just saying that it has to fit reasonably into your financial plan. If you're working the Baby Steps and are ready to put some money away for Junior's college expenses, there are some fantastic, tax-favored opportunities that give you the chance to invest for college tax-free!

Education Savings Account

The first college savings program you want to check out is the Education Savings Account (ESA). This is often nicknamed the

"Education IRA" because it works a lot like the Roth IRA. As of this book's printing, you can invest up to $2,000 (after-tax) a year into an ESA, and it grows tax-free. If you start this when your child is born and invest $2,000 a year until they're eighteen years old, you'll put in a total of $36,000. But that money, invested at the average stock market return of 12 percent, will grow to around $126,000 by the time the child starts school. And remember, that money grows tax-free. Every last dime of it can be used for education expenses.

This alone should take care of most families. The average four-year state school's tuition cost $16,436 for the 2009–2010 school year, and the average cost for a four-year private school was $35,201.[5] An ESA with $126,000 would easily cover the state schools, and it would even cover most of the private schools, for a four-year student. However, Sallie Mae's "How America Pays for College, 2010" survey found that only 15 percent of families take advantage of college savings programs like the ESA.[6] What a waste! If I can turn $36,000 into $126,000 tax-free, I'm definitely doing that!

If your child doesn't go to college, you can transfer the money to a sibling for his or her school. If you're in a position where none of these savings will go toward college, then you'll get hit with penalties and taxes. Be sure to talk through all this with your financial advisor when you set up the accounts.

Above and Beyond: The 529 Plan

If you want to save more than $2,000 per year or you don't meet the income limits for an ESA, you could move to a 529 plan. I'll be honest; I'm not a huge fan of 529 plans because there are a lot of different types, and some of them are no good. You have to be careful here and make sure that you only get a

529 that leaves you in control of the mutual funds at all times. Those are usually called "flexible" plans. That way, you can keep an eye on it and move the investments around if necessary, just like you could in an ESA or IRA.

Never buy a plan that restricts your options ("fixed" plans) or automatically changes your investments based on the age of the child ("life phase" plans). A lot of these start aggressively, but then get increasingly conservative as the child gets older. In my opinion, by the time you need the money in this kind of plan, they've cut it back so far that the whole thing has become totally screwed up. Don't let the government or plan administrators control your destiny. Remember, your money is your responsibility, so don't leave those decisions to someone else.

One Last Option: UTMA/UGMA

If you've already done an ESA and a 529, or if you make too much money to qualify for an ESA, then and only then could you research a Uniform Transfers/Gifts to Minors Act (UTMA/UGMA) plan. This plan offers you the chance to save for college with reduced taxes, but it is not as good as the other options. My guess is about 1 percent of the people who read this book will get an UTMA as part of their college planning, but it's worth mentioning just so you know all the options.

With an UTMA, the account is opened in the child's name and a custodian is named, usually a parent or grandparent. The custodian manages the fund until the child reaches age twenty-one (age eighteen for an UGMA), at which point the child can take the money and use it however they want. So basically, you're just opening up a mutual fund in your child's name, and when they are old enough, they take control of it. The tax advantage comes in the fact that, since it is in the child's name, they'll probably be in a lower tax bracket than you are and will be charged the taxes for their own bracket.

Again, though, I really don't like these plans. If, God forbid, you end up with a twenty-one-year-old drug addict, for example, you could inadvertently be handing over tens of thousands of dollars to them at a time when there's no way they can be trusted with that much money. At least with the ESA and 529, the money has to be spent on education; an UTMA/UGMA just hands your young adult a blank check. The sad truth is, that could be a nightmare in some situations.

FOUR NEVERS OF COLLEGE FUNDING

The ESA, 529, and even the UTMA/UGMA plans should cover just about any college savings goal you could possibly dream up. Sure, those plans require some advance planning, though. If you're child is graduating high school this year, you really don't have time to expect much out of an ESA! But whether you have one year or eighteen years until the first tuition payment is due, avoid these money pits in the area of college funding.

Never Use Student Loans

All the savings options we've covered just go to support my first rule of college: pay cash. If you can't pay cash, put the kid to work for a semester and then send him back to pay cash later. Student loans may look like a quick fix, but they turn into a nightmare and send college graduates out into the world with a boat anchor of debt around their necks. I wrote in *The Total Money Makeover:*

> Student loans are a cancer. Once you have them, you can't get
> rid of them. They are like an unwelcome relative who comes to stay

for a "few days" and is still in the guest room ten years later. We have spread the myth that you can't be a student without a loan. Not true! According to FinAid.org, 70% of students borrow money for school expenses. Student loans have become normal, and normal is broke. Stay away from loans; make plans to avoid borrowing.[7]

In chapter 4, *Dumping Debt*, we saw that all debt is horrible, so you can go ahead and get rid of any notion of college loans being "good debt." There's no such thing. The only "good debt" is no debt. The unending stream of payments from student loans doesn't look or feel any different than an unending stream of payments from a car loan or credit card. There's nothing "good" about that, emotionally or financially.

If Junior is graduating in the next year or two and you don't have the cash on hand for college, start talking to him right now. You don't owe your kids a free ride to the school of their choice. It is perfectly reasonable for them to take some ownership in their own education. That means *work*. There are plenty of sixteen-year-old kids bussing tables and cutting yards across the country right now to help save for college. For some, the military could be a fantastic way to serve their country and save a bunch of money for college. A lot of parents don't like to think about that option, but the truth is, there are some excellent educational opportunities for our men and women in uniform.

Bottom line: Student loans look easy on the front end, but they will absolutely destroy your graduate as he or she enters the workforce. Students on average graduate from a four-year college with over $20,000 in student loans. If you include *all* students (graduate and undergraduate), that number tops $42,000. Can you imagine what it feels like to step out of college and, on the first day of your adult life, have over $40,000 of debt on your shoulders? That's no way to start a career, and the student loan bills start coming whether you have a job or not. Don't put that kind of stress on your kids. Avoid student loans like the plague!

Never Use Insurance as a Savings Plan

If you have kids, your mailbox was probably full of crazy baby insurance offers by the time you got your newborn home from the hospital! One of the most common things we've seen is a whole life, universal life, or variable life insurance plan promoted as a way to save for your child's college education. The most common of these actually comes from a baby-food manufacturer! Seriously? The company that makes mashed carrots wants to send your child to college using crummy insurance? Horrible idea.

We talked about these types of insurance plans in chapter 7, *Clause and Effect*. Insurance is a bad way to save for retirement, and it's an even worse way to save for college. The returns stink, and that kid will spend her whole life trying save enough money in a bad insurance plan to go to college. Just like we said in the insurance chapter, you should keep your insurance and your investments separate. Don't let the emotional pull of a new baby or a college dream lead you into a bad decision.

Never Use Savings Bonds

Bonds are horrible investments, and slapping the word "college" on them doesn't make them any better. The cost of tuition at most colleges goes up around 7 percent every year, but savings bonds only earn around 4–5 percent. So with bonds, you're not even treading water; you're sinking a little deeper every year.

We talked about bonds in chapter 9, *The Pinnacle Point.* You see how these things keep popping up? Insurance, investments, college funding—they all kind of mix together, right? That's why a basic understanding of this stuff is important, even for the Free Spirit whose eyes started rolling in the back of their head several pages ago!

JOIN THE CONVERSATION

My well-being is more important than me paying for my kids to go to college. They can find scholarships and sponsors, but no one will sponsor my retirement.

—TiAnna

www.facebook.com/financialpeace

Never Use Prepaid Tuition

Prepaid tuition isn't the worst option in the world, but I still do not recommend it. I don't like prepaid tuition because you'll be exactly breaking even. When you prepay, you're paying *today's* tuition rate for your student in advance. That means your effective rate of return is the amount that the tuition goes up each year. So, since college tuition increases around 7 percent a year, you'd essentially make 7 percent on your money.

The problem with this is that I can put that money in a good mutual fund inside an ESA and make 12–14 percent return on my money. With compound interest and a higher rate of return, you'd end up with a lot more money in an ESA, and all that money can be used for *any* college expense—like books, room and board—and not just tuition. You wouldn't just have more money; you'd have a lot more options.

SIMULTANEOUS BABY STEPS

This chapter started with a warning to stick to the plan and follow the Baby Steps in order. That's important! But by now you realize that if you have kids heading to college someday, you'll be working Baby Steps 4 and 5 simultaneously. Make sure your retirement plan is up and running, and then add the college plan.

In chapter 12, *Real Estate and Mortgages*, we'll add Baby Step 6—pay off the mortgage early—on top of that, so you'll be running three Baby Steps at the same time. That's why I teach people to only start retirement planning at 15 percent of their income. You need some money left above your basic retirement funding to save for college and to knock out the mortgage. Once those two things are done, you'll have a ton of extra money to start pouring into your investments for wealth building.

We covered a lot of ground in this chapter, and I doubt you caught *everything* with just one read. That's okay. This is a lot of information, and all the letters and numbers and initials start to mix and merge together in my head, too! That's the value of having this book on your bookshelf. Review it as you hit these Baby Steps, and use it as a reference as you start to make your own retirement and college planning options. And remember that pretty much everything we discussed here can change at any time. If you're in a *Financial Peace University* class, refer back to the online resources for this lesson for the most up-to-date information. Otherwise, keep an eye on daveramsey.com, and we'll make sure you know when the big things change.

WE DID IT!

Our son, Austin, graduated from high school in 2008 and was set to attend Florida State University to study engineering. We were pumped as a family for his success—and excited by the prospect of attending football games! He had a prepaid college tuition plan and had won some scholarships, but we were still about $10,000 shy of the required amount per year. We looked into loans, but ultimately said NO. We didn't want him coming out of college with debt, and we certainly weren't going to mortgage our future.

We withdrew him and he decided on community college, instead. During his first semester, he looked into the Navy. They offered a wonderful ROTC program that would pay for college, but he chose to enlist. Austin has been in the Navy for about one year now. He has finished Basic and Naval Training and is attached to an aircraft carrier set to sail soon.

This twenty-year-old listened to his mama (who listens to Dave) and now has $10,000 in a savings account for emergencies, contributes 5 percent to a 401(k), and has started a Roth IRA. Saying no to college debt was hard, but it has turned out to be a good thing. He is studying onboard and will get his degree as he serves his country. Many of Austin's friends who chose to borrow for college have major debt already, but I see nothing but smooth sailing for a lifetime for this young sailor!

Debbie
Lakeland, FL

KEY POINTS

1. Your financial independence at retirement is up to you. Do not depend on Social Insecurity to take care of you! If it's still around when you retire, just consider that bonus money on top of the excellent saving you've done for yourself.
2. Do the Baby Steps in order. Start college funding only after you have your own retirement plan in place, and then do both Baby Steps simultaneously.
3. You don't owe your children a free ride to the college of their choice. Do what you can to help them, but do not put your own financial well-being in jeopardy. Making a child work his way through college is not child abuse!

QUESTIONS FOR REFLECTION

1. What do you think when you see retirement-aged people working in grocery stores? Is that what you want to do when you retire?
2. What motivates you to get serious about your retirement plan?
3. Why is it such a bad idea to cash in a retirement plan early in order to get out of debt faster?
4. Why do so many people use their retirement account as their emergency fund in the form of retirement loans? What is the danger of doing this?
5. Why does college funding come *after* retirement planning in the Baby Steps?
6. Would you feel guilty taking care of your own retirement plan before putting money aside for your child's college education? Why?
7. How does living on a monthly budget help you prepare for retirement?

11

WORKING IN YOUR STRENGTHS

CAREERS AND EXTRA JOBS

My grandfather was an incredible man. He was one of my heroes, actually. He entered the workforce during one of the most difficult periods in American history, the Great Depression. Life wasn't easy back then, but he enjoyed his work, loved his family, and poured himself into both. He started in the accounting department at Alcoa, an aluminum company, as a very young man, and over time grew into one of their head cost accountants. Grandpaw stayed with Alcoa for thirty-eight years, until the day he retired from the workforce. He left with a gold watch and a pension, as well as the satisfaction of knowing he devoted his entire working life to a single company he was devoted to.

Those days are gone in America. Companies, products, services, startups, and shutdowns are moving faster today than ever before. The rate of change going on in the workplace is mind-blowing! My grandfather, God love him, would be completely out of place in today's market.

Throughout this book and all through our *Financial Peace University* class, we focus almost entirely on the outgo. That is, we budget and plan how to spend and save our money. That's what the Baby Steps are all about, right? It's how we tell our money what to do once it leaves our hands. In this chapter, though, we switch gears and examine the income.

Obviously, income is important. I've always said, "If your outgo exceeds your income, eventually your upkeep will become your downfall!" That is, sometimes, we just need to make more money! But just like everything else we've been talking about, when it comes to careers, it's not *just* about money. The goal of your professional life should be to devote yourself to your passion and calling, finding somewhere and some way to make a living by working in your strengths.

THE WORLD IS CHANGING

In our culture today, there is only one constant: change. It's a paradox, right? The only thing we can count on is that we can't count on things to stay the same. Everything is up in the air! Just look at how far we've come over the past thirty years in computers and technology. I've got a thumb drive in my pocket that has more computer memory than it took to put the first man on the moon! The little eleven-inch, two-pound laptop on my desk would have been considered the world's most powerful supercomputer just a few years ago! This stuff is moving fast!

Our careers are the same way. If you dig in your heels and resist the change going on all around you, you're going to be left in the dust. The days of sitting at the same desk for thirty-eight years like my grandfather are ancient history. In fact, the Bureau of Labor Statistics found that the average job today lasts only two years. Our grandparents were still figuring out where all the restrooms were at the two-year mark, but by that point, we're already hitting the door and finding something else to do!

YOUR STRENGTHS AND WEAKNESSES

The average worker today will have ten different jobs by age forty and could have as many as twenty different jobs during his or her working lifetime. That prospect might have scared our grandparents to death. Fifty years ago, workers found security by landing a good job with a stable company and staying there forever. Today, the modern workforce finds security in understanding who they are and what they want to be doing. The focus has shifted away from the big corporations and toward the individual's strengths and passions.

How can you know where you ought to be and what you ought to be doing if you don't know who you are? If I don't know who I am, I'll just stumble blindly into a career and probably be miserable in it because I'm doing it for the wrong reasons. Money is never enough incentive to dread going to work every day. I talk about this in my book *EntreLeadership*:

> Seth Godin says, "Instead of wondering when your next vacation is, maybe you should set up a life you don't need to escape from." Business is way too hard to work at something just for money. Winning at business at times requires that you exhaust every ounce of spiritual, emotional, and physical energy you have. You won't put that effort in day in and day out, year in and year out, just for money. Money is great, but it is ultimately an empty goal. Bigger homes, bigger cars, and even more giving is just not a big enough goal to keep you creative and energized throughout your life. You have to have a passion, a higher calling, to what you engage in. Malcolm Gladwell says, "Hard work is a prison cell only if the work has no meaning."[1]

No one else can tell you what you should do with your life—not your parents, your friends, or even your spouse. It would be a neat dream of mine to have my kids come up alongside me and run my company someday. However, it would be a total nightmare if I forced them into that if it wasn't what they wanted to do for themselves. I left that door open to them, but I never pushed them through it. A couple of them are moving that way now, but it's not because I pressured them. I don't want *any* team members to work with us only because they feel forced to be here. That's a recipe for disaster in any business.

Myths About Fulfillment and Contentment

Author and speaker Marcus Buckingham has a fabulous video series called *Trombone Player Wanted*.[2] In that video workshop, he presents some myths that get stuck in people's minds early in life and then hold them back for the *rest* of their lives. The two myths that he uses to open the presentation really play into this whole discussion of strengths and weaknesses.

Myth 1: As you grow, you change.

Have you heard this one? When it comes to how you feel about your job, you may hear it like this: "Oh, don't worry. *You'll get used to it.*" What is the message there? How can we get used to something that we desperately struggle with at the very core of our being? Buckingham makes the point pretty clear that we *never* outgrow our personalities. We each have natural tendencies, strengths, and weaknesses that are bound up with who we are as people. We're not going to outgrow who we are.

If you have kids, you probably saw this stuff in them very early. By the time your child is two or three, you can really start to see what kind of personality that child will have for the rest of his or her life. Is he orderly or messy? Does she avoid confrontation? Is he sweet and sensitive, or is he a little bulldog? Those things don't change.

For example, I have one daughter who is very precise and detailed. Even when all three kids were little, she could tell if the other two had been in her room. Sometimes we thought that she could tell if the *air* was out of place! From the day we brought her home from the hospital, she has been driven by precision and rules; it's just who she is. So, of course she needs to be in a career where she can engage that part of her personality.

My other daughter is the total opposite. She's got a lot of her father in her, so she's kind of wild and crazy, loves talking to people, and feels right at home on a stage in front of several thousand people. It would be a disaster if I tried to force that one into accounting or law. She's just not wired that way, and it would crush the beautiful spirit that God put inside of her.

Myth 2: You will learn and grow the most in the areas in which you are weakest.

This is a total lie, but we buy into it from a young age because, most likely, our parents bought into it. Buckingham cites a Gallup poll that asked, "Your child comes home with the following grades: English-A, Social Studies-A, Biology-C, Algebra-F. Which grade should get your most attention?" It's not that surprising that 77 percent of parents said they'd focus almost exclusively on the one F. Heck, I know I'd focus on the F too!

But what does that do to us and to our kids? It's a way of saying that our strengths don't matter and that we should spend all our time focused on our weakest areas. I don't think that we should ignore our weaknesses, but I do believe we need to see them in perspective alongside our strengths.

Buckingham turns the issue around and says that we don't really grow in our weaknesses at all; instead, we grow in our strengths, in the areas that we already know and love the most. Sure, we *can* grow in our weaker areas through sheer force of will, but it is extremely difficult and the gains are usually pretty small. At best, we could go from "completely horrible" to "pretty pathetic." If we turned it around, though, and focused on growing in our strengths, then we can grow by leaps and bounds, because our heart and passion are already poured into those areas!

Passion Matters

When we're focused on and operating in our strengths and passions, nothing can hold us back. We'll be on fire, and everyone around us will wonder how we can work so hard without getting tired. I like how Mark Twain said it: "The secret of success is making your vocation a vacation." When you love what you do, you will work like crazy—but it will never feel like work. You'll be functioning at a high level and knowing that the work you are doing was assigned by God, because it fits perfectly with the gifts, skills, and talents He put inside of you to begin with.

Get on the Bus

Jim Collins wrote an incredible book titled *Good to Great* several years ago. In it, he examined several high-performing companies and researched how they went from "good" to "great." One of the keys he found that enabled these companies to go to the next level was their ability to get the right people in the right jobs. As Collins describes it, great companies have the ability to get the right people on the bus, get the wrong people off the bus, and most important, get the *right people* in the *right seat* on the bus.[3]

For us, it's not a matter of just being part of the right company; it's about being in the right *position* at the right company. You might absolutely love the company you work for but you're struggling with what you're currently doing. Or maybe you feel like you're outgrowing your current position and want to look into advancement. In those cases, it sounds like you're on the right bus, but you might need to change seats.

Think about the parts of your job that you absolutely love doing and do better than anyone else. Then start talking to your supervisor about how you can do more of *that* and less of the stuff that drags you down. It's a win-win if you love what you do day after day, you're happy and content, you enjoy going to work, and your boss gets the most out of you. So don't be scared to have these conversations! Most leaders would rather have you excited about coming to work every day than see you drag yourself through the door every morning and sit there like a zombie for eight hours on their dime.

JOB HUNTING

As we talk through these things, you may have realized you are in exactly the right seat on exactly the right bus. That's great! Or, you may have realized you're on the right bus, but you're in the wrong seat. No problem—just do what we talked about and start working toward your new seat. But the truth is, sometimes we're on the wrong bus. Or maybe we're just getting started with our career and we haven't boarded a bus at all! If that's you, then let's look at some practical things to know and do when you're job hunting.

Starting the Search

When you are looking for a job, you have to have a plan. Most people just mail out a stack of résumés and wait for the phone to ring. I don't care how many degrees they have; that just doesn't work. They're going to have a long wait, especially in an economy where there are more people needing jobs than there are job openings. Those are the people who end up flipping burgers three months after completing their MBA degrees. At that point, the only thing MBA stands for is "Moving Beef Around!"

You've got to see this job-hunting process from the employer's perspective. Truett Cathy, the founder of Chick-fil-A, says, "We don't hire people because *they* need a job. We hire them because *we need them.*" That is, companies don't start out looking for *you*. They have a specific *need* and they need *someone* to meet it. So your objective is to find out what they need, and then to convince them that you are the absolute best person in the world to meet that need.

Develop a Strategy

If you start your search with the simple mind-set of "I need a job," a job is all you'll get—at best. There will be no passion, no excitement. You'll punch a time clock, put in your eight hours, and collect your paycheck. That's it. Until, of course, you either burn out or your lack of enthusiasm inspires your boss to show you the door. Either way, that's no way to live.

So instead of just saying, "I need a job," try starting off with, "I need a career." A job gives you a paycheck; a career gives you a direction and a purpose for your work. With a career in mind, identify the target. Look at newspapers, online job boards, and employment agencies that specifically fill the kind of position you want. Keep in mind, though, that the best jobs are rarely found in—or filled from—job postings. The best way to get the best jobs is through personal networking. Chances are, you already know the person who will get you your next job, so start opening your eyes at the contacts you already have. Who is in a field that interests you? Who is the most well-connected person you know? How can you maximize things like Facebook to get to the person who can get you your dream job?

If you've already found a particular company you want to work for, then your mission is to learn everything you can about them. Research them; pore over their website; talk to people who work there. Spy on them! Businesses love knowing that people want to work for them.

We had more than 3,500 interviews for our open positions last year, and out of those, we hired a whopping 34 people. That's a 1 percent acceptance rate. We did the math and figured out that you'd have a better chance getting accepted to Harvard than to make it through our interview process! Why? Because we're an *awesome* place to work! People all over the country want to come work with us because we're passionate, we do excellent work, and we're on a mission! We don't waste our time with people who don't know anything about us; there are plenty of passionate people who share our vision to choose from!

You have to have an *active* job search. You can't just mail a stack of résumés every month and pray for someone to call. Get out there, shake some hands, and beat down some doors.

Every employer in the world is looking for someone who is looking for them. Nobody wants an office filled with corporate drones. I know I don't. And if one accidentally slips in, I promise you, they don't last long. Everyone else's passion and productivity either makes them so uncomfortable that they leave, or we get tired of dragging them around and we *help* them leave. We've got too much important work to do to let one lazy clock puncher slow us down!

Résumés

When it comes to contacting the company you've targeted, think of it like starting a new relationship with someone. Imagine that you met someone at a party and asked, "What do you do?" Now, do you want to hear their entire work history, the fine details of their job, and a list of references, or were you just trying to start a conversation? When we meet new people socially, we are interested in who they are and what they do, but we don't necessarily want them to give us their entire résumé with the first handshake. All that does is tell me that this person is totally focused on themselves—*me, me, me! All about me!* That's not someone I'd want to bump into at another party.

When we pound a company with a résumé, cover letter, stack of work samples, and long list of references right out of the gate, we're doing the same thing. If an employer doesn't know you yet or hasn't asked for that much information, you're taking a huge leap in assuming they are that interested in spending so much time on a total stranger. Just like meeting new friends at a party, you need to slow down and engage in a conversation. No good decision will be made at the first meeting. Slow down, and let's get to know each other first.

In his book *48 Days to the Work You Love*, career coach Dan Miller lays out a professional, courteous process for contacting a new company you're interested in.[4] He suggests a three-step plan of attack:

Step 1: Introduction Letter. This is *not* your résumé! This is your first handshake with a new friend. In this letter, you're just popping up on the company's radar. Your goal is to greet them, get your name on someone's desk, and inform them that you'll be following up soon with a résumé.

Step 2: Cover Letter and Résumé. Your cover letter should be a single page and contain three paragraphs. In the first paragraph, introduce yourself briefly and remind the company of your introduction letter. In the second paragraph, tell them why you are calling on them. Refer specifically to their need and your ability to meet that need. In the last paragraph, tell them your plan following the résumé. That is, tell them when you will be contacting them again (step 3, below) and whatever other appropriate follow-up actions you're planning. Address this letter to an *individual*, not "To Whom It May Concern." If you've done your research on the company, you'll already know whose name to address it to.

The résumé should never be more than one page. Keep it on point, don't waste time on trivia that doesn't matter, and put the most important information near the top. Tailor the résumé to the recipient; list your qualifications that meet their specific need, and emphasize the qualifications you'd like to see if you were hiring someone—like integrity, dependability, and loyalty.

I shouldn't even have to say this next point, but years of experience tell me I do. Never, ever send out a résumé and cover letter with sloppy, lazy, messy mistakes on it. Read your submission a dozen times if you have to in order to make sure it is 100 percent pristine. Even a tiny typo on the cover letter will give a negative first impression to the person reading it. Every detail matters, right down to the *subject line* you type in your e-mails. We were interviewing a candidate not too long ago who had two horrible typos in the subject line of his e-mail—and this was for a writer/editor position! Without even *opening* the e-mail, we already knew we couldn't trust this guy to edit others' writing. He blew it before we even got to "Hello."

Step 3: Phone Follow-Up. Your cover letter should tell the employer that you'll be contacting them soon by phone. Be specific in the cover letter and tell them a time and date for your call—*and then do it!* The Census Bureau reports that 98 percent of the companies in the U.S. have fewer than one hundred employees.[5] That means most places don't have big HR departments screening all the applicants. There's probably a VP or department leader making the hiring decisions, and if they start seeing this level of professionalism and courtesy from an applicant, you'll start to stand out.

Interviews

In an interview, you have to present yourself well. Never forget that you are the *product*. You're trying to sell the company on the values and benefits of that product, so make it the best one possible. Dress professionally, but try to look like you already belong there. In your research, find out what most people wear to work at that particular place, and then step it up a notch or two from there. If you're interviewing at a jeans-and-flip-flops office, showing up in a tux will make you look really out of place, right? You want the employer to be able to visualize you sitting at a desk in their atmosphere, so don't go too far above or below their "average" look.

Be on time; address everyone by name; offer a firm, confident handshake; and maintain appropriate eye contact. A lot of employers make the hiring decision in the first thirty seconds of meeting someone, so don't depend on your résumé to save you if you make a bad first impression in person. Companies don't hire résumés; they hire people.

After the interview, take the initiative to set a time to follow up. Say something like, "Would you mind if I called to follow up with you next Thursday?" They'll probably say that's fine, and then you can make it more concrete with, "Great, how's 10:00?" Then, you have an appointment. They agreed to it, so there's no reason to be scared about making that call. Just be sure to actually *do it*. If you tell them you'll follow up and then don't, they'll definitely notice. After the interview and before the phone follow-up, send them a short, handwritten thank-you note. Trust me—that's a nice touch that stands out, and most people don't do it.

PART-TIME JOBS AND SIDE BUSINESSES

No matter how well we're handling our finances, the truth is that sometimes, we just need more money. Raising your income long term is a career track issue. That is, your income over time should increase as you advance through your chosen career. But some people don't have a five-year problem; they have a *five-minute* problem! I get these calls on my radio show all the time. They say, "Dave, we're working the program. I have a great job that I love and I know I can get promotions and move up over time. But I've got bill collectors calling me *today*. I need some extra cash right now! What do I do?"

Part-Time Jobs for Short-Term Goals

For short-term goals like getting out of debt, building up your emergency fund, saving up a down payment on a house, and dropping a big chunk into a child's college fund, you may have to examine the dreaded part-time job. It's not ideal for many, especially those who already work long hours and have a family, but an extra job for a short period can do wonders to jump-start your short-term needs.

Sure, it's not glamorous, but chances are you could be delivering pizzas by the end of the week. This isn't the type of job I want you to do for years, but sometimes we've got to sacrifice to win. If throwing a few pizzas for six months could get you out of debt one year faster, wouldn't it be worth it? If you really want to live like no one else later, you may have to *work* like no one else today.

That's what I did twenty years ago when we went broke. I had a huge pile of debt and my career was in ruins. I worked like a crazy person for an intense period of time to clean up the mess. When we started our company, I did everything, went everywhere, and talked to everyone who would listen. Today, I don't have to. I get to pick what I want to do and where I want to go. I get to spend as much time with my family as I want to. I have an assistant who spends half her week telling people, "No, Dave can't come speak at your thing." I used to take all those jobs because I had to, but because I did that for a very intense period, I don't have to anymore. I worked like no one else, so now I can work like no one else.

Building a Side Business

There's absolutely nothing wrong with delivering papers or pizzas for a short time if that's what it takes to get some grease in the gears. There's no shame in that, and it shows tremendous strength of character to swallow your pride and do whatever it takes to win. However, adding extra income doesn't necessarily mean you have to take a job flopping Whoppers. You may make more money, have more fun, and discover a whole new calling in life if you think about starting up a home-based business instead.

Dan Miller says that you should build your life bouquet from the flowers that are within reach. That is, look at your life—your hobbies, interests, and passions—and see if there is a way to turn those things into an income. Wouldn't it be fabulous if you could actually make money doing the things you already love doing? Guess what? People *are* doing that. They're doing it every day. There has never been a better time in the history of America to start up your own business and build it into a full-time career!

You're looking at one home-based business success story. My company started on a card table in my living room. Before any of the books or classes or radio shows or television appearances or live events, there was Dave and Sharon Ramsey working on a little folding table in our house. We had no money, but we had passion and we weren't afraid of hard work. God took what we had and magnified it far beyond what either of us could ever have dreamed of!

Think you can't create something in your garage that could change the world? Tell that to Bill Gates, who started Microsoft in his dorm room. Tell that to Steve Jobs, who started Apple from his parents' garage. Tell that to David Green, who started Hobby Lobby from a little craft workshop he set up in his garage. Don't tell these guys it can't be done! They did it, and they did it with no resources, no real experience, and in the midst of a horrible economy, high inflation, and the raging energy crisis of the 1970s!

In my book *EntreLeadership*, I tell the story of some ladies I've gotten to know who have totally transformed their families, their finances, and their careers just by focusing on one small-business idea:

Jane DeLaney of Birmingham, Alabama, found a crumpled five-dollar bill in her pocket in 2003. She says that was the inspiration for starting her company, and she optimistically opened a business account with that five dollars. Jane and her sister Jenny began to build an online tool to help a family plan and budget their meals a week at a time. The planning takes stress away from the family and stretches the dollars spent considerably. They charge a whole $1.25 per week, or, you guessed it, five dollars per month. By 2006 Jane and Jenny had over a thousand subscribers and came to us to advertise on *The Dave Ramsey Show*. Our national ads are way too expensive for a company grossing $100,000 per year and we didn't want to sink them, so we offered to sell some of our Internet-only ads at a bargain rate.

That little bit of web advertising and Judith, their third sister, joining the company to create a marketing strategy caused an explosion. As they grew, they were able to become national advertisers on our show. Now they have over 60,000 subscribers—that is almost $4 million a year they are grossing. Jane, her sisters, and their husbands can't quit smiling. They are helping families remove stress, spend more time together, and save money. And they are getting paid very handsomely for providing this wonderful service.[6]

Their service, E-Mealz, is a smashing success, and it is a perfect example of how you can turn your own interests and passions into an income. Sure, Jane could have gotten a part-time job as a waitress to bring in some extra cash for her family, but I doubt she would be earning $4 million waiting tables!

If you have a business idea that fires you up, something that keeps you up at night dreaming, this may be the perfect time to give it a try. Like I said in *EntreLeadership*, "You are never too old. You are never the wrong color. You are never too disabled. You are never the wrong political party. There is never a big enough obstacle to keep a person with passion operating in a higher calling from winning."[7]

You Are Not Your Job

I love talking about careers. Can you tell I'm passionate about mine? But before we close this chapter, I want to say one word. I believe in hard work. I believe in throwing yourself totally into whatever passion or calling God's put on your heart. But never allow your total sense of self-worth to come only from what you do for a living. You are so much more than that.

Too often, especially with men, if you ask them *who they are*, they'll answer by telling you *what they do*. I understand that, because I am so passionate and spiritually tied to my life's calling. But I am many things that you'll never see in a class, book, or radio show. I'm a husband, a father, a disciple of Christ. Those things are just as much a part of me as my career.

So keep your life and career in perspective. But at the same time, here's an idea: When you're at work, *work hard*! And when you're at home, *play hard*! Be active and alive and intense with whatever you're doing. If you're doing something you absolutely hate, then change it! Don't go your whole life dreading a job that is sucking the life out of you. Make a plan to get where you want to be and do the things it takes to get there!

JOIN THE CONVERSATION

I left my dead-end job to start my own remodeling company. I wouldn't have been able to prior to FPU.

—Tom

www.facebook.com/financialpeace

WE DID IT!

My wife, Theresa, and I got married almost seven years ago—before we even graduated college. My parents helped pay for my college, but my wife was on a scholarship that ran out well before she was done with school. When we married, I got a great wife, but I also got some great debt! As a wedding present, my dad bought us the *Financial Peace University* Home Study program. He told me that he had started using this program, and it had made his life much easier. He said that he wished he had started this a long time ago, so he wanted to give me the chance he never had.

After my wife and I were done with our bachelor's degrees, we both went into the workforce. Theresa became a teacher at a Catholic school and I, after some jumping around, found a career at a treatment home for underprivileged youth. Needless to say, we didn't choose professions that made a lot of money! On top of that, my wife went back to school to get her master's degree in education. Soon, the debt piled up and we started looking at your program (which had honestly sat collecting dust for a while). We started the envelope system and really looked at what we *wanted* compared to what we *needed*. I got two part-time jobs and my wife got three to supplement our income. Working together, we knocked out more than $30,000 in debt in less than two years! We are now twenty-nine years old and have two wonderful kids, Mady and Jacob. We are debt-free except our mortgage and have almost $100,000 saved for retirement already. It goes to show you that with a little hard work and discipline, the sky is the limit when it comes to building wealth!

Scott
Boys Town, NE

KEY POINTS

1. The days of working for the same company for forty years are pretty much over in America. Today, most workers will have as many as twenty different jobs over their working lifetime.
2. The key to finding your true passion and calling is to first understand yourself, including your strengths and weaknesses.
3. A résumé won't get you a job. It will, at best, get you an interview.
4. You are more than your job. You must view your career in perspective with everything else in your life.

QUESTIONS FOR REFLECTION

1. If you could do anything you wanted and money was no object, what would you do? How is your current work preparing you to do that?
2. What areas of growth or education will help you along your career path?
3. Based on your unique personality, what strengths do you bring to the workplace?
4. What are the dangers of becoming a workaholic? How can it affect your life, spirit, family, and relationships?
5. If you have debt, what are some ways you could make extra money to get out of debt faster? Are there any creative, side-business ideas that could help?

12

REAL ESTATE AND MORTGAGES

KEEPING THE AMERICAN DREAM FROM BECOMING A NIGHTMARE

I love real estate. My parents were in the real estate business, so it has always been a big part of my life. I remember when I was just a little kid—seven or eight years old—answering the phone carefully, professi onally, and politely. My parents made sure we kids knew that every phone call could put food on the table! Their clients would always tell them how polite and helpful their "receptionist" was. Mom and Dad would just laugh and say, "Receptionist? That's our eight-year-old son!" This business is in my blood!

So it didn't surprise anybody when I sat for and passed my real estate agent exam three weeks after my eighteenth birthday. Two years later, at twenty, I passed the broker's exam. This world was all I knew for the first half of my life! Over the decades, I have bought and sold foreclosures, performed quick flips, and made a ton of money in real estate. I've lost a lot, too—doing stupid deals in real estate is how I went broke in my twenties. But that didn't make me mad at real estate; it just made me mad at being stupid back then.

By now, I've owned more than a thousand pieces of real estate, so I know a thing or two about how to buy and sell, and I know about the different types of mortgages that banks try to push on people under the banner of "the American dream." A home is the largest investment most Americans will ever make, so let's take some time to see how to handle that investment well.

FINALLY, COMPLETELY DEBT FREE!

By this point in the Baby Steps, life is starting to get pretty sweet, isn't it? If you've been walking along with us through the process, I want you to imagine what it would feel like as we come up to this step. You are debt-free except for the house. You have a fully funded emergency fund of three to six months' worth of expenses, which for most people is somewhere around $10,000, give or take. You are investing 15 percent of your income into 401(k)s and Roth IRAs to make sure you'll have a fabulous retirement. You are investing in your kids' college education so those tuition bills don't knock you over later. And now we come to a critical juncture in your journey:

Baby Step 6: Pay off your home early

In my years of working with families along this journey, I've seen that this is where it will either all come together or all fall apart.

This is the point where it's easy to sit back, look at how far you've come, and say, "Well, hey, that's pretty good. I can take it easy now!" Don't do it! I explained in my book *The Total Money Makeover:*

> At this point in your Total Money Makeover, you are in grave danger! You are in danger of settling for "The Good Enough." You are at the eighteen-mile mark of a marathon, and now that it is time to reach for the really big gold ring, the final two Baby Steps could seem out of your reach. Let me assure you that many have

been at this point. Some have stopped and regretted it; others have stayed gazelle-intense long enough to finish the race. The latter have looked and seen just one major hurdle left, after which they can walk with pride among the ultra-fit who call themselves financial marathoners. They can count themselves among the elite who have finished The Total Money Makeover.[1]

I don't want you to fall apart just before the finish line. I know it's hard; I know it's taken a long time to get to this point, but you are so close! Don't lose the gazelle intensity that has brought you to this point! Focus, fight, and climb your way over the biggest hurdle yet: your mortgage. Keep the momentum going by throwing every extra dollar you can squeeze out of your budget at the mortgage and get debt out of your life for good!

JOIN THE CONVERSATION

I knew a fifteen-year fixed-rate mortgage was the way to go, but now I really understand why it is so important on many levels.

—Larry

www.facebook.com/financialpeace

SELLING YOUR HOME

There are pretty much two sides of the real estate business: selling and buying. Whether you're just in it for your personal residence or you're using real estate as an investment, it all comes down to how well you can buy and sell properties. Like I said, I've bought and sold a ton, so I can help you with some pointers no matter what side of the closing table you're sitting on.

Living in a Model Home

When selling a home, you have to think like a retailer. If you were to go to a shopping mall and the floors were dirty, there was garbage lying around, the stores were cluttered with random displays and furnishings, and the shop windows were smudged with greasy fingerprints, what impression would you have of the mall and those businesses? Not a great one. The same is true for your home when you're trying to sell it. The people who walk through it aren't your friends; they're your customers.

The home has to be in near-perfect condition. From the moment you put a sign in the yard, you are no longer living in "your" home. You're living in a model home. You've got to make your children—or your husband, or your wife, or your roommates—understand that you're all mannequins in a big display window. People are going to be walking up to that display to judge the quality of the product, and if there are dirty sneakers in the corner or a week's worth of mail on the kitchen counter, you'll lose a sale pretty quickly.

Do you have pets? If you're selling a house, then the answer better be no! I don't care how cute and cuddly your kitty is; if a potential buyer walks in and sees a cat, they'll immediately think, *litter box* no matter how clean the house is. They'll probably convince themselves that the house *smells* like a litter box too. One look at Fluffy can cost you $10,000! Remember, you're thinking like a retailer; you don't see animals milling around a high-end retail store, do you? Then don't have them rubbing up against people who are looking at your house!

Here are some other easy things you can do to make a nice presentation inside the home:

- Put high-quality, 100-watt lightbulbs in all the lamps and overhead lights. Well-lit rooms look bigger and brighter.
- Clean your countertops! A buyer won't care about your fine collection of tiny ceramic teapots. Every little thing you have laying out shrinks your counter space. You want the buyer to imagine *their* things on the counters, not yours.
- Clean out the closets and the garage. You're getting ready to move, anyway. Get your clutter out of the way so the buyer can see a ton of available closet and storage space.
- Light candles in a few rooms when you know a prospective buyer is coming for a walk-through. Candlelight or a fire in the fireplace gives a fantastic feeling of warmth and comfort to set the buyer's mind at ease.
- Take a deep breath. How does the house smell? We talked about the power of smell in some retail stores in chapter 6, *Buyer Beware*. Take a lesson from those stores and bake some bread or cookies before a buyer comes over. That sweet smell will hit them as soon as they walk in the front door.
- Get your furniture out of the way. If you have a knack for overdecorating, clear out some of the clutter that someone may trip over. This isn't about *your* preferences; this is about creating a beautiful, roomy, neutral environment that *anyone* could imagine tailoring to *their* tastes, not yours.
- Dust, vacuum, and clear away cobwebs. The house has to be spotless at all times!
- Get out of the house. Buyers aren't coming to see you; they're coming to see your house. If you're there, it will feel like they're standing in *your* house. You want them to feel like they're standing in *their* house.

None of these things are expensive and none of them take a lot of time to do, but these are the keys to a strong home presentation. Most people don't bother doing half of these things, so buyers will always gravitate to those who do.

Curb Appeal and Fix-Up Dollars

It's not uncommon for a house listing to include the phrase "paint and carpet allowance." Do you know what that means? When a buyer sees that in the listing, two words immediately spring to mind: trash hole. It means the seller is too broke or lazy to clean up the house enough to make it attractive to buyers. And once the buyer knows there's a problem with the paint and carpet, they'll be looking for—and probably finding—other problems *everywhere*.

The return on investment for fix-up dollars is enormous. I've seen hundreds of sellers skimp on paint, carpet, and even basic cleaning costs because they "couldn't afford" $1,000 of simple clean-up. But here's what they don't consider. Suppose you "save" $1,000 on paint when you list the house, but because the house looks old and beat-up, it sits on the market two months longer than it would have if you painted it. If you have a $1,500 mortgage payment every month, your decision to save $1,000 on paint just cost you $3,000 in extra mortgage payments. You've got to think this stuff through and really determine what's important.

The work you do inside only matters, though, if you can get a buyer to walk through the door. That means you've got to pay a lot of attention to your home's curb appeal. A lot of buyers will make their decision from the curb or driveway before they ever even step out of the car. An unkempt lawn, crazy weeds, overgrown bushes, crooked shutters, bicycles in the yard, and cracked porch steps immediately tell buyers what to expect. It sets the tone for the whole experience, so you can't afford to blow it from the curb.

I remember one time, back when I was buying, fixing, and flipping homes, I bought this old 1970s ranch house with a totally overgrown yard. This house had gigantic bushes crawling all over it. These weren't cute little shrubs; they were trashy monster bushes that hadn't been trimmed in twenty-five years, and they were basically trying to eat the house! I told my landscaper to just cut all of it down to the dirt and replace it with some simple, small landscaping. A couple of days later, after all that mess had been chopped down and hauled off, I drove over to the house to check on the work. Can you believe that I actually drove *past* the house? I didn't even recognize it! Once we got those bushes out of the way, the house grew fifteen feet. There was this great, big beautiful home back there, but no one would ever have known if we hadn't gotten the offending bushes out of the way. From there, it just needed a coat of paint and that house sold pretty quickly.

So here's what I suggest. Before you put a sign in the yard, get everything ready as though you were having an open house. Then hop in your car, drive around the block, and pull up to your house just like a buyer would. Try to see your house through the buyer's eyes, looking for all the odds and ends that a critical eye would immediately spot. Walk up to your front porch and look around. Is the welcome mat straight? Are there cobwebs? Are your kid's dirty baseball cleats lying next to the door? Then walk in and go all the way through the house looking for things like that. Remember, buyers don't want to imagine *you* living in the house; they need to imagine *themselves* living there. Your job is to fix, get rid of, or clean up anything that would prevent them from doing that. Paint, lawn care, wallpaper, basic repairs, and touch-ups make homes sell faster and for more money, so do them!

The Real First Impression: Internet Listings

When I first started selling real estate more than thirty years ago, there was a ton of legwork involved, but at least I got to walk with buyers as they experienced a home for the first time. That has totally changed over the past fifteen years. Nowadays, most buyers have seen full slide shows, videos, and detailed listings for every house before they ever talk to an agent or drive around looking. The Internet has revolutionized the home-buying experience, and if you're not taking advantage of that convenience, you may be looking at that For Sale sign in your yard for a long, long time. You simply cannot afford to overlook the Internet when listing your house.

In 1995, only 2 percent of Americans used the Internet to look at houses. Just ten years later, in 2005, that number jumped to 77 percent![2] By 2010, it had soared all the way to the 90 percent mark.[3] That means nine out of ten buyers will know all about your house before they ever even make it to the curb. It also means a whole lot of them will *never* ring your doorbell.

That could be because the pictures online were bad, the lighting was off, the camera angles made your rooms look too small, and a million other reasons. All of a sudden, photography has become one of the biggest keys to selling your house! Every ounce of effort you've put into curb appeal now comes down to one single picture at the top of your online listing, so make sure it's a good one!

JOIN THE CONVERSATION

We are going to pay cash for our house in a few years!

—Allison Faulds

www.facebook.com/financialpeace

A Quality Agent Makes the Difference

Unless you're a seasoned pro at selling houses, I firmly believe that a quality real estate agent is worth more than they'd cost you when it comes time to sell. "For Sale by Owner," or FSBO, says something to a buyer. It says that you aren't paying commission to an agent, so you'll probably be more flexible on price. In fact, a study from the National Association of Realtors found that the median home price for sellers who use an agent is 16 percent higher than homes sold directly by an owner.[4]

Besides the money, a good agent can walk you through all the paperwork and details that most people don't understand. This is their job, and they sell dozens of homes a year as opposed to the average family, who will sell only a few times in their lifetime. But not every agent is a winner. It's like any other business; about 20 percent of the agents do 80 percent of the work. The good ones in your area will be fairly obvious.

Just look around and see who has signs all over town, who's invested in billboards, who your friends have used, and who's making the most of online services.

These are professionals offering a professional service, so you need to interview them. Don't just go with the first person you find, and don't go with your clueless nephew just because he's "family." You don't need family here; you need a pro. Your home is probably the largest investment you've ever made, so don't trust it to someone who doesn't know what they're doing.

A true professional won't mind an interview. Remember, agents get paid on commission, so if they don't sell your home, they don't get any money. That means they have an active stake in whether or not your home sells. It also means you want to see that they've sold some houses before—a *lot* of houses. If they only sold twelve houses last year, that means they only average one house a month. That's not going to cut it. I want someone who sold fifty or more houses last year!

Have them give you a full presentation of why you should go with them. Look at their track record and talk to their former clients. If my business was hiring a consultant, and we were going to pay them $15,000 for their services, they'd have to come in and convince me why they're the best of the best. It's the same for your real estate agent. Don't settle and don't cut corners when choosing one. That could be an extremely frustrating—not to mention expensive—decision.

Obviously, I'm all about saving money when you can, but this is something I don't recommend most people skimp on. Find a good agent and get your house sold! If you can't find a good one in your area, I'll even help you out. Check out the "Endorsed Local Providers" link on daveramsey.com and we'll help you find a hard-charging, high-octane agent in your community who you can trust.

BUYING A HOME

I absolutely love home ownership. It is truly the picture of the American dream for a lot of families, and it can be one of the biggest blessings of your life. Of course, it can also be a nightmare if you buy or sell poorly, get into crazy financing, buy when you're not ready, or buy some piece of garbage just because someone told you it was a good idea. Let's take a look at this stuff from a buyer's perspective.

Home Ownership Is a Great Investment

There are three main reasons why home ownership is such a great investment:

1. It's a forced savings plan.

A house is a big, big purchase—probably the most expensive thing you'll ever buy. But it is important to remember that the dollars you put into a house aren't wasted or lost forever. Buying a house is a forced savings plan. Imagine you buy a $200,000 home, either with cash or with the mortgage suggestion we'll discuss later. Even with a mortgage, you are systematically paying that mortgage down to nothing over time. After fifteen years (on a fifteen-year mortgage), you are finished with the payments and you own the house free and clear. Even if the home doesn't go up in value at all over that fifteen years, you've still forced yourself to save that $200,000. The money isn't gone; it's in the house. Plus, you've had the added benefit of living in it all that time!

2. It's an inflation hedge.

Younger Americans didn't really experience the inflation mess of the late 1970s. For the past decade, inflation has been somewhere around 3–5 percent. That's not a big deal. But when I started selling houses in 1978, inflation was raging and driving house prices up about 12 percent a year. That stinks if you're trying to buy, but it's great if you own a home and are thinking about selling. Inflation carries your home value higher and higher, and if you're a homeowner, you get to enjoy that ride. If you don't own a home, you're not only missing out on the rising values, but you're being locked out of getting into the game by the inflation-driven cost of entry.

3. It grows virtually tax free.

You remember from chapter 10, *From Fruition to Tuition,* that one of my favorite terms is "tax-free." There aren't a lot of tax-free investments available, but your home is definitely one of the best. According to current tax law, you can have a gain of $250,000 if you're single or $500,000 if you're married and pay zero taxes on the sale of your personal residence if you've lived there at least two years. So theoretically, if you find yourself in a market of exploding home values, you could end up with a tax-free gain of up to a half million dollars. That's a good deal.

Title Insurance and Land Surveys

You know from chapter 7, *Clause and Effect,* that I'm not a fan of custom insurance gimmicks. For that reason, I get a lot of questions about title insurance from people buying houses. This is one time where I'll say absolutely, positively get this special coverage. Title insurance covers you against an unclean title. You may think that could never happen to you, but you're wrong. Bad titles happen all the time, and no one ever knows that it's coming.

What makes a title "unclean"? Basically, if something gets messed up in the transfer of ownership at some point in the house's history—even several owners back—someone could pop up out of the blue and make a claim of ownership against your house. If you have title insurance, the insurance company has already done a check to make sure the title is clean, but if someone does make a claim, the insurance company essentially pays them to go away. Remember, the purpose of insurance is to transfer risk. If this happens with a property you own, it becomes the insurance company's problem, not yours.

This gets a little messy, so let me give you an example from my own real estate experience. I bought a house once from a guy who had bought it from two sisters. The two sisters had inherited it as part of the estate from their mother, who had passed away. We found out later that the two sisters had a brother, and the brother never signed off on the sale of the house even though the estate had him listed as a partial owner. The house had already changed hands twice before he popped up, and it was just the luck of the draw that he came looking for money while I owned it. But, because I had title insurance, the insurance company wrote him a big check and he went away happy.

Here's the bottom line on title insurance: I've owned more than one thousand pieces of real estate and I know what I'm doing in this business, but even I got bit by an unclean title. It happens a lot, so don't take the chance. The coverage is really cheap, but it can save you thousands of dollars. Get it.

And unless you're buying more than a standard subdivision lot, you should always get a land survey. In much of the country, the property lines are defined like this: "Well, the line runs from that old tree stump to over near that pile of rocks where little Suzie broke her arm thirty years ago." You need something a little more definitive than that! What happens, especially with old family properties, is that every generation has exaggerated the boundary line just a little bit, until eventually you think you have thirty acres when you really have twenty. That can be a big shock when you're buying or selling. Always know how much land you're getting into.

Buying Through an Agent

Traditionally, real estate agents have been more for sellers than for buyers, but that's changed a lot over the years. Today, buyer's agents are a fantastic way to find the perfect house, navigate through all the paperwork, and ultimately close on your dream home. It's like what we said when we were looking at selling: These agents do this every day. They know what to ask and what to look for, and they can navigate a buyer through a complicated buying process. Plus, it's great to have an agent standing between you and the seller. Let someone else—someone who knows what they're doing—represent you.

An agent will also have access to the Multiple Listing Service (MLS), which will revolutionize your house hunt. The MLS gives the agent (and you) a ton of information and pictures you can't get any other way. Without it, you're left at the mercy of Google, FSBO sellers, and blind luck as you drive around looking at For Sale signs.

But I should give you one warning about buying through an agent. Some agents, unfortunately, can *only* think like retailers. That's *exactly* what you want when you're selling a house, but it is exactly what you *do not* want when you're buying. Retailers think full price and don't look for a bargain. That makes sense on some level, because their biggest commissions come from selling. When they're in that mode, they want to get top dollar for every house they represent. It's tough for some agents to switch that off when they're representing a buyer. Make sure your buyer's agent is perfectly willing and competent to fight for the best deal possible for you.

JOIN THE CONVERSATION

Now I understand that "affording" a home means Baby Steps 1, 2, and 3 are out of the way!

—Ru

www.facebook.com/financialpeace

Buying Considerations

When house hunting, whether you're using an agent or flying solo, there are several things you definitely need to keep in mind. Some of this stuff is pretty basic, but again, I'm always amazed at how many people fail to do the simple things in real estate.

1. Always remember that location is king.

I'm sure you've heard the old line: homes appreciate in good neighborhoods and are priced based on three things—location, location, and location. It's a cliché, but it's true. You could take a run-down, half-caved-in trailer and put it in the middle of Mississippi or Iowa, and it wouldn't even bring $2,000. You could drop that same roach motel on the sand in Malibu Beach, and it'll bring $1 million. It's not the house; it's the little piece of dirt it's sitting on. So when you're buying, be aware of the neighborhood, the ZIP code, the school district—anything that could impact the value of the house just because of where it's located. Location is king in real estate.

2. Buy in the bottom price range of the neighborhood.

Never, *never* buy the most expensive house in the neighborhood! I've talked to more people than I can count who have fallen for this trap. I don't care how nice it is or how close it is to being your dream home; buying near the top of the neighborhood's price range is a surefire way to lose money in the long term.

Generally speaking, homes appreciate; that is, they go up in value over time. If you buy at the ceiling of your neighborhood's price range, your home simply won't appreciate as much or as fast as the others on your street. The reason? People don't drive down $200,000 streets when they're looking for a $300,000 home. Buying a nice home near the bottom of a good neighborhood's price range leaves you the most room to appreciate over time. Later, when you go to sell it, you'll have the best value in the neighborhood! I've seen houses on the low end of the range sell in a matter of days at a huge profit for the owners, while the higher-end house across the street sits unsold for months. It's a trap!

3. Look for water and a great view.

Here's another "across the street" example. If you're looking at lakefront property, the houses on the water are always a *lot* more expensive than houses across the street from the lake. Something about water shoots home values into the stratosphere! It could be a duck pond in the middle of a hayfield, but if you drop a house next to it, it will appreciate more than an identical house away from the water.

It's the same thing with a house with a view. You could build the same house at the foot of a mountain and at the top of the mountain, and the one at the top will outsell the one at the bottom all day long. Even though the one higher up is more of a pain to get in and out of, the view off the back deck will beat the pants off practically any amenity you could throw in on the other one. And if you are trying to sell a home with a great view, you need to get a good camera out there and do a 360-degree panoramic video of it for the Internet. If you put that online with the note "Imagine having this view from your back deck," you may not even need to put any pictures of the house on the listing!

4. See past the things you can change.

You can get incredible bargains on homes by overlooking out-dated carpet, ugly wallpaper, bad landscaping, and the velvet Elvis print hanging above the fireplace. These are the things you can change. You've got to look past them, and if you do, you'll be way ahead of most buyers and can land a sweet deal.

I remember one time when I was neck-deep in buying and selling foreclosures, a young couple at church asked me to help them find a deal on a house. Not too long after that, I came across a great buy on a foreclosure. The house was valued at $140,000 (this was twenty years ago), and I was able to buy it for $60,000. I gave the couple a call and said, "I got a great house for you. I can get it for way less than half price, and I'll sell it to you for $65,000. That gives me a quick $5,000, and it puts you in a great house for less than half of retail." That's a pretty good deal, right? They'd get a $140,000 house for $65,000, which means they'd save $75,000 off the value of the home. I thought we had a winner!

They met me at the property a little later and took a walk through. That young lady walked into the house, spent just a few minutes in there, and then walked back out. She said, "We can't buy it." I asked her why, and she said, "I just can't stand the carpet color!"

I was shocked. I said, "Listen, you're getting this house at $75,000 off. You could carpet the whole neighborhood and still come out ahead!" All it would take is a couple thousand dollars' worth of carpet and this could have been her dream home, but she couldn't imagine what it *could* be. So, they walked away, which was fine with me because I ended making a huge profit on it by selling it to someone else with a little more imagination!

Stay away from homes with bad floor plans, structural problems, and other things you can't do anything about. But don't let some old paint, 1970s lime-green shag carpet, or overgrown shrubbery keep you away from a great house. You want to find something ugly that you can fix; but if it's ugly to the bone, keep looking.

5. Get a home inspection and an appraisal.

Never buy a house without first getting it checked out by a certified home inspector. This is someone with the tools and knowledge to dig in and spot any potential problems or surprises, from the roof to the foundation and everywhere in between.

You'll also get an appraisal, but let me give you a word of caution here. An appraisal is just someone's opinion of the home's value. It's a better opinion than the home's current owner has because it's based on actual market value instead of emotion and family history—but it is still an opinion. Most appraisers understand that, but others get their egos a little too involved in the process. As a result, there are some really bad appraisers out there who believe they independently determine a house's value and that their word is law. It's not. It's just an opinion.

6. Avoid mobile homes and timeshares.

Never buy mobile homes or timeshares. These two things have practically no appreciable value. Financially speaking, a mobile home is like a car that you live in—it goes down in value from the moment you move in. You will never sell it for what you paid for it, and in a lot of cases, you won't be able to sell it at all. It's a horrible, horrible idea.

Timeshares are just as bad. From the second you sign your name on a timeshare contract, you are stuck with it forever. You will never be able to sell it, because there is no secondary market for timeshares. Honestly, you can't even give the things away, because the annual upkeep and maintenance fees are so ridiculous. Before you get sucked into one, ask yourself if you're ready to own it for life. Most of the time, a timeshare is a sure-fire way to write endless annual checks in maintenance fees for a vacation most people don't take every year. Stay away.

UNDERSTANDING MORTGAGE OPTIONS

There are a ton of different types of mortgage options available to buyers these days. I don't recommend most of them, but it's good for you to have a general understanding of the different options you'll see as you get ready to buy a house. Once we cover the options, we'll talk about my recommendation for how to buy.

Conventional Mortgages

Conventional mortgages are generally backed through Fannie Mae, or the Federal National Mortgage Association (FNMA). You've probably heard "Fannie Mae" discussed on the news a lot over the past few years, because bad loans through Fannie

Mae were partly responsible for the economic mess that hit the country in 2008.

Fannie Mae loans are privately insured against default, and they're usually packaged together and sold as bonds. Generally speaking, conventional mortgages offer a very generic, very structured process for financing a home. You can get them for set terms, like fifteen or thirty years, there are different options available, and most require some kind of down payment, usually around 5–20 percent.

If you take out a conventional mortgage without an adequate down payment of at least 20 percent, the bank will require private mortgage insurance (PMI). That covers the bank's loss in case the house is foreclosed on. You'll have to pay the PMI premiums yourself, and they usually run about $70 a month per $100,000 borrowed. Once you pay the loan down to 80 percent loan-to-value, though, you can usually have the bank drop the PMI. Or, if the home value goes up enough to bring you above the 80 percent mark, you can get an appraisal and have the PMI removed. There are a few exceptions to this, so talk to your mortgage company to find out exactly what they require to drop PMI. That's something a lot of people don't consider, but it might be something you can do *today* to save money on your mortgage every month.

Federal Housing Administration (FHA)

FHA loans are insured by the Department of Housing and Urban Development (HUD). This basically means that FHA loans are backed by the government, so if you get foreclosed on, the government insures the bank that they won't lose money on you. These loans allow a small down payment, as low as 3 percent, and are especially targeted at lower-priced homes. A lot of first-time buyer programs use the FHA in some way, but these loans are more expensive than conventional, and I don't recommend them.

Department of Veterans Affairs (VA)

VA loans are insured by the Department of Veterans Affairs and designed to be a benefit for our country's brave veterans. These loans allow vets to buy a home with practically nothing down and nothing out of pocket. However, there are a lot of fees involved with a VA loan, and the interest rate is usually a lot higher than you'd get with a conventional. I personally think the government could have done a better job setting up the VA plan, because I think it's great to honor our servicemembers this way. However, as it is, I don't recommend the VA loan. The conventional is almost always the better way to go.

Owner Financing

One of the most interesting options is owner financing. This means you work a deal with the seller and you pay him back directly over time, which actually makes him the mortgage holder. The cool thing with this option is that you can get creative with how you work out the arrangement. You and the seller can essentially make up your own plan, and as long as you both agree to it and stick to the plan, pretty much anything goes.

If you happen to be in an owner-financed arrangement right now, here's a suggestion. While mortgage rates are down, you could make your mortgage holder an offer for an early buy-out. That is, if you owe $100,000, you could offer him $75,000 in cash to pay off the loans. That would give him $75,000 *today*, instead of getting monthly payments for the next several years, and it would immediately knock $25,000 off your loan. Then you could go to the bank and get a conventional loan at a good, low rate for that $75,000, and everybody wins. See how cool this option can be? Just be creative!

HORRIBLE MORTGAGE OPTIONS TO AVOID

Just like everything else in the financial realm, there are a ton of awful products in the area of real estate and mortgages. Some of these may be less common now that banks have reacted so strongly to the recent economic mess, but they're still out there and just as dangerous as ever.

Adjustable Rate Mortgages (ARM)

One of the worst financial products of all time has to be the adjustable rate mortgage (or ARM). ARM loans hit the scene in the early 1980s when interest rates were through the roof. This was back when I was selling real estate, and we were trying to sell houses at 17–19 percent fixed rates. Because rates were high overall, banks had to start offering higher interest rates on deposits and money market accounts in order to attract new business. So, it wasn't uncommon for a bank to pay out around 12 percent on a money market. However, at the same time, they had a lot of older mortgage loans on the books in the 6–8 percent range. So, let's see. They were paying out 12 percent on savings accounts, but they were only making 6–8 percent on old loans, and all this was happening while new homes were selling at 17–19 percent. Can you see the problem here? The banks needed to make more money!

So they came up with the ARM. If they could get buyers into an adjustable rate, they thought that they could protect themselves from getting stuck with a bunch of lower-interest loans on the books after interest rates went up again. The point to remember is that the ARM plan is not here to help you; it was designed during a financial crisis to help the bank stay in business in an environment where rates were climbing. It essentially transfers the risk of higher rates *off* of the bank and *onto* you! And especially these days, with rates incredibly low, there's only one direction those rates are going to adjust, and that's *up*. Don't get caught with an ARM. If you're in one, refinance out of it *today*!

You'll often see "interest only" options tacked onto ARMs. Interest-only loans are terrible for the obvious reason: you're only paying the interest! You could make your payment like clockwork for thirty years and never pay a dime of principal! It's a con to try to get you into a house you can't afford with a payment that looks manageable. Stay far, far away from this one.

Reverse Mortgages

The reverse mortgage absolutely blows my mind. It's a way to say to our seniors, "Congratulations on working your whole life to get out of debt. Now we'd like to give you the opportunity to systematically go back into debt deeper and deeper every month until you die." No thanks.

The idea behind a reverse mortgage is that a homeowner can take monthly payments from a bank against the equity in their paid-for home, which effectively puts them deeper into debt every month. On top of this being an obviously bad idea debt-wise, there are also a lot of scams and fraud in the area of reverse mortgages. This one can literally unravel a life of hard work. Don't even think about it. And make sure your aging parents don't fall for it, either! I don't care if they see their favorite actor from the 1960s pitching this garbage on TV! It's still garbage!

Accelerated or Bi-weekly Payoff

An accelerated payoff plan is a good idea on the surface. In this plan, you make half a mortgage payment every two weeks instead of making one a month. So, over the course of the year, you make twenty-six half payments, or thirteen whole payments. That means you're just paying one extra mortgage payment every year, which obviously pays the loan off faster.

I want you to pay your mortgage off as quickly as possible, but you can do it on your own. There's no reason to pay a bank anything extra in the form of fees for this option. Just make extra principal payments regularly and you can get the same benefit.

The Tax Advantage Myth

I often have people call my radio show and argue with me because I tell people to get totally out of debt—house and all—as quickly as possible. These financial goobers say something like, "Dave, it's stupid to pay off your house because of the tax advantage. I'll lose my tax deduction if I pay off my house." The problem with this theory is that the math doesn't work. It's just a myth that everyone spreads but no one sits down to do the math. Well, I did, and I talked about it in *The Total Money Makeover:*

> If you have a home with a payment of around $900, and the interest portion is $830 per month, you have paid around $10,000 in interest that year, which creates a tax deduction. If, instead, you have a debt-free home, you would, in fact, lose the tax deduction, so the myth says to keep your home mortgaged because of the tax advantages.
>
> This situation is one more opportunity to discover if your CPA can add. If you do not have a $10,000 tax deduction and you are in a 30-percent bracket, you will have to pay $3,000 in taxes on that $10,000. According to the myth, we should send $10,000 in interest to the bank so we don't have to send $3,000 in taxes to the IRS. Personally, I think I will live debt-free and not make a $10,000 trade for $3,000.[5]

I'm always amazed at "financial people" who can't do math.

THE BEST WAY TO BUY

That gives you a short-and-sweet rundown of the main options for financing a house. There's still one option, though, that we haven't discussed—and that is by far the best option available.

100-Percent-Down Plan

I'm talking about what I call the "100-Percent-Down Plan." Translation: Pay cash for the whole house! People tell me all the time that this approach is unrealistic. Really? Then why do I have so many young couples come up to me at live events and call in to my radio show to tell me they just wrote a check for their first house after living on rice and beans for five years?

Don't tell me it can't be done! I talk to these people every day. Sure, it's not "normal," but who wants to be normal?

One of my favorite radio calls of all time was a twenty-seven-year-old guy from Cleveland. He told me that he grew up with a granddad who told him if he ever borrowed money, he'd kill him! That sounds a little extreme, but this kid took it to heart. He got married at age twenty-three, and he and his wife had a combined income of $80,000. They lived in a tiny apartment above a sweet elderly lady's garage. They took odd jobs here and there, drove old cars, didn't take fancy vacations, and didn't blow all their money like all their twentysomething friends. They lived comfortably on $30,000 and saved $50,000 a year for four years. By the time he called me, they were both twenty-seven, had just written a $150,000 check for their first home, and had $50,000 cash to furnish it.

Now, how set is this guy? I did the math on this deal and figured out what the mortgage payments would have been on that $150,000 house if he had financed it like a "normal" person. The payments would have been a little over $1,200 a month on a fifteen-year fixed-rate loan at 6 percent. If all this couple ever does is pay *themselves* that $1,200 that they *would have been* sending to the bank every month for all those years, they will retire with just under $15 million! These superstars put their backs into this stuff for four years, and now they're set for life. I love stories like that!

But maybe you can't go all the way for whatever reason. That's fine, but don't resolve yourself to the "normal" plan of a thirty-year loan with a tiny down payment. What if you put 50 percent down and put the rest on a fifteen-year mortgage, but paid it off in six like a car? People who win with money refuse to live the status quo. Dig in your heels and get creative!

Ready to Buy?

If you don't have $200,000 in the bank to pay cash for a house today, that's okay. You've got time. Even if you never pay cash for a house, you still need to only buy when you're ready. How do we define ready? Let's look at the Baby Steps. If you are not out of debt and don't have a full emergency fund of three to six months' worth of expenses, you aren't ready to buy a house. Buying a house when you can't afford it is one of the best ways to ruin your life. Home ownership brings with it a ton of risk, from faulty water heaters to a bad roof. If you don't have savings to cover this stuff, you'll be running back to credit cards and equity loans when something "unexpected" comes up.

If you're working the debt snowball or haven't finished your emergency fund, you should rent. There is absolutely nothing wrong with renting for a little while. People will tell you, "Rent? No way! That's just flushing money down the toilet! It's always better to own!" No, it's not. Broke people should not buy houses. That's a recipe for disaster. The money you pay in rent while you're cleaning up your debt and saving up your emergency fund and down payment demonstrates patience. Look, I don't want you renting forever as a way of life; I just want you to be ready before you buy! Make a goal to hit Baby Step 3 and then save up a big down payment as quickly as possible! I love home ownership, but it will kill you if you're not ready for it.

If You MUST Take Out a Mortgage

Let me be clear: I hate debt. I will never borrow another penny the rest of my life. I save up and pay for things now. But if you're going to buy a house with a mortgage, and if you're truly ready to buy a house, then this is the one time I won't get mad at you for borrowing. So if you're going to do it, let's at least make sure you do it right.

Here's the rule: Only get a fifteen-year fixed-rate conventional mortgage with at least 10 percent down and a payment that is no more than 25 percent of your take-home pay. There are three main parts to this little formula:

1. Only get a fifteen-year, fixed-rate conventional mortgage.

Remember, we're not messing around with ARMs, VA loans, or interest-only garbage. Focus only on conventional fixed-rate options, and never—*never*—get a mortgage term longer than fifteen years. The "normal" thirty-year loan is a train wreck. We covered this in the *Dumping Debt* chapter, but it's important, so let's look at the example again. A $225,000 mortgage at 6 percent interest has a payment of $1,899 on a fifteen-year loan. If you went with a thirty-year loan, your payment would be $1,349, so you'd save $550 a month. But here's the heart-breaker: In exchange for that $550 a month, you'll be in debt an extra fifteen years and you'll end up paying $143,000 *more* than if you got a fifteen-year loan to begin with! You could almost buy a whole other house for what you'd lose in interest!

2. Put at least 10 percent down.

If you can't put at least 10 percent down, that's a sure sign that you aren't ready to buy a house. I'd prefer you put 20 percent or more down, though. That gives you a more solid position and it keeps you out of PMI territory.

3. Your payment should be no more than 25 percent of your take-home pay.

If more than a fourth of your take-home pay is eaten up by your house payment, you'll essentially be what is known as "house poor." That just means you have too much of your monthly cash flow tied up in mortgage payments. Even though you should be debt-free with a full emergency fund before you buy, a house payment of 35–50 percent of your pay can put a serious strain on your family and prevent you from hitting Baby Steps 4–6 like we've talked about.

So many people get in an enormous financial mess because they buy a house when they're not ready or they take out a terrible loan with ridiculous rates and horrible terms. Especially when home prices are down, interest rates are low, and maybe within months of getting married, the pressure to buy a house can be overwhelming. "Gotta buy a house! Gotta buy a house! Gotta buy a house!" No, you don't. I want you to have a house; I just don't want your house to have you!

Here's what happens. You're familiar with Murphy's Law, right? Whatever can go wrong *will* go wrong. Well, when you buy a house with no money and without knowing what you're doing, Murphy will move into your spare bedroom. And he won't be alone; he'll bring his three cousins—Broke, Desperate, and Stupid—with him. They will own your life. What you thought was a blessing will quickly turn into a curse. What you thought was the American dream will turn into a nightmare. Don't let that happen. Remember, review, and apply what we talked about in this chapter, and then when it's time to move, buy a new house, buy your *first* house, or sell the house you're in, you can do it with confidence and know for sure that it's a blessing.

WE DID IT!

I don't even know where to begin. We've accomplished so much in these past three years, it's hard to put into words. It started back in March 2007 when my company went through a layoff and I thought I would be unemployed by the end of that month. Luckily that didn't happen, but that was the wake-up call I needed to change our ways as a family. We were "normal" with a mortgage, car payment, and student loans totaling $115,000 in debt.

After the job scare, I was introduced to Dave Ramsey's program by a co-worker. The next week, our church just happened to host its first *Financial Peace University* class. My wife and I graduated FPU in June 2007 and began our journey to freedom. It took us three years, five garage sales, and the sale of my precious 1996 Camaro, but we finally did it. We paid off $115,000 in three years on a $75,000/year income and are COMPLETELY DEBT-FREE, house and everything!

I am thirty-eight years old and my wife is thirty-six, and we won't have a house payment for the rest of our lives! If that wasn't amazing enough, after working your program for two years, we realized our marriage and communication had improved, but we hadn't taken very good care of ourselves along the way. So with our knowledge of how to budget money and communicate with each other, we decided to apply those same techniques to our weight problem. In a little over a year, my wife lost an incredible one hundred pounds and I lost eighty pounds!

To celebrate all of our accomplishments and show our family members who had been making fun of us these past three years that this stuff really does work, we treated everyone to a Florida vacation free of charge. We paid for it in cash (and got a nice discount as a result)! Guess who wasn't making fun of us anymore? Thank you, Dave!

Jeff
Greenfield, IN

KEY POINTS

1. When selling a home, think like a retailer.
2. When buying a home, think like an investor.
3. Don't dismiss the idea of paying cash for a house. People do it all the time!
4. If you absolutely must take out a mortgage, only get a fifteen-year fixed-rate conventional mortgage with at least 10 percent down and a payment that is no more than 25 percent of your take-home pay.

QUESTIONS FOR REFLECTION

1. What does it mean to be "house poor"? Have you ever been in that position?
2. Why is it okay to rent for a while? When would be a good time to rent instead of buy?
3. What are some dangers in thirty-year mortgages, adjustable rate loans, and home equity loans? If you're in one of these, how can you get out quickly?
4. If you absolutely must take out a mortgage, what are the guidelines to make sure you don't get caught in a mess?
5. According to the mortgage guidelines we reviewed, how much house can you actually afford? Do you feel you'd be content with this level of home?
6. What would it feel like to pay off the mortgage once and for all? How would that affect your retirement?

13

GIVE LIKE NO ONE ELSE

UNLEASHING THE POWER OF GENEROUS GIVING

I've been blessed with three great kids—two daughters and a son. Daniel is the youngest of the bunch, but like his sisters, he's all grown up and out of the house now. That can be kind of tough for a parent, you know? Sometimes it's weird to look at this strapping young man, because in the back of my mind, I can still see him as a little kid in Spider-Man pajamas, running around the house, sliding into home base everywhere.

I remember one time in particular, a long time ago, I was up early doing my Bible study. It was about 5:30 in the morning, and I was reading through John's Gospel. It was one of those passages that I'd read a thousand times, and it was earlier than I usually got up, so I admit I probably wasn't as tuned in as I could have been. But I was up, had the coffee going, and was doing my best to keep my commitment to a daily prayer and Bible study time.

That's when I heard the sound that makes every parent wince. *Ka-blink. Ka-blink. Ka-blink.* It was the telltale sound of a five-year-old coming down the stairs, dragging his security blanket—at 5:30 in the morning. Daniel rounded the corner to my study and gave me a great big smile that showed the gap where his front teeth were missing. "Good morning, Daddy!"

I'm always happy to see my kids, but it was early, and I knew a happy five-year-old awake at 5:30 in the morning turned into a tired, grouchy five-year-old by 5:30 in the afternoon. This wasn't going to end well. Besides, I was *trying* to do my Bible study! But Daniel walked up anyway and said, "Daddy, can I sit with you?" So I put him on my lap and he gave me a big kiss and said, "Daddy, I love you." That's good. Life doesn't get much better than that.

I went back to my reading, and a few minutes later, I just got flooded with emotion. Tears started running down my face as I sat there reading Scripture with Daniel on my lap. He asked what was wrong, and I said, "I was just reading John 3:16. It says here that God loved the world so much that He sent His only Son." I looked in his eyes and said, "Daniel, you're my only son. I can't even *fathom* what God must have gone through giving His Son for the sake of the world."

That's when it hit me. I had read these verses before, but something in that moment unlocked the most important, fundamental spiritual and financial principle there is: We are made in God's image . . . and God is a *giver*. Giving is the key that unlocks our full potential—in our life *and* in our money.

UNDERSTANDING THE GREAT MISUNDERSTANDING

Throughout this book, we have covered six Baby Steps that walk you right up to edge of incredible wealth and security for your family. Once you reach this point, you're out of debt with three to six months' worth of expenses in the bank for emergencies. You're investing 15 percent of your income into retirement, maxing out your children's college fund, and you are sitting in a paid-for house. That sounds a lot like financial peace, doesn't it? But you're not done yet. We still have one more Baby Step to cover:

Baby Step 7: Build wealth and give a lot of it away

Seeing these two things together—building wealth and giving it away—is confusing to some people. Many believe that you can't do both, that if you have wealth, it's because you're selfish and have hoarded every dollar you've earned. In my book, *More Than Enough*, and in my *Financial Peace University* classes, this tension is what I call "the great misunderstanding."

JOIN THE CONVERSATION

Now that my finances are in order, I like to buy lunch for co-workers who are struggling with having enough money for food.

—Kris

www.facebook.com/financialpeace

Fistful of Dollars

The great misunderstanding is a paradox; it's the mistaken belief that in order to have more, we have to hold on more tightly. Imagine standing on a street corner with $1,000 cash in your hand. What's our natural, human tendency? We clench our fingers around that cash and hold on for dear life! Society tries to tell us that the secret to getting more is to hold on to what we have, and so we make a fist around our money. But there's a problem with that. If I clench my fist around that $1,000, none of it will leave; but at the same time, my hand's not open to receive any more. I've put up a wall that keeps my money from getting away *and* keeps more money from coming in.

There's a bigger problem, though. What's going on in our spirits when we do that? The clenched fist is the international sign of anger, but even a dog understands the warmth and reception of an open hand. It's like Golda Meir once said, "You can't shake hands with a clenched fist."

Antoine Rivaroli said, "There are men who gain from their wealth only the fear of losing it." We've all met those people. It's like the more money they have, the more paranoid they are about losing it. And so they clench their fists, dig in their heels, and totally separate themselves from the world around them. When that happens, no money is flowing out (giving), and no more money can flow in. They get stopped up, like a pond where no water can get in or out. What grows in a pond that's stopped up? Scum. That's what happens to people who refuse to let go of their money; they're scummy.

Owners and Managers

Not too long ago, my company made a big charitable contribution to a ministry we had been working with. I usually do all my giving at home, but this was one of the rare times when we were making a corporate contribution. We had planned for it and, of course, we had budgeted for it. Since it was a work thing, I didn't write the actual check myself; a lady in our accounting department did it as part of her normal duties. When it came time to make the donation, how hard do you think it was for her to write a check with all those zeros? How much trouble did she have handing over that much money? None at all. It didn't faze her one bit; writing that check was just an item on her to-do list for that day. The money flowed right through her without a pause because she was just doing what the owner (me) told her to do with the money. It didn't even occur to her to wrap her fingers tightly around that money, because it wasn't hers to begin with. It's always easier to give *someone else's* money away, because we feel no attachment to it.

The Bible says, "The earth is the LORD's, and the fulness thereof."[1] You know what that means? God is the *owner*. He owns it all—not a tithe, not a love offering, not our leftovers; *He owns it all*. When we view our wealth like that, then suddenly, giving becomes easy because we're not giving *our* money away at all. We're just asset managers for the Lord, doing what the owner (God) tells us to do with the money.

It's easy to get confused about this, though. When we think of ourselves as the owner, it becomes very, very difficult to open our hands enough to pass any wealth on to others. We're like two-year-olds, balling up our fists and yelling, "Mine! Mine!" But when we act as managers, we can gratefully receive what God passes to us, enjoy the use of that money to take care of our families, and then pass that money on to help others—because that's what the owner said to do. He's entrusting that money to us and allowing us to use it for ourselves and our families, but He's also trusting us to manage His money the way He wants.

Reclaiming Genuine Stewardship

If you grew up in or around church, you've heard the word "steward" or "stewardship." It's definitely become a "Christian" word. In fact, in a lot of churches, "stewardship campaign" is code for, "We're getting ready to build a new building!" If you hear your pastor use that term, grab your wallet; he's getting ready to ask for some money—and that's not necessarily a bad thing.

But if you go back in history, you'll find that "steward" is not a Christian term at all. It's an Old English term that means "one who manages another's financial affairs." Think about what the world was like in the thirteenth or fourteenth century, like in the movie *Braveheart*. There were realms, and within each realm, there was a castle. Inside the castle lived the lord of the realm, the guy who owned everything—all the land, farms, buildings, businesses, commerce, etc. He lived in the biggest, nicest castle in the realm.

Nearby, you'd see another large estate that was *almost* as nice as the lord's. This is where the lord's steward lived. The steward was the person who actually managed all of the lord's assets. The steward managed all the crop rotations, labor, taxes, banking, marketplace—*everything*. He didn't own any of it, but he was responsible for it all because the lord had entrusted it to him.

So when the King James translators were working on the first English version of the Bible in 1611, they came to this concept of biblical ownership and our role as managers, and they immediately understood. That's why the word "steward" appears in the King James Bible so much; it was a common, easily understood term that immediately emphasized *managership*, not *ownership*.

THE OWNER'S REASONS FOR GIVING

I'm a pretty purpose-driven individual, and the thought of doing something just because someone told me to do it without any good explanation never sat right with me. So when I first met God as an adult and started going to church, I questioned *everything*. The first time I heard the pastor say I should give a tenth of my income to the church, I thought, *Riiiiight. That sounds like a pretty good deal for you.* It took me a while to process this stuff, and I know I'm not alone. Before I gave the church my money, I needed to understand why God asks us to give so often. Maybe you're the same way, so let's take a look at this.

God Doesn't Need Your Money

My first thought was basic: God must need my money. That makes sense, doesn't it? I know I'm not the only pew warmer who has had that thought. I mean, it takes money to run a church. Someone's got to pay the light bill in the sanctuary. Someone's got to pay the pastor. Staffing and facilities and mission trips get expensive, so it makes sense that God needs my money to do all those things, right?

Looking back on those thoughts I had early on makes me laugh now, but the truth is, that's where most of us start. Now that I've been walking with God for a couple of decades, I have a different view of things. We just said that God is the owner; He owns it *all*. This is God! He said, "And the stars also," and BOOM—the whole galaxy came into being! He knit every cell in my body together; He knows every hair that is (and used to be) on my head; He has provided absolutely everything I've ever had or ever will have. God *does not need* my money.

At that point, I changed a little bit and thought that maybe the church needed my money. I believed that my giving was simply my duty as a Christian. God said to do it, so that's why I was supposed to do it. It's like I was a good little Christian Boy Scout: "I'll do my best to give to God and country and church. I'm going to keep the rules because the rules are the rules and I'm a good rule-keeper." There's not much grace or wonder in that point of view, is there? That attitude just made me a junior Pharisee, someone only interested in rules for rules' sake. That's not the giving spirit that God wants, either.

Made in His Image

It was years into this process before I had that breakthrough I mentioned at the start of this chapter. At that point in my life, I was tithing, I was doing my duty and going through the motions, but the whole reason for it hadn't clicked yet. Then, with my son on my lap at 5:30 in the morning one day, I realized that God wants me to give because I am made in His image—and *He's a giver.*

I believe that God puts us through the mechanical act of giving—even when we don't fully understand the reasons why—because the act of giving changes us. It crushes our hearts and reforms us into something that looks and acts a little bit more like Christ. You can't say you're a follower of Christ when you're not giving. You can't walk around with the clenched fist and tell people about how amazing Jesus is. There's a disconnect. They won't believe you because your whole attitude is one of selfishness, fear, and greed. Remember, the clenched fist is the sign of anger. Jesus never talked to people about the love and grace of God with His hands balled up into fists!

Every time I open my hand to put money in the offering plate at church, or to support a missionary, or to leave a huge tip for a struggling single mom waiting tables, it shifts how I see things. Every time I spend a weekend serving other people instead of skiing on the lake, it changes my heart a little bit. Over time, all those changes add up as we become more and more like Christ. Because we are designed in God's image, we are happiest and most fulfilled when we are giving and serving.

Giving Makes Us Less Selfish

It's pretty tough to be a selfish giver. You can't open your wallet and your calendar to other people while still being a selfish jerk. The opposite is true too: You can't be a selfish jerk if you're giving to and serving other people. So, in a sense, choosing to be a giver is the same as choosing *not* to be a selfish jerk!

Unselfish people have more of a tendency to prosper in relationships and wealth. You know who makes the best fathers, mothers, business partners, merchants, bosses, team members, clients, or salespeople? Unselfish people. These are the people you can trust and the ones you actually want to spend time with and do business with. The only place greedy people prosper is on television. In the real world where you and I live, that's not how it works. If you want to build wealth and have fantastic relationships, you've got to give.

I'm not just talking about giving in a church setting, either. Sure, I believe that Christians ought to give to their local churches like the Bible says, but I also think Christians and everyone else in the world should be actively giving and serving in their communities. You want to change someone's whole outlook on life? The next time you're traveling during the holidays, leave a hardworking waitress a $100 tip on a $5 tab. There's only one reason she'd be waiting tables on Christmas Eve: she needs the money! Think about what you could do in that person's life with a simple act. You don't need the credit or the thank-you. Just leave Ben Franklin on the table and say, "Merry Christmas." Then go hide in the parking lot and watch through the window as she sees what you've left. That's some of the most fun you can have with money!

If you start doing stuff like this, crazy things will start happening in your life. You'll be energized, more creative, more passionate, and more excited about life. Something inside of you will be unlocked and you may have no idea what's happening to you. I can tell you what's happening: you were *made* to be a giver, and when you start living up to that potential, you start becoming more and more of what you were made to be. This stuff is life changing! Albert Schweitzer may have said it best, "I don't know what your destiny will be, but one thing I know: The only ones among you who will be really happy are those who will have sought and found how to serve."

INSTRUCTIONS FOR GIVING

I've already told you that, as a young Christian, I had a lot of questions about giving. I was starting from scratch, so I had to do a lot of digging and spend a lot of time in prayer about this stuff. As I've walked people through this for a long time now, I've found that most people have the same questions I had early on. Let's take a look at the most common ones; maybe you've asked yourself these questions, too.

What Is a Tithe, Anyway?

The word "tithe" isn't a spiritual term. It's like "steward," in that it was just a regular, run-of-the-mill word that the church kind of took over. "Tithe" is actually a math term; it simply means a tenth. A pastor told me once that he allows his congregation to give a 5-percent tithe. I laughed a little and said, "Well, okay, but that's a *five*, not a *tithe*! You can't tenth a twentieth."

The instruction to give a tenth of your increase is biblical, dating all the way back to Genesis 14:18, where Melchizedek felt God's call to give Abram a tenth of everything he had. Later, in Genesis 28:22, Jacob also felt God's call to give a tenth of his increase to the Lord. The affirmation of the tithe and the command to obey it appears throughout both the Old and New Testaments, and it always refers to a tenth of your increase. So farmers gave a tenth of their crops, hunters gave a tenth of their meat, and so on.

There are a lot of denominational differences in how different traditions approach the tithe. In fact, a lot of Christians believe that the tithe is a holdover from the Law and therefore they don't have to observe it. I personally disagree with this, though, because the tithe appears before the Law, and it is affirmed in the New Testament by Jesus in Matthew 23:23 and Luke 11:42. Whether your church tradition teaches tithing or not, this is absolutely not a salvation issue. It's a matter of biblical interpretation, and honestly, it's between you and God. I'm not here to be your conscience or to play the part of the Holy Spirit; I'm just telling you what I've discovered about giving and tithing.

I will say, however, that people often ask me when in the Baby Steps they should start giving their tithe. Well, just look at where "Giving" is on the budget form in the back of this book—it's the top line! I believe that giving should be a part of your financial plan all through the Baby Steps. The Bible tells us to give a tithe. If you're a believer, that means you give it off the top all the way through. Of course, once you work the Baby Steps and you're out of debt and building wealth, you'll be free to give like crazy above and beyond the tithe, and that's a fantastic goal!

Who Gets the Tithe?

The tithe should go to your local church, which provides the same function as the Old Testament storehouse. You see the storehouse come up a lot in Proverbs, Nehemiah, and other places in the Old Testament. Since Israel was largely an agricultural economy, a good percentage of the tithe was given as crops. Those crops went to the storehouse, which was used to feed the poor, widows, orphans, and the priests.

That not only gives today's Christians a model of where the tithe goes; it also shows our churches some priorities in how to use their resources. The call to take care of widows and orphans is pretty obvious; I don't think any of us would object to that, but I do think we should broaden our perspective a little bit. A 2009 report from the U.S. Commerce Department and the Census Bureau found that more than half of households below the poverty line are single-mom households.[2] That same report found that more than 15 million children are living in severe poverty. I believe that the call to take care of widows and orphans should include taking care of single moms and the kids who have no dad around. And in this day and age, this should definitely include our brave military families who are getting by while Mom or Dad is deployed serving our country.

Not only did the storehouse take care of widows and orphans, but it also made sure the priests were well fed. Today's translation: we should pay our pastors well. I've looked at the compensation models for hundreds or thousands of churches across the country, and I can tell you one thing for sure: we're not paying our pastors what they are worth. We expect our pastors to be world-class speakers, scholars, writers, counselors, leaders, and administrators. We expect them to be on call 24/7, and we feel neglected if—heaven forbid—the head pastor doesn't personally show up when we spend a night in the hospital. And in exchange for these unreasonable expectations, churches by and large pay their pastors as little money as possible—far, far less than these men and women could make in the normal job market with the skill set we demand in our ministers.

I've heard speaker and author John Maxwell say that American churches are losing up to 1,500 pastors *every month*. Why? Because they are overworked, underappreciated, and underpaid. They're burning out! But many people think that pastors should "suffer for Jesus" or that they "shouldn't be in it for the money." That's bull. Those are excuses that broke, cheap Christians make for not giving and for not paying their pastors what they're worth. These men and women work *hard*. Pay them well.

Sometimes I'll hear someone say that they don't give a tithe to their local church because the church doesn't handle money well. This one scares me. I always respond, "So you can't trust them with your money, but you're trusting them with your children's souls?" Listen, if you can't trust your church with your money, then you have two choices: Lead the charge to fix the problem or find another church. Personally, I think you could get in there and help shake things up. Maybe you could start a *Financial Peace University* class at church and help the members and leaders get a handle on their own finances. Maybe you could encourage your leaders to take a look at our *Momentum* program, which teaches entire congregations to apply God's Word to their lives and frees the local church to answer God's call to kingdom work. You could do a lot of things, but whining shouldn't be one of them. We have enough whiney Christians sitting on the sidelines. Either get in the game or stop complaining![3]

Do I Tithe on the Gross or on the Net?

One of the most common questions I get about giving is, "Do I tithe on the gross or on the net?" Well, let me tell you something *gross*. According to studies performed by the group Empty

Tomb, the average Christian today gives less than 3 percent of their income. So we're called to give 10 percent, almost nobody does, a lot of Christians give nothing, and the average gift is less than 3 percent. Does gross or net really matter? If I can convince you to do *either*, we'll be way ahead of the game!

Is an Offering the Same Thing as a Tithe?

Often in church, we're guilty of confusing an offering with the tithe. They're really two totally distinct things. The Bible calls us to give a tithe of our first fruits. That is, we give 10 percent right off the top. An offering is a separate gift, offered over and above the tithe. That's why you'll usually hear your church talk about "tithes *and* offerings." They're not the same.

I believe that Christians should tithe no matter where they are in the Baby Steps. That's why, when you look at our budgeting forms, the "Giving" line is always at the top. If you're a Christian, that top line should be your tithe—your first fruits. But an offering needs to be in line with the rest of your budget. People like to quote the biblical story of the widow's mite as proof that people should give everything they have, no matter how broke they are.[4] That's a total misuse of that story. We assume a lot of things about that widow that may or may not be true. We don't know, because we don't have those details. The passage just gave us that one snapshot of that one moment in her life.

What we do know, though, is that the Bible tells us crystal clearly, "If anyone does not provide for his own, and especially for those of his household, he has denied the faith and is worse than an unbeliever."[5] That means you've got to get out of debt, have emergency savings in the bank, take care of your retirement and your kids' college expenses, and put yourself in a position to give like crazy way above your tithe.

I know a lot of people have this burning desire to give, and that is fantastic. But I also know several people who feel guilty about doing *anything* for themselves and their families instead of giving that money to someone else. That's unhealthy. I've met sweet widows who are late on their house payments but current on their church building fund pledges. That's completely backward. The Bible calls us to take care of our own household first. If you do the Baby Steps we've covered in this book, you'll get there in no time; and then, you can give from a position of strength that will blow your mind!

Should I Give Everything Away?

We've talked a lot in this book about building wealth. You may have noticed that I am in no way ashamed of that fact. I have absolutely no guilt at all over the fact that I've become financially successful over the years. I have worked my tail off and I've truly been blessed, and I thank God for that. But like Andrew Carnegie said, "Surplus wealth is a sacred trust to be managed for the good of others." You see, I don't just hoard my wealth for myself; I'm also very intentional about giving not just my tithe, but giving far above the tithe to a handful of ministries and charities that my family supports.

We don't give everything away, and we don't spread it so thin among a million different charities that we're not really making a difference in any one of them. We've picked a small collection of ministries that we really believe in, and we invest heavily in the work they're doing. That way, we're making a huge difference in a few places instead of making practically no difference in a million places.

I often get letters and e-mails from people who have a problem with the fact that I've become wealthy. They don't care how much my wife and I have given away; they're still bothered by the fact that I have nice things. I believe that represents a toxic attitude about wealth and giving. I talked about it in my book *More Than Enough*:

> Our Dr. Jekyll and Mr. Hyde culture gives us one message and then turns on us. We are taught that becoming wealthy is the peak of success. Everything is measured in wealth. Go for it! Grab all you can! If you just gather enough stuff, you will not only be happy, you will also "be somebody!" Our culture pushes us to build wealth, to gather stuff and power, then our culture turns on us and blames all the problems of the world on "rich" people. The have-nots are always blaming every evil out there on the haves. If you are a have-not "you must be lazy or dumb," but then when you work your fingers to the bone and build wealth some bonehead is always around to act like everything is your fault. "All those rich people don't really care about anything but money; they should give it all away to help the poor."
>
> Proper giving is understanding that we don't give everything away and start over because when we do we lose the power to help. The weak can't lift what the strong can. . . . If you want to be a powerful giver you should view your wealth as the goose and give the golden eggs. If you give away the goose, the golden eggs are gone and so is your ability to help others. Those of you who think "those nasty rich people should be made to give up the wealth they have earned" are not only stupid, but your short-sightedness kills the goose, and the poor are not really helped.[6]

A big goose can lay some big eggs, and those big eggs can take care of a lot of churches, widows, and orphans. Keep the goose, and give the eggs generously and wisely.

CONCLUSION

Over the past twenty years, we've led more than a million families through our *Financial Peace University* class, which unpacks all of the Baby Steps, information, and practical application we've covered throughout this book. We have more than four million listeners tune in to *The Dave Ramsey Show* every week on radio stations across the country, walking with us on this crusade. We've had several million more read my other books and attend our live events to really take hold of everything we've been discussing. I'm not bragging here. I really say that just to let you know that the stuff I teach isn't new, and it isn't some crackpot theory about how I *think* money works. It's a time-proven system that's been tested by millions and millions of other families, and it's changing lives on the East Coast, on the West Coast, and everywhere in between.

This stuff works, and I didn't invent any of it. I just packaged it well! I truly believe that the material I teach is God's and Grandma's way of handling money. God worked these lessons out in my own life through fire and adversity. I'm so hardheaded, I probably couldn't have learned them any other way! Once all my assumptions about wealth were totally stripped away as I went broke in my twenties, once I literally had nothing left but my family and a willing spirit, God picked me up and led me down this path of discovery. On that journey, I learned things about God, money, relationships, and my life's calling that have completely blown me away.

It's pretty incredible what God can do with a willing spirit. This stuff changed my life, and I pray it changes yours too. I can walk with you and point the way, but it's up to you to take the first step.

WE DID IT!

I cannot possibly explain enough how thankful we are for this class. I've heard people say it a thousand times, but you have truly helped change our lives in unbelievable ways. Since the moment we turned eighteen and were "privileged" enough to get our very own credit cards, I felt empowered by the number of cards I had (as many as nine at one point), and I felt like I could have *anything* I wanted. In my naivete, I remember at one point saying that I didn't understand why people complained about not being able to have things when it is so "easy" to get a credit card and just charge it!

A few years later, after getting married (most of those expenses on credit cards), still carrying student loans, two car payments, and close to $30,000 in credit card debt, I found Dave on the radio. I became hooked. After about a year of listening, I convinced my husband to take *Financial Peace University* at our church. I was always the one to handle the finances in our five years of being together, so it wasn't easy, but he went along—and now he is hooked, too!

We tell everyone we can about your program and how wonderful and freeing it is to be DEBT-FREE! We have since paid off everything but the house and are *finally* in a situation in which I can stay at home with my three kids. It never felt possible before, and it breaks my heart now when I hear other moms say that they would love to stay home with their kids, but they can't afford it. Yes, you can!

Aside for the freedom of being debt-free, the message of giving went a long way with us. We now have more money than ever, yet spend so much less on ourselves and find such a thrill in giving away to others who need it. The dreaded *tithing* word finally has meaning, and we are faithful givers and truly enjoy doing it. We have direction and goals—attainable goals—and my husband and I are more connected in our thoughts and our dreams.

Thank you, Dave!

Kristy
Sylvania, OH

KEY POINTS

1. The great misunderstanding, the paradox, is that we believe the way to have more is to hold on to what we have more tightly.
2. A steward is a manager, not an owner.
3. Give the first 10 percent of your income to your church or favorite charity.
4. Offerings are over and above the tithe.

QUESTIONS FOR REFLECTION

1. Why don't we give as much as we'd like to at times?
2. How do you feel when you give? Can you think of one or two times you've made a big difference in someone's life with a generous gift?
3. Has anyone ever surprised you with a meaningful act of giving? How did that make you feel?
4. How does viewing yourself as a manager of God's resources affect your thinking and behavior about money?
5. What is your reaction to the analogy of the goose with the golden eggs? What's the point of that way of thinking?
6. Have you ever considered the giving aspect of our being made in the image of God? How does that change your understanding of giving?

AFTERWORD

I've said several times in this book that personal finance is only 20 percent head knowledge. The other 80 percent is *behavior*. This book gives you the head knowledge, but no book alone can do much to change behavior. I believe that the properly led small group is hands down the best method I've ever seen for doing that. There's just something powerful about sitting face to face with other families and working through this stuff together. When you go through this material with other men and women, the shame and mystery behind the financial curtain start to melt away. You see that you're really not alone, no matter where you are in your financial journey. Everybody makes mistakes. Everybody has done stupid things with money. Everybody is capable of winning. Sometimes that's hard to see if you're just sitting home alone, reading a book.

That's why we started the *Financial Peace University* class in the first place. When I went broke, Sharon and I were so ashamed that we didn't want anyone else to know what a wreck our lives had become. That was such a huge mistake. I believe that if we had come alongside other families and been honest about what was going on, all of that fear and guilt would have been washed away by the love, support, and prayers of other people who were facing the same stuff.

If you have not attended a *Financial Peace University* class, you should. We have classes in pretty much every city all around the country. It is truly thirteen weeks that can change your life. And if you have gone through the class, I encourage you to do it again! FPU is a lifetime membership, so you can go through as many times as you want. You could even start a new class in your area and help other families experience the peace you've discovered! In my two decades of doing this, actually playing a role in someone else's success is the most rewarding part of the job. By leading a class, you can experience that *right now*. Trust me—it's a great way to spend one night a week.

Find out more at daveramsey.com.

NOTES

SUPER SAVING

1. Lynda Edwards, "Save for a Rainy Day? Most Prefer to Borrow," Bankrate.com, November 1998, http://www.bankrate.com/gookeyword/news/sav/19981120.asp.
2. 1 Timothy 6:10.
3. Hebrews 12:11, NIV (2011).
4. Dave Ramsey, *Financial Peace Revisited* (New York: Viking Penguin, 2003).

RELATING WITH MONEY

1. "Money Talks Quell Conflict," *Florida Today*, May 18, 2003.
2. Citibank study cited in *The Gleaner*, July 15, 2001.
3. Gary Smalley, *Making Love Last Forever* (Dallas: Word Publishing, 1996).
4. United States Department of Commerce, *Poverty in the United States in 1997*.
5. Proverbs 22:6, NKJV.
6. Proverbs 22:7, NRSV.
7. Wendy Wang and Rich Morin, "Home for the Holidays . . . and Every Other Day," *Pew Research Center Publications*, November 24, 2009, http://pewresearch.org/pubs/1423/home-for-the-holidays-boomeranged-parents?src=prc-latest&proj=peoplepress.
8. "Lower Wages, Lack of Job Opportunities Means More Americans Delaying 'Adulthood,'" *Science Daily*, April 28, 2010, http://www.sciencedaily.com/releases/2010/04/100427101217.htm.
9. Leonard Sax, "What's Happening to Boys?" *Washington Post,* March 31, 2006, http://www.washingtonpost.com/wp-dyn/content/article/2006/03/30/AR2006033001341.html.
10. Henry Cloud, PhD, and John Townsend, PhD, *Boundaries* (Grand Rapids, MI: Zondervan Publishing House, 1992), 25.

CASH FLOW PLANNING

1. Luke 14:28–30, NKJV.
2. Eric Halperin, Lisa James and Peter Smith, "Debit Card Danger," Center for Responsible Lending, January 25, 2007, http://www.responsiblelending.org/overdraft-loans/research-analysis/Debit-Card-Danger-report.pdf.
3. 1 Timothy 5:8, NKJV.

DUMPING DEBT

1. "Getting Paid in America" Survey Results. National Payroll Week 2008, http://www.nationalpayrollweek.com/documents/2008FinalSurveyResults.pdf.

2. Census Bureau and Pitney Bowes Business Insight, 2010. Cited in *Directions Magazine*, June 2010 newsletter, http://www.directionsmag.com/images/newsletter/2010/06_week2/Exeter_tables.pdf.

3. Richard Barrington, "2011 Credit Card Facts & Statistics—Free Infographic Report," from Index Credit Cards website, January 10, 2011, http://www.indexcreditcards.com/finance/creditcardstatistics/2011-report-on-credit-card-usage-facts-statistics.html.

4. Proverbs 22:7, NRSV.

5. Jay MacDonald, "Dealing with Deadbeat Friends or Family Members." From the BankRate website, May 26, 2006, http://www.bankrate.com/brm/news/pf/20060519a1.asp.

6. Proverbs 17:18, CEV.

7. Dave Michaels, "Should Texas Gamble on Slots?" *Dallas Morning News*, February 22, 2005.

8. Warren Smith, "Anti-lottery Activism Needed Now." *Charlotte World*, April 4, 2005, http://www.worldnewspaperpublishing.com/news/FullStory.asp?loc=TCW&ID=1351.

9. Damon Carr, "Automobiles Can Drive You BROKE." *Final Call*, November 8, 2005, http://www.finalcall.com/artman/publish/article_2267.shtml

10. Carnegie Mellon University, "Brain Scans Predict When People Will Buy Products." *ScienceDaily*, January 4, 2007, http://www.sciencedaily.com/releases/2007/01/070103201418.htm.

11. Vicki Mabrey, "Credit Card Debt? Tell It to the Judge," *ABC News Nightline*, January 20, 2006, http://abcnews.go.com/Nightline/PersonalFinance/story?id=1526505.

12. "The Case for Economic Education." Junior Achievement, August 2004, www.ja.org.

13. Dave Ramsey, *The Total Money Makeover*, 3rd ed. (Nashville: Thomas Nelson, 2009), 44.

14. Proberbs 6:1, 4–5, NKJV.

15. Ramsey, *The Total Money Makeover*, 121.

CREDIT SHARKS IN SUITS

1. "What's In Your FICO Score," http://www.myfico.com/CreditEducation/WhatsInYourScore.aspx.

2. "Mistakes Do Happen: A Look at Errors in Consumer Credit Reports," Executive Summary, National Association of State PIRGs, June 2004, http://www.uspirg.org/home/reports/report-archives/financial-privacy--security/financial-privacy--security/mistakes-do-happen-a-look-at-errors-in-consumer-credit-reports.

3. Ibid.

4. Ibid.

5. Anne Kadet, "Who Profits Most from Debt? Debt Collectors," *SmartMoney* magazine, January 23, 2007, http://www.smartmoney.com/borrow/debt-strategies/who-profits-most-from-debt-debt-collectors-20685/.

6. Ibid.

7. "Debt Collection Puts on a Suit," *BusinessWeek Online*, November 14, 2005, http://www.businessweek.com/magazine/content/05_46/b3959128.htm.

8. Kadet, "Who Profits Most from Debt? Debt Collectors."

BUYER BEWARE

1. John De Graaf, David Wann, and Thomas H. Naylor. *Affluenza*, 2nd ed. (San Francisco: Berrett-Koehler, 2005), 165.
2. Ibid, 154.
3. Ibid, 155.
4. David Bauder, "More TVs Than People in Average Home," Breitbart Website, September 21, 2006, http://www.breitbart.com/article.php?id=D8K9ER580&show_article=1.
5. Mindy Fetterman and Jayne O'Donnell, "Just Browsing at the Mall? That's What You Think." *USA Today*, September 1, 2006, http://www.usatoday.com/money/industries/retail/2006-09-01-retail-cover-usat_x.htm.
6. Proverbs 31:10–11, NKJV.

CLAUSE AND EFFECT

1. Dave Ramsey. *The Total Money Makeover*, 1st ed., (Nashville: Thomas Nelson, 2003), 73.
2. "Income Stable, Poverty Rate Increases, Percentage of Americans Without Health Insurance Unchanged," U.S. Census Bureau News, August 30, 2005.
3. "Why Disability" booklet, published by National Underwriter.
4. "Aging Services: The Facts," American Association of Homes and Services for the Aging, www.aahsa.org, 2007.
5. "Few Seniors Have Long-Term Care Insurance," *Kaiser Health News*, December 14, 2010, http://www.kaiserhealthnews.org/Features/Insuring-Your-Health/Michelle-Andrews-on-long-term-care-policies.aspx.
6. From phone interview with Dr. Paul Keckley, conducted by Richard Speight, May 9, 2007.
7. Mark 6:4–6, *The Message*.
8. "Identity Theft: The Aftermath 2006," Identity Theft Resource Center, www.idtheftcenter.org.
9. Ibid.

THAT'S NOT GOOD ENOUGH!

1. "Haggle with Your Plumber, Doctor, or Chimney Sweep," MSN Money, March 16, 2003.
2. Ibid.
3. Roger Fisher and William L. Ury. *Getting to Yes: Negotiate Agreement Without Giving In* (Chicago: Nightingale Conant).
4. Dave Ramsey. *Financial Peace Revisited* (New York: Viking Penguin, 2003), 164.

THE PINNACLE POINT

1. Ecclesiastes 11:2, NIV (1984).
2. Ramsey, *Financial Peace Revisited*, 146.
3. Kathy Rebello, Peter Burrows, and Ira Sager, "The Fall of an American Icon," *Business Week*, February 5, 1996, http://www.businessweek.com/1996/06/b34611.htm.

4. Kris Axtman, "How Enron Awards Do, Or Don't, Trickle Down," *Christian Science Monitor*, June 20, 2005, http://www.csmonitor.com/2005/0620/p02s01-usju.html.
5. Ramsey, *Financial Peace Revisited*, 129.

FROM FRUITION TO TUITION

1. "The 2010 Retirement Confidence Survey: Confidence Stabilizing, But Preparations Continue to Erode." Retirement Confidence Survey sponsored by the Employee Benefit Research Institute, 2010.
2. Ramsey, *The Total Money Makeover*, 3rd ed., 155.
3. "Getting Paid in America" Survey Results. National Payroll Week 2008, http://www .nationalpayrollweek.com/documents/2008FinalSurveyResults.pdf.
4. Ramsey, *The Total Money Makeover*, 168–69.
5. "How America Pays for College, 2010." A national study conducted for Sallie Mae by Gallup. https://www1.salliemae.com/about/news_info/research/how_america_pays_2010/.
6. Ibid.
7. Ramsey, *The Total Money Makeover*, 171.

WORKING IN YOUR STRENGTHS

1. Dave Ramsey, *EntreLeadership* (New York: Howard Books, 2011), 114.
2. Marcus Buckingham, *Trombone Player Wanted*, Short Film Series, directed by Marcus Buckingham (The Marcus Buckingham Company, 2006).
3. Jim Collins, *Good to Great: Why Some Companies Make the Leap . . . and Others Don't* (New York: Harper Collins, 2001).
4. Dan Miller, *48 Days to the Work You Love* (Nashville: B&H Publishing Group, 2010).
5. "County Business Patterns." 2003 U.S. Census Bureau report, http://www.census.gov/ prod/2005pubs/03cbp/cbp03-1.pdf.
6. Ramsey, *EntreLeadership*, 123.
7. Ibid, 119.

REAL ESTATE AND MORTGAGES

1. Ramsey, *The Total Money Makeover*, 184.
2. Walter Molony, "Home Buyer and Seller Survey Shows Rising Use of Internet, Reliance on Agents," National Association of Realtors News Release, January 17, 2006, http://archive.realtor.org/article/ home-buyer-seller-survey-shows-rising-use-internet-reliance-agents.
3. "How Do Buyers Shop for Homes?" *Better Homes and Gardens Real Estate*, www .bhgrealestate.com/Learn/Buying-and-Selling/How-Do-Buyers-Shop-For-Homes-.html.
4. Molony, "Home Buyer and Seller Survey Shows Rising Use of Internet, Reliance on Agents."
5. Ramsey, *The Total Money Makeover*, 187.

GIVE LIKE NO ONE ELSE

1. Psalm 24:1, KJV.

2. "Income, Poverty, and Health Insurance Coverage in the United States: 2009," issued September 2010 by the U.S. Department of Commerce, Economics and Statistics Administration, and the U.S. Census Bureau, http://www.census.gov/prod/2010pubs/p60-238.pdf.

3. Find out how to start a *Financial Peace University* class or bring *Momentum* to your church in the online resources for this FPU lesson or at daveramsey.com.

4. Luke 21:1–4.

5. 1 Timothy 5:8, NKJV.

6. Dave Ramsey, *More Than Enough* (New York: Penguin Books, 1999), 268–69.

FINANCIAL MANAGEMENT FORMS

Welcome to the wonderful world of cash flow management! By filling out just a few forms, your new financial plan will start to unfold right in front of you. You'll immediately identify problem areas and learn how to shut the valve of wasteful spending, because you'll know exactly where all of your dollars are going!

It will probably take a little while to complete the forms the first time. After that initial startup, however, you'll get better and better until budgeting becomes second nature.

Complete the whole set of forms to get started. Then, you'll only need to do the "Monthly Cash Flow Plan" (Form 5), "Allocated Spending Plan" (Form 7) or the "Irregular Income Plan" (Form 8) once a month. This should only take about 30 minutes a month once you get in the habit.

You'll also want to update the whole set of forms once a year or whenever you experience a dramatic positive or negative financial event (such as receiving a large inheritance or paying for a major house repair).

Use the examples on the following pages as a guide. You can download all the forms in a printable PDF format from the website, and you can even use the online budgeting tool as a replacement for the "Monthly Cash Flow Plan" (Form 5).

Are you ready? It's time to make those dollars dance! Go for it!

QUICKIE BUDGET

This form will help you get your feet wet in the area of budgeting. It is only one page and should not be intimidating as you get started. The purpose of this form is to show you exactly how much money you need every month in order to survive. We won't get into the details of your credit card bills, student loans and other consumer debts here. This is just to give you a starting point as you begin to take control of your money.

There are four columns on this form:

1 *Monthly Total*
- This column shows you how much you are spending on necessities each month.
- If you do not know the amount, write down your best estimate.
- If an estimate is grossly inaccurate, then you may have never even noticed how much you were spending in that area before now. Don't beat yourself up about this!

2 *Payoff Total*
- Write down how much money is required to completely pay off that item.
- This line only appears in the relevant categories (mortgage, car debt, etc.).

3 *How Far Behind?*
- If your account is past due in any category, write down how many days you are behind.
- If you are up-to-date, simply write a zero or "N/A" (not applicable) in this column.

4 *Type of Account*
- Write in how this area is paid—by check, automatic bank draft, cash, etc.
- Early in the program, you will see the benefits of using cash for certain items. Challenge yourself by identifying categories for which you can use cash only.
- The asterisks (*) on the form indicate areas in which a cash-based approach could be helpful.

QUICKIE BUDGET

Item	Monthly Total	Payoff Total	How Far Behind	Type of Account
GIVING	_____		_____	_____
SAVING	_____		_____	_____
HOUSING				
First Mortgage	_____	_____	_____	_____
Second Mortgage	_____	_____	_____	_____
Repairs/Mn. Fee	_____		_____	_____
UTILITIES				
Electricity	_____		_____	_____
Water	_____		_____	_____
Gas	_____		_____	_____
Phone	_____		_____	_____
Trash	_____		_____	_____
Cable	_____		_____	_____
*Food	_____		_____	_____
TRANSPORTATION				
Car Payment	_____	_____	_____	_____
Car Payment	_____	_____	_____	_____
*Gas & Oil	_____		_____	_____
*Repairs & Tires	_____		_____	_____
Car Insurance	_____		_____	_____
*CLOTHING	_____		_____	_____
PERSONAL				
Disability Ins.	_____		_____	_____
Health Insurance	_____		_____	_____
Life Insurance	_____		_____	_____
Child Care	_____		_____	_____
*Entertainment	_____		_____	_____
OTHER MISC.	_____		_____	_____

TOTAL MONTHLY NECESSITIES_____

MAJOR COMPONENTS OF A HEALTHY FINANCIAL PLAN

	Action Needed	Action Date
Written Cash Flow Plan	_____	_____
Will and/or Estate Plan	_____	_____
Debt Reduction Plan	_____	_____
Tax Reduction Plan	_____	_____
Emergency Funding	_____	_____
Retirement Funding	_____	_____
College Funding	_____	_____
Charitable Giving	_____	_____
Teach My Children	_____	_____
Life Insurance	_____	_____
Health Insurance	_____	_____
Disability Insurance	_____	_____
Auto Insurance	_____	_____
Homeowner's Insurance	_____	_____

I (We) _____, (a) responsible adult(s), do hereby promise to take the above stated actions by the above stated dates to financially secure the well-being of my (our) family and myself (ourselves).

Signed:_____ Date:_____

Signed:_____ Date:_____

CONSUMER EQUITY SHEET

Item / Describe	Value	−	Debt	=	Equity
Real Estate	_____		_____		_____
Real Estate	_____		_____		_____
Car _____	_____		_____		_____
Car _____	_____		_____		_____
Cash On Hand	_____		_____		_____
Checking Account	_____		_____		_____
Checking Account	_____		_____		_____
Savings Account	_____		_____		_____
Money Market Account	_____		_____		_____
Mutual Funds	_____		_____		_____
Retirement Plan 1	_____		_____		_____
Retirement Plan 2	_____		_____		_____
Cash Value (Insurance)	_____		_____		_____
Household Items	_____		_____		_____
Jewelry	_____		_____		_____
Antiques	_____		_____		_____
Boat	_____		_____		_____
Unsecured Debt (Negative)	_____		_____		_____
Credit Card Debt (Negative)	_____		_____		_____
Other	_____		_____		_____
Other	_____		_____		_____
Other	_____		_____		_____
TOTAL	_____		_____		_____

INCOME SOURCES

Source	Amount	Period/Describe
Salary 1	_____	_____
Salary 2	_____	_____
Salary 3	_____	_____
Bonus	_____	_____
Self-Employment	_____	_____
Interest Income	_____	_____
Dividend Income	_____	_____
Royalty Income	_____	_____
Rents	_____	_____
Notes	_____	_____
Alimony	_____	_____
Child Support	_____	_____
AFDC	_____	_____
Unemployment	_____	_____
Social Security	_____	_____
Pension	_____	_____
Annuity	_____	_____
Disability Income	_____	_____
Cash Gifts	_____	_____
Trust Fund	_____	_____
Other	_____	_____
Other	_____	_____
Other	_____	_____
TOTAL	_____	

LUMP SUM PAYMENT PLANNING

Payments you make on a non-monthly basis, such as insurance premiums and taxes, can be budget busters if you do not plan for them every month. Therefore, you must annualize the cost and convert these to monthly budget items. That way, you can save the money each month and will not be caught off-guard when your bi-monthly, quarterly, semi-annual or annual bills come due. Simply divide the annual cost by 12 to determine the monthly amount you should save for each item.

Item Needed	Annual Amount		Monthly Amount
Real Estate Taxes	_____	/ 12 =	_____
Homeowner's Insurance	_____	/ 12 =	_____
Home Repairs	_____	/ 12 =	_____
Replace Furniture	_____	/ 12 =	_____
Medical Bills	_____	/ 12 =	_____
Health Insurance	_____	/ 12 =	_____
Life Insurance	_____	/ 12 =	_____
Disability Insurance	_____	/ 12 =	_____
Car Insurance	_____	/ 12 =	_____
Car Repair/Tags	_____	/ 12 =	_____
Replace Car	_____	/ 12 =	_____
Clothing	_____	/ 12 =	_____
Tuition	_____	/ 12 =	_____
Bank Note	_____	/ 12 =	_____
IRS (Self-Employed)	_____	/ 12 =	_____
Vacation	_____	/ 12 =	_____
Gifts (including Christmas)	_____	/ 12 =	_____
Other _____	_____	/ 12 =	_____

MONTHLY CASH FLOW PLAN

Every single dollar of your income should be allocated to some category on this form. When you're done, your total income minus expenses should equal zero. If it doesn't, then you need to adjust some categories (such as debt reduction, giving or saving) so that it does equal zero. Use some common sense here, too. Do not leave things like clothes, car repairs or home improvements off this list. If you don't plan for these things, you're only setting yourself up for failure later.

Yes, this budget form is long. It's really long. We do that so that we can list practically every expense imaginable on this form to prevent you from forgetting something. Don't expect to put something on every line item. Just use the ones that are relevant to your specific situation.

Every main category on this form has subcategories. Fill in the monthly expense for each subcategory, and then write down the grand total for that category. Later, as you actually pay the bills and work through the month, use the "Actually Spent" column to record what you really spent in each area. If there is a substantial difference between what you budgeted and what you spent, then you'll need to readjust the budget to make up for the difference. If one category continually comes up over or short for two or three months, you'll need to adjust the budgeted amount accordingly.

Notes:
• An asterisk (*) beside an item indicates an area for which you should use a cash envelope system.

• The emergency fund should get all the savings until you've completed your full emergency fund of three to six months of expenses (Baby Step 3).

• Don't forget to include your annualized items from the "Lump Sum Payment Planning" sheet (Form 4), including your Christmas gift planning.

MONTHLY CASH FLOW PLAN

Budgeted Item	Sub Total	TOTAL	Actually Spent	% of Take Home Pay
CHARITABLE GIFTS		_____	_____	_____
SAVING				
Emergency Fund	_____		_____	
Retirement Fund	_____		_____	
College Fund	_____	_____	_____	_____
HOUSING				
First Mortgage	_____		_____	
Second Mortgage	_____		_____	
Real Estate Taxes	_____		_____	
Homeowner's Ins.	_____		_____	
Repairs or Mn. Fee	_____		_____	
Replace Furniture	_____		_____	
Other _____	_____	_____	_____	_____
UTILITIES				
Electricity	_____		_____	
Water	_____		_____	
Gas	_____		_____	
Phone	_____		_____	
Trash	_____		_____	
Cable	_____	_____	_____	_____
*FOOD				
*Grocery	_____		_____	
*Restaurants	_____	_____	_____	_____
TRANSPORTATION				
Car Payment	_____		_____	
Car Payment	_____		_____	
*Gas and Oil	_____		_____	
*Repairs and Tires	_____		_____	
Car Insurance	_____		_____	
License and Taxes	_____		_____	
Car Replacement	_____	_____	_____	_____
PAGE 1 TOTAL	_____	_____		

MONTHLY CASH FLOW PLAN

Budgeted Item	Sub Total	TOTAL	Actually Spent	% of Take Home Pay
*CLOTHING				
*Children	_____		_____	
*Adults	_____		_____	
*Cleaning/Laundry	_____	_____	_____	_____
MEDICAL/HEALTH				
Disability Insurance	_____		_____	
Health Insurance	_____		_____	
Doctor Bills	_____		_____	
Dentist	_____		_____	
Optometrist	_____		_____	
Medications	_____	_____	_____	_____
PERSONAL				
Life Insurance	_____		_____	
Child Care	_____		_____	
*Baby Sitter	_____		_____	
*Toiletries	_____		_____	
*Cosmetics	_____		_____	
*Hair Care	_____		_____	
Education/Adult	_____		_____	
School Tuition	_____		_____	
School Supplies	_____		_____	
Child Support	_____		_____	
Alimony	_____		_____	
Subscriptions	_____		_____	
Organization Dues	_____		_____	
Gifts (incl. Christmas)	_____		_____	
Miscellaneous	_____		_____	
*Blow Money	_____	_____	_____	_____

PAGE 2 TOTAL _____

MONTHLY CASH FLOW PLAN

Budgeted Item	Sub Total	TOTAL	Actually Spent	% of Take Home Pay
RECREATION				
*Entertainment	_____		_____	
Vacation	_____	_____	_____	_____
DEBTS (Hopefully -0-)				
Visa 1	_____		_____	
Visa 2	_____		_____	
Master Card 1	_____		_____	
Master Card 2	_____		_____	
American Express	_____		_____	
Discover Card	_____		_____	
Gas Card 1	_____		_____	
Gas Card 2	_____		_____	
Dept. Store Card 1	_____		_____	
Dept. Store Card 2	_____		_____	
Finance Co. 1	_____		_____	
Finance Co. 2	_____		_____	
Credit Line	_____		_____	
Student Loan 1	_____		_____	
Student Loan 2	_____		_____	
Other _____		_____		_____
Other _____		_____		_____
Other _____		_____		_____
Other _____		_____	_____	_____
_____				

PAGE 3 TOTAL		_____	_____	
PAGE 2 TOTAL		_____	_____	
PAGE 1 TOTAL		_____	_____	
GRAND TOTAL		_____	_____	
TOTAL HOUSEHOLD INCOME		_____		
		ZERO		

RECOMMENDED PERCENTAGES

How much of your income should be spent on housing, giving, food, etc.? Through experience and research, we recommend the following percentages. However, you should remember that these are only recommended percentages. If you have an unusually high or low income, then these numbers could change dramatically. For example, if you have a high income, the percentage that is spent on food will be much lower than someone who earns half of that.

If you find that you spend much more in one category than we recommend, however, it may be necessary to adjust your lifestyle in that area in order to enjoy more freedom and flexibility across the board.

Item	Actual %	Recommended %
CHARITABLE GIFTS	_____	10–15%
SAVING	_____	5–10%
HOUSING	_____	25–35%
UTILITIES	_____	5–10%
FOOD	_____	5–15%
TRANSPORTATION	_____	10–15%
CLOTHING	_____	2–7%
MEDICAL/HEALTH	_____	5–10%
PERSONAL	_____	5–10%
RECREATION	_____	5–10%
DEBTS	_____	5–10%

ALLOCATED SPENDING PLAN

This form goes into deeper detail than the "Monthly Cash Flow Plan" (Form 5). Here, you will allocate—or spend—all of your money from each individual pay period.

There are four columns on this form, representing the four weeks in a given month. You will use one column for each week you get paid. If you are married and your spouse earns an income, you will both use this same form. For weeks in which you both receive a paycheck, add those two incomes together and use a single column.

Now, go down the list and allocate each expense to a specific payday, using your bills' due dates as a guide. For example, if your phone bill is due on the 22nd and you get paid on the 15th and 30th, then you know that you would probably pay that bill from your income on the 15th. The point is to anticipate your upcoming expenses and income and plan accordingly.

Beside each line item, you'll see two blanks separated by a slash (/). Put the expense to the left of the slash and the remaining income from that pay period to the right of the slash. As you work your way down the column, the income remaining should diminish until you reach a perfect zero at the bottom of the list. If you have money left over at the end of the column, go back and adjust an area, such as savings or giving, so that you spend every single dollar.

NOTES:

1. If you have an irregular income, such as self-employment or commissions, you should use the "Irregular Income Planning" sheet (Form 8) instead of this "Allocated Spending Plan."

2. If you know that you have an impulse spending problem, you may want to allocate more money to the "Blow" category. That way, you are at least setting up some spending boundaries.

3. An asterisk (*) beside an item indicates an area for which you should use a cash envelope system.

ALLOCATED SPENDING PLAN

PAY PERIOD: ____ /____   ____ /____   ____ /____   ____ /____

ITEM:
INCOME _____   _____   _____   _____

CHARITABLE ____ /____   ____ /____   ____ /____   ____ /____

SAVING
   Emergency Fund ____ /____   ____ /____   ____ /____   ____ /____
   Retirement Fund ____ /____   ____ /____   ____ /____   ____ /____
   College Fund ____ /____   ____ /____   ____ /____   ____ /____

HOUSING
   First Mortgage ____ /____   ____ /____   ____ /____   ____ /____
   Second Mortgage ____ /____   ____ /____   ____ /____   ____ /____
   Real Estate Taxes ____ /____   ____ /____   ____ /____   ____ /____
   Homeowner's Ins. ____ /____   ____ /____   ____ /____   ____ /____
   Repairs or Mn. Fees ____ /____   ____ /____   ____ /____   ____ /____
   Replace Furniture ____ /____   ____ /____   ____ /____   ____ /____
   Other _____ ____ /____   ____ /____   ____ /____   ____ /____

UTILITIES
   Electricity ____ /____   ____ /____   ____ /____   ____ /____
   Water ____ /____   ____ /____   ____ /____   ____ /____
   Gas ____ /____   ____ /____   ____ /____   ____ /____
   Phone ____ /____   ____ /____   ____ /____   ____ /____
   Trash ____ /____   ____ /____   ____ /____   ____ /____
   Cable ____ /____   ____ /____   ____ /____   ____ /____

*FOOD
   *Grocery ____ /____   ____ /____   ____ /____   ____ /____
   *Restaurants ____ /____   ____ /____   ____ /____   ____ /____

ALLOCATED SPENDING PLAN *(continued)*

TRANSPORTATION
    Car Payment   ____ / ____   ____ / ____   ____ / ____   ____ / ____
    Car Payment   ____ / ____   ____ / ____   ____ / ____   ____ / ____
  * Gas and Oil   ____ / ____   ____ / ____   ____ / ____   ____ / ____
  * Repairs and Tires   ____ / ____   ____ / ____   ____ / ____   ____ / ____
    Car Insurance   ____ / ____   ____ / ____   ____ / ____   ____ / ____
    License and Taxes   ____ / ____   ____ / ____   ____ / ____   ____ / ____
    Car Replacement   ____ / ____   ____ / ____   ____ / ____   ____ / ____

*CLOTHING
  * Children   ____ / ____   ____ / ____   ____ / ____   ____ / ____
  * Adults   ____ / ____   ____ / ____   ____ / ____   ____ / ____
  * Cleaning/Laundry   ____ / ____   ____ / ____   ____ / ____   ____ / ____

MEDICAL/HEALTH
    Disability Insurance   ____ / ____   ____ / ____   ____ / ____   ____ / ____
    Health Insurance   ____ / ____   ____ / ____   ____ / ____   ____ / ____
    Doctor   ____ / ____   ____ / ____   ____ / ____   ____ / ____
    Dentist   ____ / ____   ____ / ____   ____ / ____   ____ / ____
    Optometrist   ____ / ____   ____ / ____   ____ / ____   ____ / ____
    Medications   ____ / ____   ____ / ____   ____ / ____   ____ / ____

PERSONAL
    Life Insurance   ____ / ____   ____ / ____   ____ / ____   ____ / ____
    Child Care   ____ / ____   ____ / ____   ____ / ____   ____ / ____
  * Baby Sitter   ____ / ____   ____ / ____   ____ / ____   ____ / ____
  * Toiletries   ____ / ____   ____ / ____   ____ / ____   ____ / ____
  * Cosmetics   ____ / ____   ____ / ____   ____ / ____   ____ / ____
  * Hair Care   ____ / ____   ____ / ____   ____ / ____   ____ / ____
    Education/Adult   ____ / ____   ____ / ____   ____ / ____   ____ / ____
    School Tuition   ____ / ____   ____ / ____   ____ / ____   ____ / ____
    School Supplies   ____ / ____   ____ / ____   ____ / ____   ____ / ____
    Child Support   ____ / ____   ____ / ____   ____ / ____   ____ / ____

ALLOCATED SPENDING PLAN

Alimony ____/____ ____/____ ____/____ ____/____
Subscriptions ____/____ ____/____ ____/____ ____/____
Organization Dues ____/____ ____/____ ____/____ ____/____
Gifts (incl. Christmas) ____/____ ____/____ ____/____ ____/____
Miscellaneous ____/____ ____/____ ____/____ ____/____

*BLOW $$ ____/____ ____/____ ____/____ ____/____

RECREATION
 * Entertainment ____/____ ____/____ ____/____ ____/____
 Vacation ____/____ ____/____ ____/____ ____/____

DEBTS (Hopefully -0-)
 Visa 1 ____/____ ____/____ ____/____ ____/____
 Visa 2 ____/____ ____/____ ____/____ ____/____
 MasterCard 1 ____/____ ____/____ ____/____ ____/____
 MasterCard 2 ____/____ ____/____ ____/____ ____/____
 American Express ____/____ ____/____ ____/____ ____/____
 Discover Card ____/____ ____/____ ____/____ ____/____
 Gas Card 1 ____/____ ____/____ ____/____ ____/____
 Gas Card 2 ____/____ ____/____ ____/____ ____/____
 Dept. Store Card 1 ____/____ ____/____ ____/____ ____/____
 Dept. Store Card 2 ____/____ ____/____ ____/____ ____/____
 Finance Co. 1 ____/____ ____/____ ____/____ ____/____
 Finance Co. 2 ____/____ ____/____ ____/____ ____/____
 Credit Line ____/____ ____/____ ____/____ ____/____
 Student Loan 1 ____/____ ____/____ ____/____ ____/____
 Student Loan 2 ____/____ ____/____ ____/____ ____/____
 Other _____ ____/____ ____/____ ____/____ ____/____
 Other _____ ____/____ ____/____ ____/____ ____/____

IRREGULAR INCOME PLANNING

Many people have an "irregular" income, which simply means that their compensation fluctuates from month to month. This is especially common for the self-employed, as well as commission-based salespeople. While this makes it more difficult to predict your income, you are still responsible for doing a monthly budget!

The "Monthly Cash Flow Plan" (Form 5) should remain a crucial part of your plan, as it lays out exactly how much money you need to bring home each month to survive and prosper. However, instead of doing the "Allocated Spending Plan" (Form 7), you will use this "Irregular Income Planning" sheet.

On this form, simply look at the individual items from your "Monthly Cash Flow Plan" sheet and prioritize them by importance. Ask yourself, "If I only have enough money to pay one thing, what would that be?" Put that at the top of your list. Then, ask yourself, "If I only have enough money to pay one more thing, what would that be?" That's number two. Keep this up all the way down the list.

With your list in place, you're ready to get paid. If you get a $1,500 paycheck, you will spend that $1,500 right down the list until it is gone, recording the cumulative amount spent in the "Cumulative Amount" column. At that point, you're finished spending, no matter what remains unpaid on the list. That's why the most important things are at the top of the list, right?

Be prepared to stand your ground. Things usually have a way of seeming important when they are only urgent. For example, a once-in-a-lifetime opportunity to see your favorite band perform live may seem important, but in reality, it is only urgent, meaning that it is time-sensitive. Urgency alone should not move an item to the top of this list!

Item	Amount	Cumulative Amount

BREAKDOWN OF SAVINGS

After you have fully funded your emergency fund, you can start to save for other items, such as furniture, car replacement, home maintenance or a vacation. This sheet will remind you that every dollar in your savings account is already committed to something. For example, it's a bad idea to take money away from car repairs to pay for an impulse Hawaiian vacation, even if you pay cash for it. What would you do if the car broke down the week you got back home? However, it can be okay to re-assign the dollars to another category, as long as you do it on purpose and it doesn't put you in a pinch in another category. Keep up with your breakdown of savings every month, one quarter at a time.

Item	*Balance By Month*		
	_____	_____	_____
Emergency Fund (1) $1,000	_____	_____	_____
Emergency Fund (2) 3–6 months	_____	_____	_____
Retirement Fund	_____	_____	_____
College Fund	_____	_____	_____
Real Estate Taxes	_____	_____	_____
Homeowner's Insurance	_____	_____	_____
Repairs or Mn. Fee	_____	_____	_____
Replace Furniture	_____	_____	_____
Car Insurance	_____	_____	_____
Car Replacement	_____	_____	_____
Disability Insurance	_____	_____	_____
Health Insurance	_____	_____	_____
Doctor	_____	_____	_____
Dentist	_____	_____	_____
Optometrist	_____	_____	_____
Life Insurance	_____	_____	_____
School Tuition	_____	_____	_____
School Supplies	_____	_____	_____
Gifts (incl. Christmas)	_____	_____	_____
Vacation	_____	_____	_____
Other _____	_____	_____	_____
Other _____	_____	_____	_____
TOTAL	_____	_____	_____

DEBT SNOWBALL

Now it's time to knock out that debt! List your debts in order, from the smallest balance to the largest. Don't be concerned with interest rates, unless two debts have a similar payoff balance. In that case, list the one with the higher interest rate first. As you start eliminating debts, you'll start to build some serious momentum. These quick wins will keep you motivated, so you'll be able to stay on track.

The idea of the snowball is simple: pay minimum payments on all of your debts except for the smallest one. Then, attack that one with gazelle intensity! Every extra dollar you can get your hands on should be thrown at that smallest debt until it is gone. Then, you attack the second one. Every time you pay a debt off, you add its old minimum payment to your next debt payments.

So, as the snowball rolls over, it picks up more snow. Get it?

Redo this sheet every time you pay off a debt so that you can see how close you're getting to total debt freedom. Keep the old sheets for encouragement—or to wallpaper the bathroom in your debt-free house someday!

The "New Payment" is the total of the previous debt's payment PLUS the current debt's minimum. As these payments compound, you'll start making huge payments as you work down the list until you can eventually call Dave's radio show and scream, "I'M DEBT FREE!"

DEBT SNOWBALL

Item	Total Payoff	Minimum Payment	New Payment
_____	_____	_____	_____
_____	_____	_____	_____
_____	_____	_____	_____
_____	_____	_____	_____
_____	_____	_____	_____
_____	_____	_____	_____
_____	_____	_____	_____
_____	_____	_____	_____
_____	_____	_____	_____
_____	_____	_____	_____
_____	_____	_____	_____
_____	_____	_____	_____
_____	_____	_____	_____
_____	_____	_____	_____
_____	_____	_____	_____
_____	_____	_____	_____
_____	_____	_____	_____
_____	_____	_____	_____

PRO RATA DEBTS

"Pro rata" means the fair share, or the percent of your total debt each creditor represents. This will determine how much you should send them when you cannot make the minimum payments. Even if you cannot pay your creditors what they request, you should pay everyone as much as you can. Send the check for their pro rata share, along with a copy of your budget and this form, every month. Do this even if the creditor says they will not accept it.

Do you need to use the pro rata plan?

First, use your monthly cash flow plan to determine your total disposable income. Simply write down your income on the line at the top of the form. Then, write down the total you spend on necessities (not including consumer debt) each month. Subtract the necessity expense from the income, and you are left with your disposable income. This is the money you have to put toward your debts.

Second, add up your total amount of debt, not including your home, and write that in the blank provided. Below that, write in the total of the minimum monthly payments on all your debts. If the total of your minimum payments is greater than your total disposable income, you need to use the pro rata plan.

How to Use This Form

This form has six columns:

1. Item: the name and type of the account.

2. Total Payoff: the total amount due on the account.

3. Total Debt: the combined total of all your debts.

4. Percent: the portion of the total debt load that each account represents. You can calculate this by simply dividing the Total Payoff by the Total Debt for each line.

5. Disposable Income: the amount of money you have left after paying necessities.

6. New Payment: the amount that you will now send to each creditor. Simply multiply the numbers in each line's Percent and Disposable Income columns for this figure.

The pro rata plan helps you to meet your obligations to the best of your ability. Your creditors will not like receiving less than their required minimum payments. However, if you keep sending them checks, they'll most likely keep cashing them.

PRO RATA DEBTS

Income _____   Total Debt: _____

Necessity Expense − _____   Total Minimum Payments: _____

Disposable Income = _____

Item	Total Payoff		Total Debt		Percent		Disposable Income		New Payment
_____	_____	/	_____	=	_____	X	_____	=	_____
_____	_____	/	_____	=	_____	X	_____	=	_____
_____	_____	/	_____	=	_____	X	_____	=	_____
_____	_____	/	_____	=	_____	X	_____	=	_____
_____	_____	/	_____	=	_____	X	_____	=	_____
_____	_____	/	_____	=	_____	X	_____	=	_____
_____	_____	/	_____	=	_____	X	_____	=	_____
_____	_____	/	_____	=	_____	X	_____	=	_____
_____	_____	/	_____	=	_____	X	_____	=	_____
_____	_____	/	_____	=	_____	X	_____	=	_____
_____	_____	/	_____	=	_____	X	_____	=	_____
_____	_____	/	_____	=	_____	X	_____	=	_____
_____	_____	/	_____	=	_____	X	_____	=	_____
_____	_____	/	_____	=	_____	X	_____	=	_____
_____	_____	/	_____	=	_____	X	_____	=	_____
_____	_____	/	_____	=	_____	X	_____	=	_____
_____	_____	/	_____	=	_____	X	_____	=	_____
_____	_____	/	_____	=	_____	X	_____	=	_____
_____	_____	/	_____	=	_____	X	_____	=	_____
_____	_____	/	_____	=	_____	X	_____	=	_____

MONTHLY RETIREMENT PLANNING

Too many people use the READY-FIRE-AIM approach to retirement planning. That's a bad plan. You need to aim first. Your assignment is to determine how much per month you should be saving at 12% interest in order to retire at 65 with the amount you need.

If you save at 12% and inflation is at 4%, then you are moving ahead of inflation at a net of 8% per year. If you invest your nest egg at retirement at 12% and want to break even with 4% inflation, you will be living on 8% income.

Step 1: Annual income (today) you wish to retire on: _____

Divide by .08 _____

(Nest egg needed) equals: _____

Step 2: To achieve that nest egg, you will save at 12%, netting 8% after inflation. So, we will target that nest egg using 8%.

Nest Egg Needed $ _____

Multiply by Factor X _____

Monthly Savings Needed = _____

Note: Be sure to try one or two examples if you wait 5 or 10 years to start.

8% FACTORS (SELECT THE ONE THAT MATCHES YOUR AGE)

Your Age	Years to Save	Factor	Your Age	Years to Save	Factor
25	40	.000286	45	20	.001698
30	35	.000436	50	15	.002890
35	30	.000671	55	10	.005466
40	25	.001051	60	5	.013610

MONTHLY COLLEGE PLANNING

In order to have enough for college, you must aim at something. Your assignment is to determine how much per month you should be saving at 12% interest in order to have enough for college.

If you save at 12% and inflation is at 4%, then you are moving ahead of inflation at a net of 8% per year.

Step 1:   In today's dollars, the annual cost of the college of your choice is:

Amount per year $ _____

X 4 years = $ _____

(hint: $15,000 to $25,000 annually)

Step 2:   To achieve that college nest egg, you will save at 12%,
netting 8% after inflation. So, we will target that nest egg using 8%.

Nest Egg Needed $ _____

Multiply by Factor   X _____

Monthly Savings Needed   = _____

Note: Be sure to try one or two examples if you wait 5 or 10 years to start.

8% FACTORS (SELECT THE ONE THAT MATCHES YOUR CHILD'S AGE)

CHILD'S AGE	YEARS TO SAVE	FACTOR	CHILD'S AGE	YEARS TO SAVE	FACTOR
0	18	.002083	8	10	.005466
2	16	.002583	10	8	.007470
4	14	.003247	12	6	.010867
6	12	.004158	14	4	.017746

CREDIT CARD HISTORY

CARD NAME	NUMBER	ADDRESS	PHONE #	CLOSED	WRITTEN CONFIRMATION REQUESTED	WRITTEN CONFIRMATION RECEIVED
Visa	1234 561989 12	1234 Poplar Grove, suite 130	123-456-7890	09/21/06	09/21/06	11/21/06

INSURANCE COVERAGE RECAP

TYPE	COMPANY	PLAN ID#	POLICY #	ACCOUNT	AGENT	PHONE #
Term life	ABC Insurance	1234 567989 12	1234 567989 12	$450,000	John Smith	456-7890

HOW TO FIGURE YOUR NEW PAYMENT

Use this worksheet to estimate the monthly mortgage payment on a 15-year loan compared to a 30-year loan.

_____ / 1,000=_____ X_____ = _____

SALES PRICE   #1,000'S   FACTOR   MONTHLY PAYMENT

Example: Sales Price - $150,000, 15 years at 6%

$150,000   150   8.44 $1,266

_____ / 1,000 = _____ X _____ = _____

SALES PRICE   #1,000'S   FACTOR   MONTHLY PAYMENT

MONTHLY PAYMENT PER $1,000 IN LOAN AMOUNT

Rate	15-Year	30-Year	Rate	15-Year	30-Year
4.5%	7.65	5.07	8.5%	9.85	7.69
5.0%	7.91	5.37	9.0%	10.15	8.05
5.5%	8.17	5.68	9.5%	10.44	8.41
6.0%	8.44	6.00	10.0%	10.75	8.78
6.5%	8.71	6.32	10.5%	11.05	9.15
7.0%	8.99	6.66	11.0%	11.37	9.52
7.5%	9.28	7.00	11.5%	11.68	9.90
8.0%	9.56	7.34	12.0%	12.00	10.29

SHOULD I REFINANCE?

This worksheet helps you decide whether or not it would make sense to refinance your current mortgage to a lower-interest loan.

_____ − _____ = _____

Current principal and   New principal   Monthly savings
interest payment   and interest payment
(not including taxes & insurance)

_____ / _____ = _____

Total closing costs   Monthly savings   Number of months
                                                                  to break even

Will you stay in your home longer than the number
of months to break even? If so, you are a candidate for a refinance.

Example: Refinance on a $150,000 Mortgage at 8% to 6.5%

$1,434 current payment − $1,307 new payment = $127 savings

$2,300 closing cost divided by $127 savings = 18 months

ESTIMATED CLOSING COSTS TABLE

Loan Amount	Closing Costs	Loan Amount	Closing Costs	Loan Amount	Closing Costs
30,000	1,500	60,000	1,775	90,000	1,950
35,000	1,550	65,000	1,800	95,000	1,975
40,000	1,600	70,000	1,825	100,000	2,000
45,000	1,650	75,000	1,850	150,000	2,300
50,000	1,700	80,000	1,900	200,000	2,600
55,000	1,725	85,000	1,925	250,000	2,900

HOW TO FIGURE THE CHANGE IN YOUR ARM

Your Adjustable Rate Mortgage (ARM) adjusts based on the movement of an index. You can find your index in your original note or mortgage. The most commonly used index is the Treasury Bill (T-Bill). The one-year ARM uses the one-year T-Bill, the three-year ARM uses the three-year T-Bill, and so on. Other commonly used indexes are the LIBOR and the 11th District Cost of Funds.

First, find out what index you use and when it is adjusted.

Next, find out (also from your loan paperwork) what margin was assigned to your loan (usually 2.59).

Basically, your ARM adjusts as the index moves.

The index is usually published daily in *The Wall Street Journal*.

So, if you have a one-year ARM that adjusts with the one-year T-Bill and a margin of 2.59 (which is typical), then, at the one-year anniversary of your closing, you would look up the one-year T-Bill in *The Wall Street Journal*. Add the T-Bill to your margin and you have your new rate (if it is not capped).

Example: T-Bill 4.41 plus margin 2.59 = 7% new interest rate.

Name of Index

Used by your ARM: _____   Index Adjustment   _____

Date that it is adjusted: _____   Margin   _____

New Interest Rate   _____

WARNING: *Almost all ARMs start below margin the first year, guaranteeing a payment increase at anniversary unless rates DROP.*

CREDIT REPORT INFORMATION

The FACT Act amendments to the Fair Credit Reporting Act require the nationwide credit bureaus to provide consumers, upon request, one free personal credit report in any 12-month period.

You may contact the Central Source online at www.annualcreditreport.com or by calling toll free (877) FACT ACT. Free copies are also available if you have been denied credit in the past 60 days and the creditor used their services.

EXPERIAN
Phone: (888) 397-3742

Website: www.experian.com

EQUIFAX CREDIT BUREAU
Phone: (800) 685-1111

Website: www.equifax.com

TRANSUNION CREDIT BUREAU
Phone: (800) 888-4213

Website: www.transunion.com

FEDERAL TRADE COMMISSION
Phone: (202) 326-2222

Address: 600 Pennsylvania Avenue, N.W.
                Washington, D.C. 20580

Website: www.ftc.gov

Publishes a brief, semi-annual list (March and September) on card pricing by the largest issuers for $5 per copy. Offers a number of free credit-related publications.